To Fiona,

Happy cooking!

Come Home to Supper

Love,

Grandma & Papa

Christmas, 2013

Come Home to Supper

OVER 200 SATISFYING
CASSEROLES, SKILLETS,
AND SIDES (DESSERTS, TOO!)
TO FEED YOUR FAMILY
WITH LOVE

CHRISTY JORDAN

WORKMAN PUBLISHING · NEW YORK

Library of Congress Cataloging-in-Publication Data is available.

ISBN: 978-0-7611-7490-5

Design by Sarah Smith
Cover photo courtesy of Hoffman Media copyright © 2013
Cover photo concept by Melissa Martin
Back cover photos copyright © Ben Fink Photography
Additional photography credits on page 308

Workman books are available at special discounts when purchased in bulk for
premiums and sales promotions as well as for fund-raising or educational use.
Special editions or book excerpts can also be created to specification.
For details, contact the Special Sales Director at the address below,
or send an email to specialmarkets@workman.com.

Workman Publishing Co., Inc.
225 Varick Street
New York, NY 10014-4381
workman.com

WORKMAN is a registered trademark of Workman Publishing Co., Inc.

Printed in the United States of America
First printing November 2013

10 9 8 7 6 5 4 3 2 1

To Ricky, Brady, and Katy Rose:
God set our little family together,
and I sure am glad He did!

♥

CONTENTS

Something to Come Home To

I WAS RAISED IN A TIME OF TRADITION. My family had rituals that we followed each day, each month, each year, because that is what our ancestors had taught us. At the end of summer we'd go to the orchard to pick apples. Fall meant spending a day walking behind Papa Reed's tractor as he turned the soil in his garden, picking up potatoes and putting them in buckets. Christmas Eve meant dinner at the Sanders' house in Huntsville, Alabama, and Christmas Day meant dinner at the Reed farm in Toney. In the spring, we got new dresses and dyed eggs for Easter and in the summer we held huge family reunions and spent the entire day reconnecting with long-lost cousins from other parts of the state.

And each night, no matter the time of year or season, we sat down to supper.

We were often joined by guests: Police officers who worked with my dad, friends from school, even other families dropped by from time to time. Mama would quickly set another place and not hear of them refusing her impromptu invitation. "Oh, we've got plenty, come on and sit down" would be her gentle chide, and a few whiffs of her cooking left even the busiest person completely lacking the willpower to turn her down.

Today's world makes sitting down to supper feel so difficult. We scatter in different directions each morning and are pulled in even more throughout the day. Your son needs to go to soccer practice, a meeting is running late, you forget to pick something up from the cleaners, and the list goes on. It's no wonder that the brightly lit drive-through promising inexpensive quick eats and no cleanup seems to call out so strongly. Worse yet are the evenings where bags are passed out in the car and the food is finished before arriving home, so that everyone just walks in the door and scatters again to their respective rooms (I speak from firsthand experience here).

But then we've missed *it*. We've scattered only to scatter again. Our loved ones have gone out into the world for that entire day and we missed our chance to see who they became as a result. Miss just a few of those days and we risk waking up in a house with people we no longer recognize. We grow apart and lose our strength as a family.

That is why coming home to supper is important. My favorite way to end the day is to gather around the dinner table with my family, holding hands as we give thanks for our meal and for each other, and then to pass the plates and fill our glasses as we talk about our days and I learn who my children became during their time away.

Our suppers together are the anchor that keeps us from drifting apart.

My mama told me a wonderful parenting secret when my firstborn was still a toddler. She said, "Christy, you have to sit down to supper every night and then just let them talk. You'll be amazed what they'll tell you. That is where you'll learn about their friends, what is going on in school, what they're struggling with. They'll open up and not even realize it—if you just sit down to supper together."

Believe me, I've had many of those drive-through paper-bag nights myself, and I'm not about to judge. We do what we have to do and sometimes that may mean eating on the run. But I hope this book will help you to make those nights few and far between.

These are the suppers I make for my family. They don't require a lot of time in the kitchen and they certainly don't require a large grocery budget. They're kid friendly and in most cases easily customizable for your own dietary needs and preferences.

The thing that bothers me about the food world today is that sometimes it seems we have entire channels dedicated to teaching folks how to cook the perfect filet mignon while we're sitting at home trying to come up with one more thing to do with a pound of ground beef. Filet mignon is great, but what we really need to know is how to keep a family of four fed and happy.

In this book, you'll find a whole slew of ground beef recipes that will work for those long days when you leave in the morning and won't be back until just before supper time. You'll see plenty of recipes for the slow cooker (indicated with an SC symbol), as well as tips and tricks for buying and using this workhorse appliance. You'll find lots of one-dish casseroles, skillet meals, and things you can make ahead of time, and you'll also find recipes and suggestions for pulling off the bigger meals as well. I've made sure to include plenty of chicken dishes, too, because from speaking to you I found that it is the meat served more often than any other in your homes. And you'll find plenty of recipes for pork, other cuts of beef, seafood, and a generous helping of simple sides. Dinner breads and make-ahead desserts round it all out.

I set out to write the one cookbook that I myself would use the most when it came to planning suppers for my family—I hope you'll find it as useful as I intended it to be. Please keep in mind, though, that the recipes in this book and the meals you and I make are really just a way to bring our families and friends together. Because, at the end of the day, the supper table is where we teach our families where they came from and they let us know where they hope to go. Values, heritage, history, dreams, and encouragement are passed around with the serving platters and roots grow a little deeper with each bite. We may have high hopes and aspirations when we set off into the world each morning, but if you really want to make the world a better place, end the day by coming home to supper.

—Christy Jordan

Come Home to Supper

1

Beef

My grandfather, Papa Reed, was a farmer. When I was growing up, he'd gift each of his children's families with a calf at Christmastime. We'd pile into Daddy's truck and go to the butcher to have him fill all of our coolers with ground beef, roasts, steaks, and stew meat. With the deep freezer full, we had beef aplenty for months after that. I still look to this versatile, flavorful meat when it comes to satisfying my cravings for hearty meals.

With times lean and our food budget stretched tight as a drum, having beef in the freezer was a considerable blessing to my family. I know it was a huge relief to my mother, who could whip up all manner of delicious suppers using beef as her key ingredient.

My stomach growls even now as I remember walking through the front door to the smell of Mama's roasts, hamburger steaks, and stews. Come to think of it, we never actually "walked" home. If we knew one of Mama's suppers was waiting on us, we ran!

Steak Fajitas

SERVES 4

This was one of my favorite dishes to order at Mexican restaurants until I began making it at home. Turns out fajitas are so simple to make, and they have even more flavor when prepared in this zesty lime marinade. In making them I also discovered a little trick: Transferring the beef to the freezer for a few minutes after marinating it makes it much easier to slice into thin strips.

FOR THE MARINADE

2 tablespoons fresh or bottled
   lime juice

3 tablespoons vegetable or olive oil

2 teaspoons minced garlic

1 teaspoon ground cumin

1 pound beef flank steak

1 large onion, cut into thin strips

2 bell peppers, stemmed, seeded,
   and cut into thin strips

8 to 10 large flour tortillas or
   Maria's Flour Tortillas
   (page 230)

Fresh cilantro leaves, sour cream, chopped tomatoes, and shredded cheese of your choice, for serving (optional)

1 Place the lime juice, 2 tablespoons of the oil, the garlic, and cumin in a gallon-size ziplock bag and shake to combine. Add the beef and let marinate in the refrigerator for at least 1 hour or up to 8 hours.

2 Thirty minutes before you plan to cook the beef, transfer the bag from the refrigerator to the freezer.

3 Remove the beef from the marinade (discard the marinade), transfer it to a cutting board, and slice it into ¼-inch-thick strips. Place the remaining tablespoon of oil in a large skillet and heat it over medium-high heat until it thins, 2 to 3 minutes. Add the beef and reduce the heat to medium. Cook, stirring often to prevent the beef from burning or sticking, until it is browned on the outside and no longer pink in the center, 7 to 10 minutes. Remove the beef from the skillet and set it aside.

4 Add the vegetables to the skillet and cook them over medium heat until they

Beef Kabobs

are lightly browned and slightly tender (you want to make sure they retain their crispness), 4 to 5 minutes.

5 To serve, divide the beef evenly among the tortillas. Top each serving with vegetables and the cilantro, sour cream, tomatoes, and cheese, if desired.

Beef Kabobs

MAKES 8 TO 12 KABOBS

Any supper becomes a special occasion when you serve these succulent beef kabobs. I like to customize mine for each person by loading them up with their favorite veggies. I prefer sweet cherry tomatoes, hearty rounds of zucchini, thick wedges of onion, and mushrooms. My husband and son stick with tomatoes and chunks of potato. If I have veggies left over, I make entire kabobs of only those vegetables to use as sides. I just cook them alongside my beef kabobs, as they are done in the same amount of time.

2 pounds top sirloin
1 recipe All-Purpose Marinade
   (page 284)
2 large onions, cut into wedges
1 pound cherry tomatoes, bell
   peppers (stemmed, seeded,
   and cut into 1-inch pieces),
   small mushrooms, and/or other
   vegetables of your choice

1 Using kitchen shears, cut the beef into bite-size cubes. Place the beef in a gallon-size ziplock bag and add 1 cup of the marinade. Let the beef marinate in the refrigerator for at least 1 hour or up to 8 hours.

2 Thirty minutes before you plan to cook the kabobs, preheat the oven to 350°F. Place 8 to 12 wooden skewers in a bowl and cover them with water to soak.

3 Remove the skewers from the bowl and thread the beef and vegetables onto them, placing at least one vegetable between the pieces of beef. Place the beef kabobs on an ungreased rimmed baking sheet and bake, turning every 10 minutes, until the beef is lightly browned on the outside and slightly pink in the very center, about 30 minutes. Serve hot.

Beef and Broccoli

SERVES 4

I have an old friend whose favorite dish is beef and broccoli. When she had to cut back on spending, Chinese takeout was the first luxury to go, so I set out to come up with a recipe that would taste even better than the restaurant version. She says this has ruined her for takeout now. The best part is that it feeds more, making it a great money saver!

3 tablespoons vegetable oil

2 tablespoons cornstarch

¼ teaspoon ground black pepper

1 pound top sirloin, cut into thin strips

1 pound fresh broccoli, cut into small florets (about 4 cups)

2 teaspoons minced garlic

¼ cup soy sauce

Hot cooked rice, for serving

1 Heat 2 tablespoons of the oil in a large skillet over medium-high heat. Place the cornstarch and pepper in a medium-size bowl and stir to combine. Add the beef strips to the bowl and stir to coat.

2 Transfer the coated beef strips to the hot skillet and cook, stirring often to prevent sticking, until the meat is lightly browned and no longer pink in the center, 4 to 5 minutes. Remove the beef from the skillet and set it aside.

3 Reduce the heat to medium and add the remaining tablespoon of oil, the broccoli, and the garlic. Cook, stirring frequently, until the broccoli is tender, 3 to 4 minutes.

4 Return the beef to the skillet along with the soy sauce and ⅓ cup water. Cook, stirring often, until the sauce thickens, 3 to 4 minutes.

5 Serve over the hot cooked rice.

Hamburger Steaks

SERVES 4

G rowing up, my siblings and I always loved Mama's hamburger steaks. There was nothing like coming home to the smell of onions bubbling in a skillet

No Sweat, You Got This!

Ever feel like you're in a speeding car with no one behind the wheel? Yeah, some days are like that. Sitting in the passenger side, careening down the road, and doing your best to brace for whatever is gonna happen next.

I don't know about you, but I prefer a bit more safety in cars and in life.

So take a deep breath and slide behind that wheel. Either we control our emotions or they control us, and emotions are terrible drivers.

Now slowly pull out into the day at your own pace, no need for your heart to be frantic.

Put a smile on your face—you got this! ♥

along with generous hamburger steak patties, knowing we were in for a hearty and delicious supper. I liked mine with extra onions, my brother and sister liked theirs without any at all, and Daddy liked whatever Mama put on his plate.

2 pounds ground beef

2 tablespoons vegetable oil

½ cup all-purpose flour

1 large sweet onion, such as Vidalia, thinly sliced

1 cup beef broth (see Note, page 23)

1 Shape the ground beef into four doughnut-shaped ½-inch-thick patties (the hole in the center will allow the patties to cook evenly and will fill in as the patties shrink during cooking).

2 Heat the oil in a large nonstick skillet over medium heat. Dip each patty into the flour, making sure to coat both sides, then place the patties in the skillet. Cook until browned, 3 to 5 minutes on each side.

3 Move the patties to one side of the skillet and add the onion on the other.

Cook the onions, stirring, until they are lightly browned, 2 to 3 minutes.

4 Spread the hamburger patties back out among the onions and pour the beef broth into the skillet. Cover and continue cooking until the meat is no longer pink in the center, about 10 minutes. Serve hot.

Janice's Stuffed Bell Peppers

SERVES 4

There are tons of ways to make stuffed bell peppers and I've never found one I didn't like. This recipe from my mother is my go-to because it is so simple to make and so delicious. I like to make a double batch on the weekend and serve some for supper one night, saving a few to reheat for lunches throughout the week. They also freeze really well—just let them come to room temperature, cover, and freeze them for up to three months (see the Note on page 8 for reheating instructions).

When my garden is in season, I use green bell peppers that I grow myself. At other times, though, I just buy whatever bell peppers are on sale.

Cooking spray
1 cup uncooked white rice
1 teaspoon salt
1 pound ground beef or turkey
1 small onion, chopped
1 teaspoon chopped garlic
2 teaspoons chili powder
½ teaspoon ground black pepper
1 can (10 ounces) condensed tomato
    soup
4 medium-size bell peppers
1 cup shredded Cheddar cheese,
    plus more to sprinkle on top

1 Preheat the oven to 350°F. Coat an 8-inch square baking dish with the cooking spray.

2 Place 2 cups of water in a medium-size saucepan over medium-high heat. Rinse the rice in a colander and add the rice to the water. Bring just to a boil, then reduce the heat to low, cover, and allow the rice to simmer until all the water is absorbed, about 15 minutes. Set aside.

Janice's Stuffed
Bell Peppers

3 Fill a large pot with water, add the salt, and bring to a boil over high heat.

4 Meanwhile, heat a large skillet over medium heat. Place the ground beef, onion, and garlic in the hot skillet and cook until the meat is browned, about 10 minutes. Drain off and discard the grease, then add the chili powder, black pepper, tomato soup, and reserved rice and stir to combine. Reduce the heat to low and let simmer for 10 minutes.

5 While the mixture is simmering, cut off the tops of the bell peppers and scoop out the seeds with a spoon. Drop the bell peppers into the boiling water and simmer for 5 minutes. Carefully remove the peppers with tongs, draining the water as you do so, and place them in the prepared baking dish, cut side up.

6 Add 1 cup of the Cheddar cheese to the beef mixture and stir until combined. Spoon the mixture into the peppers and top each with additional cheese.

7 Bake the peppers until heated through and the cheese is melted, 10 to 15 minutes. Serve warm.

NOTE: To reheat frozen peppers, simply place them in a baking dish straight from the freezer and put them into a cold oven. Turn the oven to 350°F and bake the peppers until they're heated through, about 30 minutes.

Hobo Packets
SERVES 4

Do you sometimes feel as though you are running a short-order kitchen? If so, hobo packets will make that job easier. These delicious meals-in-one, complete with meat and veggies, are assembled in foil packets, with everyone having their own little packet meal when they're done! I just put together the patties, set them in the packets, and lay out the other ingredients so each person can design his or her own meal. My kids love getting to make their own dinner and there is very little work for us adults.

This recipe can be modified to use boneless chicken breasts or even pork chops in place of the beef, but ground beef is my personal favorite because of its convenience and cost. If you have a vegetarian in the house, just omit the meat and use more veggies!

2 pounds ground beef

1 medium-size onion, sliced into rings

4 medium-size russet potatoes, unpeeled, scrubbed, and cut into bite-size chunks

1 pound carrots, sliced into bite-size pieces

Salt and pepper to taste

½ cup All-Purpose Marinade (page 284; optional)

1 Preheat the oven to 350°F.

2 Divide the ground beef into four ½-inch-thick patties and place each in the center of a large sheet of aluminum foil. Divide the onion rings, potatoes, and carrots among the patties, placing them on top of the meat. Season with salt and pepper and add 2 tablespoons of marinade to each packet, if using. Fold and seal the packets well.

3 Place the packets on a baking sheet and bake until the meat is cooked through and the vegetables are tender, 45 minutes to 1 hour.

4 To serve, carefully open each packet and allow the steam to vent. Adults usually eat right out of their packet, but for kids I remove the contents to a plate, as the packets are very hot.

"I am determined to be cheerful and happy in whatever situation I may find myself. For I have learned that the greater part of our misery or unhappiness is determined not by our circumstances but by our disposition."

— *Martha Washington*

Beef Patties with Ketchup Gravy (SC)

SERVES 4

This dish takes some of my go-to budget-friendly ingredients and combines them in a delicious one-pot meal. When made in a slow cooker, this is a wonderfully effortless meal to come home to (but I've given you stovetop directions, too). I dearly love ketchup, so this mild-tasting gravy is right up my alley!

½ sleeve saltine crackers
(about 18 crackers)

1 large egg

2 pounds ground beef

⅔ cup ketchup

1 tablespoon dried Italian seasoning

1 medium-size onion, chopped

1 bell pepper, stemmed, seeded, and chopped

2 cups hot cooked rice, for serving

1 If using a traditional oven, preheat it to 325°F.

2 Crush the saltines and place them in a large bowl. Add the egg and ground beef and mix well with your hands. Form the beef mixture into four ½-inch-thick patties. Place the patties in a 6-quart slow cooker or a Dutch oven.

3 In a small bowl, stir together the ketchup, Italian seasoning, and ⅓ cup water. Pour the ketchup mixture over the beef in the pot and top with the onion and bell pepper.

4 *If using a slow cooker:* Cover and seal the pot and cook until the beef patties are tender and no longer pink in the center, 7 to 8 hours on low, 3 to 4 hours on high. *If using a Dutch oven:* Cover, place over medium heat, and cook 1½ hours.

5 Serve the patties over the hot cooked rice with the gravy spooned on top.

Mama's Meat Loaf
PAGE 12

Mama's Meat Loaf

SERVES 4 TO 6

This is a delicious all-around meat loaf that turns out great whether you serve it as is or use it for my Meat Loaf with All the Trimmings (below). Either way, it comes out flavorful and moist every time.

2 pounds ground chuck

1 can (8 ounces) tomato sauce

½ cup cracker crumbs or quick-cooking oatmeal

2 large eggs, beaten

½ cup chopped onion

⅓ cup chopped bell pepper

1 clove garlic, diced

1 teaspoon salt

½ teaspoon ground black pepper

¼ cup ketchup

1 Preheat the oven to 400°F.

2 In a large bowl, combine the ground chuck, tomato sauce, cracker crumbs, eggs, onion, bell pepper, garlic, salt, and black pepper, and mix well (use your hands!). Form into a loaf, pressing firmly to compact it (this helps seal in the juices).

3 Pat the meat loaf into a loaf pan and bake until it is browned and juices run clear, about 1 hour. Remove the meat loaf from the oven and, keeping it in the pan, spread the ketchup over the top. Return it to the oven for 10 minutes more.

4 Drain any grease off the meat loaf and let it rest for 10 minutes before serving.

Meat Loaf with All the Trimmings sc

SERVES 4

Meat loaf is a working family's classic meal. This recipe allows you to serve meat loaf with two completely different sides, and two completely different flavors, too!

The meat loaf is prepared in a slow cooker and is separated from the vegetables, which are cooked in foil packets on top of the meat. The finishing touch is a nice thick layer of ketchup baked on top of the meat just before serving.

An entrée and two sides with only one vessel to wash when you're done—I didn't think it was possible to improve a classic, but we just did!

Cooking spray

1 recipe Mama's Meat Loaf
    (page 12), uncooked

3 to 4 medium-size red potatoes,
    unpeeled, scrubbed, and cut into
    wedges

½ teaspoon kosher salt

Ground black pepper to taste

Dried herbs, such as dill or parsley,
    or dried Italian seasoning
    (optional)

¼ cup (½ stick) butter

1 bell pepper, stemmed, seeded and
    cut into thin strips (see Note)

1 small sweet onion, such as Vidalia,
    sliced into rings (see Note)

1 yellow squash, cut into 1/4-inch-
    thick slices (see Note)

½ cup ketchup

❶ Coat the bottom and sides of a 6-quart oval slow cooker with cooking spray. Pat the meat loaf into the bottom of the slow cooker, pressing firmly to compact the loaf (this helps seal in the juices).

❷ Place the potatoes in the center of a large piece of aluminum foil. Sprinkle with ¼ teaspoon of the salt, some black pepper, and the seasoning of your choice, if desired, and place 2 tablespoons of the butter on top. Fold the foil to form a sealed packet.

❸ Place the bell pepper strips, onion rings, and squash slices in the center of another large piece of aluminum foil. Sprinkle with the remaining salt, some black pepper, and the seasoning of your choice, if desired, and place the remaining 2 tablespoons of butter on top. Fold the foil to form a sealed packet.

❹ Place a piece of foil on top of the meat loaf in the slow cooker. Set the vegetable packets side by side on top of the foil. Cover and cook until the veggies are tender and the meat juices run clear, 7 to 8 hours on low, 3 to 4 hours on high.

❺ Fifteen minutes before serving, preheat the oven to 400°F. Using oven mitts, carefully remove the vegetable packets

Slow Cooker 101

According to a Hamilton Beach study conducted in 2011, 80 percent of consumers who own a slow cooker use it weekly. And nearly half of those people have more than one—a clear testament to how handy and useful these humble appliances are! Since this book is filled with supper recipes that I cook on a regular basis, you're going to find a lot of slow-cooker recipes included throughout (look for this icon: SC).

Other than my hand mixer, my slow cooker is absolutely the most useful counter-top appliance in my kitchen. I use it several times a week, at least! It's not just for main dishes either; it's also great for desserts and sides. I have so many wonderful slow-cooker recipes that I have actually acquired *five* slow cookers (of varying sizes) and use each of them regularly.

Everyone who knows my work schedule knows that often a slow cooker is my secret to getting supper on the table. So when folks are about to buy a new slow cooker, I am often asked for advice. Here's what I tell them:

HOW TO CHOOSE A SLOW COOKER

If your slow cooker is more than ten years old, I recommend purchasing a new one. As the older models age, they often don't heat as well as they used to. And if you have a slow cooker with a nonremovable crock, replace it *quickly*—those are no longer considered safe to use.

You can pick up a great new slow cooker for anywhere from $30 to $60. There are a few key things to look for when considering which one to buy.

First, consider the various features. **Programmable slow cookers** are a great option for always-on-the-go families. You can program your cook time and then set the slow cooker to switch automatically to warm when cooking is done; it will hold your food at the perfect temperature until you get home, and will prevent overcooking.

New slow cookers have a range of **temperature options.** I love that they typically have a "warm" option in addition to the standard low and high cooking temperatures. If I'm going to be home working all day, I like to get supper done by early afternoon and then switch it to warm until the family gets home.

My favorite slow cookers are travel-friendly ones with a **clamp-down, sealing lid.** I've always enjoyed toting soups, stews, and even desserts to events in my slow cooker, but whenever I did this in the past, I always arrived with a big mess on my hands. Nowadays, many slow cookers come with a rubber seal around the lid and clamps that hold the lid down, sealing in the contents and letting you travel without a single spill. I've also found that sealing and clamping the lid before cooking helps the contents cook faster.

I prefer an **oval-shape slow cooker** to a round one. A whole chicken or roast just fits more easily in this oval shape.

Slow cookers come in **a variety of sizes.** The six-quart is the number one most popular—and for good reason. When you're cooking for four to six people (or fewer people but with leftovers in mind), it's ideal.

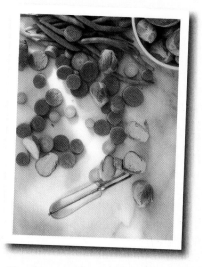

The four- to five-quart is the second most popular size. It's perfect for desserts and smaller meals, especially if you're just cooking for two.

The two-quart size is great for making a full meal for one or a small meal for two. I use mine to make spaghetti sauce, and let it simmer in the pot all day long.

My favorite is a six-quart Stay or Go Portable Slow Cooker by Hamilton Beach. It has the clamp-down lid, rubber seal, programming functions, and room for a satisfying meal that will easily feed four to six. Mine also comes with a meat probe that allows you to check the internal temperature of a piece of meat. Although I've never used it, I'm sure it would be handy! This is the one countertop appliance I simply cannot live without.

from the slow cooker. Set the packets aside. Using oven mitts or tongs, carefully pull back the foil from the top of the meat loaf. Spread the ketchup over the top of the meat loaf.

6 Transfer the crock with the meat loaf to the oven and bake until the ketchup is thickened and browned around the edges, about 10 minutes.

7 To serve, scoop out helpings of meat loaf onto each plate, along with portions of both sides.

NOTE: You can use a 12-ounce bag of your favorite frozen vegetable blend in place of the fresh veggies.

Meatballs (and Their Many Uses!)

MAKES ABOUT 100 MEATBALLS

Frozen cooked meatballs can be a supper-time lifesaver because they heat up quickly and there are so many ways to use them. I regularly prepare batches of this recipe—which makes *a lot* of meatballs!—and store a bunch in the freezer. When I need a quick meal, I simply place fifteen to twenty frozen meatballs in a pot and add one of the sauces on pages 283–284. I cook them over medium heat until heated through and serve them with rice, egg noodles, or another cooked pasta or grain.

Although this recipe calls for ground beef, turkey meatballs are yummy (and more healthful), too.

5 pounds ground beef

1½ cups quick-cooking oats or cooked rice

2 large eggs

1 can (16 ounces) tomato sauce or 2 cups ketchup

1 tablespoon salt

½ tablespoon ground black pepper

1 Preheat the oven to 350°F. Line 2 baking sheets with aluminum foil.

2 Place all of the ingredients in a large bowl and mix well with your hands until combined.

3 Scoop out and form the meat mixture into balls approximately 1 inch in diameter. Place as many meatballs as will comfortably fit on the prepared baking sheets, leaving about 1 inch or so between them. (Store the remaining meat mixture, covered, in the refrigerator.)

4 Bake the meatballs until cooked through and no longer pink in the center (cut one in half to check), about 30 minutes. Remove the baking sheets from the oven and set the meatballs aside to cool (unless using immediately). Replace the foil on each baking sheet.

5 Form, bake, and cool the remaining meat mixture in batches as directed. Once cool, place them in freezer bags and store them in the freezer for up to 3 months.

Meatball Subs

To make these into delicious meatball sub sandwiches, divide 12 baked meatballs evenly among four 6-inch sub rolls. Top with one recipe Simple Marinara Sauce (page 284) or 1½ cups (12 ounces) of your favorite store-bought marinara sauce, warmed on the stovetop, and 1 cup of shredded mozzarella cheese.

Spaghetti and Meatballs

SERVES 4

In the course of writing my books, I've ended up having to travel from time to time for various reasons, which naturally means eating lots of dinners out. No matter how nice the restaurant or how many stars the chef has, nothing on the road ever tastes as good as a meal in my own home. The kids know that spaghetti is a favorite of mine, so this is a recipe they make for me the night I get back. Of course, I keep the meatballs in the freezer to make it easy for them.

1 package (16 ounces) spaghetti
15 to 20 frozen meatballs (homemade, page 16, or store-bought)
4 cups store-bought spaghetti sauce or 1 recipe Simple Marinara Sauce (page 284)

1 Bring a large pot of salted water to a boil over high heat, add the spaghetti, and cook according to package directions. Drain the spaghetti in a colander and set it aside.

2 Meanwhile, place the frozen meatballs in a large pot over medium heat and pour the sauce over them. Cook, stirring frequently, until the meatballs are heated through and the sauce is bubbling, 15 to 20 minutes.

3 Serve over the hot spaghetti.

Easy Stroganoff

SERVES 4

No cookbook would be complete without this ultimate comfort food. Who can go wrong with meatballs in a creamy sauce served over hot egg noodles? This recipe always brings back childhood memories of being in my grandmother's kitchen when she made this for my siblings and me. Now I realize that the reason she probably made it for us was the ease of preparation! Whatever her reason, the results were always the same—our smiling faces as we dug in to this delicious dish!

1 package (16 ounces) egg noodles

15 to 20 frozen meatballs (homemade, page 16, or store-bought)

1 recipe Cream of Mushroom Soup (page 282) or 1 can (10.5 ounces) condensed cream of mushroom soup

½ cup milk

2 tablespoons Worcestershire sauce (optional)

¼ teaspoon kosher salt

⅛ teaspoon ground black pepper

1 Bring a large pot of salted water to a boil over high heat, add the egg noodles, and cook according to package directions. Drain the noodles in a colander and set them aside.

2 Meanwhile, place the frozen meatballs in a large pot and pour the soup over them. Add the milk, Worcestershire sauce, if using, and salt and pepper, and stir constantly over medium heat, until the Stroganoff is heated through and bubbly, 25 to 30 minutes.

3 Serve over the hot cooked noodles.

Smothered Steak sc

SERVES 4

Round steak is normally a pretty tough cut of meat, but when cooked slow and low in this tasty sauce, it becomes perfectly tender while still maintaining that steak "bite" we love so much. Soy sauce is the secret to bringing out the wonderful flavor of the beef in this dish. If you'd like to load up on veggies, toss in two to three carrots cut into bite-size pieces and one sliced bell pepper. I like to serve this with Roasted Asparagus (page 171) and creamy mac and cheese (page 166).

> 3 tablespoons all-purpose flour
> ½ teaspoon salt
> ¼ teaspoon ground black pepper
> ¼ teaspoon garlic powder
> 2 pounds round steak
> 1 medium-size onion, diced
> 2 cups chopped fresh tomatoes or
>   1 can (14.5 ounces) diced
>   tomatoes in juice
> ¼ cup soy sauce
> 4 cups hot cooked rice, for serving

1 If using a traditional oven, preheat it to 325°F.

2 Place the flour, salt, pepper, and garlic powder in a gallon-size ziplock bag. Seal the bag and shake well to combine.

3 Using kitchen shears, cut the round steak into bite-size pieces. Add them to the bag, seal it, and shake well to coat.

4 Pour the contents of the bag into a 4-quart slow cooker or a 5-quart Dutch oven with a lid. Sprinkle the onion on top of the meat and pour the tomatoes and soy sauce over all. Stir to combine.

5 *If using a slow cooker:* Cover and seal the pot and cook until the meat is fork tender, 7 to 8 hours on low, 3 to 4 hours on high. *If using a Dutch oven:* Cover the pot and bake until the meat is fork tender, about 2 hours.

6 Spoon the meat over the hot cooked rice and serve.

Enjoy Life—There Are No Refunds

A while back I decided to surprise my family by renting a large cabin in the Smoky Mountains. I invited my brother and sister-in-law, their two children, and my mother- and father-in-law for a big old family getaway.

To make the trip even more special, we kept it a secret from the kids. I spent weeks imagining their surprised faces at finding out where we were going and then being greeted by their cousins and grandparents upon arrival. I'd been looking forward to the weekend for quite some time and was thrilled when it was finally time to pack up. As soon as my husband, Ricky, got off work Friday, we loaded up the car (dog and all) and set off. It was such fun to have the kids guess where we were headed for the first hour of the drive, and then finally doing the big reveal!

But you know what they say about the best-laid plans....

About two hours into our trip we realized that the winter storm we were driving through was something we just couldn't ignore. Long story short: We had to turn around and go back home. Although Ricky's parents had managed to reach the cabin, the road leading to its mountaintop perch had since been covered in snow and ice; they were relying on hope and sun to be able to get down the following day. Ricky's brother and his family had to turn back and go home as well.

The kids were heartbroken, and we made the

trip home in silence, with tears from the peanut gallery in the backseat.

The bright side of this situation was obvious: We were lucky we weren't stuck on the mountain or on dangerous roads where we could easily have had a wreck. Still, I have to admit, I'd much rather have been in that cabin on a mountaintop looking out over the snow. I hid my disappointment as one thought kept reverberating through my mind: Our little weekend getaway wasn't going to happen and there were no refunds. All that money I'd spent renting the cabin was just gone, and we would never get it—or those three days—back.

Then a question came to me: How were those three days any different from any other three days? No matter where we were, at home or in a cabin on a mountain, there were still no refunds on this weekend.

The next day I woke up with renewed determination. While we didn't get to spend time together in a cabin, we still got to spend time *together*. Ricky and I took the kids to a nearby town for the day and helped our son earn a new Boy Scout badge. We made brownies and shopped for groceries as a family. In between, the

kids petted our newly adopted dog so much it's a wonder she didn't get bald spots. And we had a nice little time in our warm little house.

As a result of our "ruined" weekend, I awakened to the realization that whether you're at home or on vacation, *each day is a one-shot deal*. Instead of pining for a view from someone else's window, take a moment to appreciate the view from your own. We may not be in a rented cabin, but that doesn't mean we can't spend just as much quality time with our children in our own living room.

Make the most of today. Use it up, wear it out, squeeze every last ounce of "good" out of it. Even if you aren't financially invested in it, there are still no refunds. ♥

Ground Beef Stew (SC)

SERVES 4 TO 6

This is one of my favorite stews because it's so flavorful and easily adapted to whatever I have in my pantry and freezer. A lot of people like to make a stew toward the end of the week as a way of using up any leftover vegetable side dishes. In the old days, folks even used to keep a "stew bowl" in their refrigerator or freezer and put any leftovers in it just to use in recipes such as this.

I have one special ingredient here that I do hope you'll try: Spicy Hot V8 vegetable juice. It's what gives this stew such a full-bodied flavor without my having to add a gazillion different spices. Don't worry, though, it doesn't make it hot at all, just adds a delicious underlying flavor.

Cooking spray (optional)

1 to 2 pounds ground beef or turkey

2 to 3 carrots, diced

1 medium-size onion, chopped

5 potatoes, peeled and diced

2 cups frozen green beans

1 can (29 ounces) diced or crushed tomatoes, with their liquid

2 to 3 cups Spicy Hot V8 vegetable juice

2 cups beef broth (see Note)

1 teaspoon salt or to taste

¼ teaspoon ground black pepper

1 Heat a large skillet over medium heat. (If using turkey, spray the pan lightly with cooking spray.) Add the ground meat and cook, stirring and chopping with a wooden spoon to break it into small, crumbled pieces, until fully browned, about 10 minutes.

2 Drain the meat well and place it in a 6-quart stockpot with a lid or a slow cooker. Add the carrots, onion, potatoes, green beans, tomatoes, vegetable juice, beef broth, salt, and pepper to the pot.

3 *If using a stockpot:* Bring the mixture to a boil over medium heat, stirring often, then reduce the heat and simmer, uncovered, stirring every 15 minutes until the vegetables are tender, 1 hour. *If using a slow cooker:* Cover and seal the pot and cook until the vegetables are tender, 7 to 8 hours on low, 3 to 4 hours on high. Serve hot.

NOTE: Bouillon cubes are an economical and space-saving substitution for canned broth. Simply dissolve 1 cube in 1 cup of hot water and use as you would regular broth.

Slow-Cooker FAQs

How long should it cook?

Most slow-cooker recipes will cook in three to four hours on high and seven to eight hours on low. Resist the urge to raise the lid unless your recipe clearly directs you to do so—it will result in significant heat loss and add approximately twenty minutes to your cooking time.

Do I really need a liner?

Nope. A lot of people like to use these because they make cleanup easy, but they're really not necessary. Most slow-cooker crocks have such a thick glaze, they're simple to hand wash. Any cooked-on debris comes off if it's allowed to soak for just a few minutes.

I see liners as an additional expense, but if you enjoy them, then by all means use them. They will work just fine with my slow-cooker recipes.

What meats do well in a slow cooker?

Naturally tough cuts with a lot of connective tissue, such as chuck roasts and short ribs, are great candidates for slow cooking. The right recipe can make the toughest meat fall-apart tender when it's cooked low and slow with a savory, well-seasoned gravy.

Less "challenging" meats, such as chicken and pork chops, are also excellent when cooked this way. Think of your slow cooker not so much as a countertop appliance but a small oven.

How much do I fill it?

A slow-cooker pot should always be filled at least halfway but have at least one inch of breathing room at the top. Underfilling can cause the food to overcook, while overfilling can cause it to boil over and spill. Keep in mind that unlike in an oven or on a stovetop, liquids don't evaporate during slow cooking; this means less liquid will be needed when preparing slow-cooker recipes.

Teach Your Kids to Cook

Back in the old days, Mom stayed home to look after the house and kids while Dad went to work. This meant kids got to help out in the kitchen and watch Mom cook, learning valuable life skills as they did so. It also meant that supper was generally ready when Dad got home from work so the entire family could sit down together.

Times they are a-changing.

I'm not saying change is bad. It's just that change is change and we have to find new ways to adapt.

For the past few generations, many mothers haven't been home to cook and many children haven't had anyone there to show them how. As a result, we're losing both the ability to cook and the recipes that we've traditionally passed down through our families. Each day more and more adults find themselves out in the world wishing they had paid better attention in their high school home economics class!

This is a big motivation behind my website—the knowledge that there are so many people desperately trying to learn to cook for themselves or their families. I have received countless emails from men and women of all ages, thanking me and telling me that Southern Plate taught them how to cook.

I hope in this book you'll find more recipes to inspire you. I know you work hard and I know you're tired and I know your grocery budget is more in line with ground beef than lobster. But I do hope you'll get your kids in the kitchen with you and bring back the tradition of passing along your knowledge, skills, and recipes. Preparing a meal is best done as a family whenever possible. Allowing kids to help out builds in them a sense of confidence, passes on a needed skill, and allows you to spend even more time together. Spouses are no exception—although I admit that I'm far happier when my husband offers to help with the dishes than when he offers to help with the meal! ♥

Coca-Cola Roast sc

SERVES 4

We love our Coca-Cola where I'm from and we love to cook with it, too! Some call it soda, some call it pop, but in my neck of the woods you'll be asked "You wanna Coke?" And if you answer yes, the follow-up question is "What kind?"

In this recipe Coke acts as a wonderful tenderizer for the meat and lends a delicious flavor to the final sauce. Feel free to use whatever brand you prefer.

1 chuck roast (3½ to 5 pounds)

1 pound baby carrots

4 to 5 medium-size potatoes, peeled and cubed

1 recipe Cream of Mushroom Soup (page 282) or 1 can (10.5 ounces) condensed cream of mushroom soup

1 can (12 ounces) Coca-Cola or other cola

1 If using a traditional oven, preheat it to 325°F.

2 Place the roast in the bottom of a 6-quart slow cooker or Dutch oven and add the carrots and potatoes. Pour the soup and Coke over all.

3 *If using a slow cooker:* Cover and seal the pot and cook the roast until tender, 8 hours on low, 4 hours on high. *If using a Dutch oven:* Cover the pot and bake until the roast is tender, 2½ hours.

4 To serve, place the roast and veggies on a serving platter, slice, and serve with the gravy alongside.

Tuscany Pot Roast and Vegetables sc

SERVES 4

The white vinegar in this dish is just enough to add a gentle tang, and Italian seasoning really enhances the flavor of the vegetables and meat. Don't forget to add your beef gravy, though, so that roast has something yummy and good to simmer in!

1 chuck roast (3½ to 5 pounds)

5 to 6 carrots, cut into chunks

5 to 6 medium-size russet potatoes, peeled and cubed

1 recipe Basic Beef Gravy (page 285) or 1 jar (12 ounces) beef gravy

½ cup white vinegar

2 tablespoons dried Italian seasoning

1 If using a traditional oven, preheat it to 325°F.

2 Place the roast in a 6-quart slow cooker or Dutch oven with a lid and add the carrots and potatoes.

3 In a medium-size bowl, mix together the beef gravy, white vinegar, and Italian seasoning. Pour the gravy mixture over the roast.

4 *If using a slow cooker:* Cover and seal the pot and cook the roast until tender, 8 hours on low, or 4 hours on high. *If using a Dutch oven:* Cover the pot and bake until the roast is tender, 2½ hours.

5 To serve, place the roast and veggies on a serving platter, slice, and serve with the gravy alongside.

"Treasure each other in the recognition that we do not know how long we shall have each other."

—*Joshua Liebman*

Always Tender Roast and Vegetables SC

SERVES 4

When I was growing up my mother always made a special dinner for each member of our family on his or her birthday. We got to pick out our favorite meal, start to finish, and she'd have it ready and waiting when we got home for supper. I always picked pot roast, cooked slow and low in a thick beef gravy with root vegetables.

Is Your Roast Tough?

I love a good roast that is so tender you can cut it with the gentle pressure of a fork. If your roasts aren't turning out like this, there are usually two solutions to the problem.

1. Don't cook a roast in water. Usually when folks tell me their roast is tough, it turns out they are cooking it in water. Pot roast is a cheaper cut of meat and needs a good sauce, such as beef gravy or cream soup, to help tenderize it as it cooks.

2. Cook it a little bit longer. It's easy to make the mistake of removing a roast when it's just done, but extra time is needed to allow the meat to become tender. Cooking your roast even thirty minutes longer than usual can make a big difference. As long as you're cooking "slow and low," such as in a slow cooker or a 325°F oven, this extra cook time will allow the connective tissues in the meat to break down, resulting in a fork-tender roast.

My time-honored pot roast recipe is versatile: Though I prefer to cook it in my slow cooker, a heavy-lidded Dutch oven works just as well. I'm sharing this one and a few variations in these pages; each is slightly different from the next. I alternate between them whenever I make roasts, and I'm always surprised at the difference in flavors just a slight tweak in ingredients can make.

1 chuck roast (4 to 5 pounds)
1 teaspoon kosher salt
¼ teaspoon ground black pepper
4 to 6 large carrots (see Note)
6 medium-size russet potatoes
     (see Note)
1 medium-size onion (optional)
1 recipe Basic Beef Gravy
     (page 285) or 1 jar (16 ounces)
     beef gravy

1 If using a traditional oven, preheat it to 325°F.

2 Place the roast in a 6-quart slow cooker or Dutch oven with a lid and sprinkle the salt and pepper on top.

3 Peel and cut the carrots and potatoes into bite-size chunks and place them on top of the roast. Peel and quarter the onion, if using, and add it to the pot. Pour the beef gravy over all.

4 *If using a slow cooker:* Cover and seal the pot and cook until the roast is tender, 8 hours on low, 4 hours on high. *If using a Dutch oven:* Cover the pot and bake until the roast is tender, 2½ hours.

5 To serve, place the roast and vegetables on a serving platter, slice, and serve with the gravy alongside.

NOTE: It doesn't matter how many carrots or potatoes you use, as long as everything fits in your pot! I try to add extra carrots because my son loves them, especially when cooked in this delicious gravy.

Steak Tips Over Rice sc

SERVES 4

I began making this dish when Ricky and I first got married, then often through those lean years of early marriage and young kids because it is so economical and tasty. Stew meat is the secret to these fall-apart tender "steak tips." I often find packages of them marked down, and I freeze them and toss them in the slow cooker on busy days to simmer all day long. Serving these on hectic evenings as part of a rice bowl makes for a quick meal that everyone enjoys.

> 1½ pounds beef stew meat or chuck
>   roast, cut into bite-size pieces
> 1 large onion, sliced into rings
> 1 recipe Basic Beef Gravy
>   (page 285) or 1 jar (12 ounces)
>   beef gravy
> 1 teaspoon kosher salt
> ½ teaspoon ground black pepper
> 4 cups hot cooked rice, for serving

Always Tender Roast
and Vegetables
PAGE 26

What Is Stew Meat?

Stew meat is a general term for bite-size pieces of beef—usually on the tough side—that have been trimmed from roasts and steaks. It is sold in packages and is usually found next to roasts in your grocery. You can make your own high-quality stew meat by purchasing a chuck roast and cutting it into bite-size pieces using a knife or kitchen shears.

1 If using a traditional oven, preheat it to 325°F.

2 Combine the beef and onion in a 4-quart slow cooker or a Dutch oven with a lid. Cover with the beef gravy and sprinkle with the salt and pepper.

3 *If using a slow cooker:* Cover and seal the pot and cook until the meat is fork tender, 7 to 8 hours on low, 3 to 4 hours on high. *If using a Dutch oven:* Cover and bake until the meat is fork tender, 2 hours.

4 Spoon over the hot cooked rice to serve.

Tomato-Less Beef Stew SC

SERVES 4 TO 6

I worked up this recipe especially for my aunt Sue, who makes the world's best pound cake but can't eat tomatoes. How are those two related? Well, beyond me just putting them in a sentence together I reckon that's about it, but you can get her pound cake recipe in my first cookbook (wink).

I like to add a marinade like Dale's Steak Seasoning or Moore's Original Marinade to the stew because it's an easy way to round out the flavor. If you don't have these marinades where you live, you can make your own using my recipe on page 284.

1 cup all-purpose flour

2 pounds beef stew meat, cut into bite-size pieces

2 tablespoons vegetable oil

4 cups beef broth (see Note, page 23)

½ cup Dale's Seasoning or Moore's Original Marinade or All-Purpose Marinade (page 284)

5 medium-size potatoes, unpeeled, scrubbed, and cubed

4 large carrots, sliced into ½-inch chunks

1½ cups frozen pearl onions or 1 large onion, chopped

1 tablespoon dried Italian seasoning

1 teaspoon kosher salt

1 teaspoon ground black pepper

1 If using a traditional oven, preheat it to 325°F.

2 Place the flour in a large bowl, add the meat, and stir to coat. Transfer the coated meat, shaking off the excess flour, to a plate.

3 Place the oil in a large skillet and set over medium-high heat. Add the meat and cook, stirring often, just until browned on all sides, about 5 minutes.

4 Transfer the browned meat to a 6-quart slow cooker or heavy Dutch oven with a lid and add the beef broth, marinade, potatoes, carrots, onions, Italian seasoning, salt, and pepper.

5 *If using a slow cooker:* Cover and seal the pot and cook until the meat and vegetables are tender, 7 to 8 hours on low, 3 to 4 hours on high. *If using a Dutch oven:* Cover and bake until the meat and vegetables are tender, 2 hours.

6 Transfer the stew to a large serving dish and serve.

"It is neither wealth nor splendor; but tranquility and occupation which give you happiness."

—*Thomas Jefferson*

Lasagna

Lasagna (SC)

SERVES 6 TO 8

I love how my grandmother says "Italian." Instead of its more common pronunciation, she says it like "Eye-talian," as in "That Eye-talian food sure is good!"

Well, this is one of my Eye-talian recipes. It's very easy—you don't even have to boil the noodles! Everyone who's eaten this at my house requests the recipe; there is no telling how many times I've printed it out for folks over the years. It yields a delicious lasagna, rich with cheeses and meat.

2 pounds ground beef or turkey

½ teaspoon salt

¼ teaspoon ground black pepper

Double recipe of Simple Marinara
    Sauce (page 284) or 2 jars
    (24 ounces each) spaghetti sauce

1 container (16 ounces) cottage
    cheese

2 cups shredded mozzarella cheese

1 box (8 to 9 ounces) lasagna
    noodles, uncooked

1 If using a traditional oven, preheat it to 350°F.

2 Heat a large skillet over medium heat. Place the beef, salt, and pepper in the skillet and cook, using a wooden spoon to break it into small pieces, until fully browned, about 10 minutes. Drain off the grease. Stir in the sauce and set aside.

3 Place the cottage cheese and mozzarella in a medium-size bowl and stir until well combined.

4 Spoon one third of the sauce mixture into a 6-quart slow cooker or Dutch oven. Add a layer of uncooked noodles, breaking them as needed to make them fit. Top the noodles with one third of the cheese mixture. Repeat this layering twice more, reserving a small amount of sauce for the very top.

5 *If using a slow cooker:* Cover and seal the pot and cook on low until the pasta is tender, 6 to 8 hours. *If using a Dutch oven:* Bake, covered, for 1 hour.

6 Using a long, sharp knife, carefully cut the lasagna into squares while still in the pot and then remove the servings to a platter or individual plates with a spatula.

One-Skillet Chili "Bake"

SERVES 3 TO 4

This recipe is what I refer to as perfect "man food." It is hearty and filling, can be made spicier if you like, and involves very little effort on your part. What's more, it is eaten with chips, so you can go back to your caveman roots and ditch the utensils (my kids love that part!).

> 1 pound ground beef
> 1 can (15 ounces) red kidney beans
> 1 can (10 ounces) Ro*Tel Original or
>   1 can (12 ounces) diced tomatoes,
>   plus 1 can (4 ounces) chopped
>   green chiles (see Note)
> ½ cup uncooked white rice
> 2 tablespoons chili powder
> 1 cup shredded Cheddar cheese
> Tortilla chips or corn chips, for
>   serving

1 Heat a large skillet over medium heat. Place the beef in the skillet and cook, stirring to break it up, until it is no longer pink, 8 to 10 minutes. Drain off and discard any grease.

2 Add the kidney beans, Ro*Tel, rice, chili powder, and 1 cup of water and stir well to combine. Continue cooking, uncovered, over medium heat just until the mixture begins to bubble, then reduce the heat to low and simmer, covered, until the rice is tender, 20 minutes.

3 Uncover the skillet, top the beef mixture with the cheese, and cook until the cheese melts, 3 to 5 minutes. Scoop out onto plates and eat with the tortilla chips.

NOTE: You'll end up with a good bit more tomatoes and green chiles if you need to substitute for the Ro*Tel, but the proportions are the same and the extra won't make a difference in the dish's outcome.

Keep Cooked Ground Beef on Standby!

I love to stock up on ground beef whenever I find a good sale on it. I often buy twenty to thirty pounds at a time and brown it in a skillet in large batches. Once each batch is done cooking, I drain it and allow the beef to cool before placing it in ziplock freezer bags. These days I freeze about two cups per bag (which equals roughly one pound—ideal for most recipes), but when my kids were younger and ate less, I usually froze only one cup per bag.

Having ground beef already cooked and tucked away in my freezer is one of my greatest time-savers. Casseroles and spaghetti can be made in a flash without the mess and time of having to brown the beef. And if I find I'm having extra people for supper, I just pull out two bags instead of one.

Texas Straw Hat

SERVES 4

Like a lot of my recipes, this one is also easy to tailor to what you have on hand. Don't go out buying special ingredients if you don't already have them! Feel free to add drained diced tomatoes or tomato sauce in lieu of the tomato paste, or leave out the thyme and just add a little extra chili powder instead. Cook it until it is nice and thick, layer it with the other ingredients, and you've essentially just made yourself a Frito chili pie (my husband's grandmother always called it Texas straw hat, so we like to keep up that tradition).

1 pound ground beef

1 cup chopped onion

1 can (6 ounces) tomato paste

2 teaspoons chili powder

1 teaspoon Worcestershire sauce

¼ teaspoon dried thyme

½ teaspoon salt

⅛ teaspoon ground black pepper

1 bag (10 ounces) corn chips or tortilla chips

2 cups shredded Cheddar cheese

1 Heat a large skillet over medium heat. Place the ground beef in the skillet and cook, stirring to break up the beef, until it is no longer pink in the center, 8 to 10 minutes. Drain well.

2 Add the onion, tomato paste, chili powder, Worcestershire sauce, thyme, salt, and pepper to the skillet along with 1 cup water and stir well to combine. Cook over medium heat until the mixture begins to bubble, 7 to 10 minutes, then reduce the heat to low and simmer, stirring occasionally, until thickened, about 15 minutes.

3 Divide the corn chips among individual plates, spoon the meat mixture on top, top each with cheese, and serve.

Spaghetti Lover's Soup

SERVES 4 TO 6

Seeing as how spaghetti is one of my favorite meals, it's only fitting that leftover spaghetti sauce be recycled into another one of my favorite meals. This dish is quick and easy to throw together, hearty, aromatic, and absolutely delicious from start to finish. It's excellent served with salad and breadsticks. I think of it as an Italian-style chili, and I've never met a soul who didn't love it.

Using leftover spaghetti sauce with meat really stretches the dollars here since there is no need to add additional meat. If you like though, you can substitute a jar of sauce for the leftover and make it meatless.

2 cups Simple Marinara Sauce (page 284) or other spaghetti sauce with meat
2 cans (14 ounces each) diced tomatoes, with their juice
2 cans (15 ounces each) kidney beans, drained and rinsed
2 carrots, diced
1 stalk celery, diced (optional)
1 tablespoon dried Italian seasoning
2 to 3 ounces dried spaghetti

1 Place the spaghetti sauce, tomatoes, kidney beans, carrots, celery, and Italian seasoning in a medium-size stockpot, add

2 cups water, and stir well to combine. Bring just to a boil over medium heat, then reduce the heat to medium-low and let simmer until the vegetables are tender, about 30 minutes.

2 Break the spaghetti into 1-inch segments and add it to the pot. Continue cooking until the pasta is tender, about 10 minutes more. Serve hot.

Italian Bow-Tie Soup

SERVES 4 TO 6

My mother absolutely insisted that I include this recipe in the book because it is just so easy to throw together and she finds herself making it almost weekly. I love that you can have everything on hand, so it takes less than 5 minutes to put together but tastes like you've spent hours.

3 cans (14.5 ounces each) chicken broth

2 cans (14.5 ounces each) whole Italian-style tomatoes, with their liquid

1 teaspoon dried Italian seasoning

1½ cups uncooked mini bow-tie pasta

15 to 20 frozen meatballs, homemade (see page 16) or store-bought

2 cups frozen mixed vegetables

½ cup chopped onion

1 Place a Dutch oven over medium heat. Place the chicken broth, tomatoes, and Italian seasoning in the pot and bring the mixture to a boil.

2 Add the pasta, meatballs, vegetables, and onion, reduce the heat to medium-low and let simmer, uncovered, until the pasta is tender and the meatballs are heated through, about 15 minutes. Serve hot.

Taco Soup

SERVES 4 TO 6

On SouthernPlate.com, I've referred to this soup as "The World's Easiest Supper." I first made it about ten years ago when a friend passed along the recipe—we instantly fell in love with it. Even if this soup hadn't been so incredibly quick and easy, the flavor would have won me over on its own. Bursting with my favorite Mexican seasonings, sweet bits of corn, and juicy tomato, it's sure to be a hit. You're just not going to believe how great it tastes!

I like to stir a little sour cream into my bowl, and my husband sprinkles cheese all over his. Brady and Katy Rose just gobble it down plain.

This recipe is also delicious made with shredded chicken. Sometimes I buy a cooked rotisserie chicken, eat some of it for my lunch, and shred the rest to use in this soup for supper.

1 pound ground beef or turkey

1 large onion, chopped

2 cans (15 ounces each) kidney
  beans, drained and rinsed

1 can (15 ounces) whole kernel corn,
  drained

1 can (10 ounces) Ro*tel Original or
  1 can (12 ounces) diced tomatoes,
  plus 1 can (4 ounces) chopped
  green chiles (see Note, page 34)

1 can (15 ounces) tomato sauce

1 packet (1.25 ounces) taco
  seasoning mix

1 packet (1 ounce) ranch dressing
  mix

Shredded Cheddar cheese,
  for serving (optional)

Chopped fresh tomato, sour cream,
  sliced avocado, and chopped
  onions, for serving (optional)

1 Heat a large skillet over medium heat. Place the ground beef in the skillet and cook, stirring with a wooden spoon to break it up, until it is cooked through and no longer pink, about 10 minutes. Add the onion and cook, stirring occasionally, until it is translucent, 2 to 3 minutes. Drain off any grease and transfer the beef mixture to a medium-size stockpot.

2 Add the kidney beans, corn, Ro*Tel, tomato sauce, taco seasoning mix, ranch dressing mix, and 1½ cups water and stir to combine. Bring to a boil over medium-high heat, then reduce the heat to low and allow to simmer for 15 minutes.

3 Serve in bowls with the cheese and toppings alongside.

Little Moments, Big Memories

Some people say it's the little things that we'll remember most, the small moments that will cling to our heart.

Walking into a room and having a child look up and smile.

Drinking that cup of coffee slowly while watching the clouds stretch across the sky.

The responses to a thousand questions of "How was your day?"

Drives where you noticed the world around you instead of just counting cars and minutes at a light.

Hearing our alternate names of "Mama," "Grandmama," "Daddy," or "Grandpa."

Some people say it's the little things that we'll remember most when we look back, and that sounds like wisdom to me.

So I think I'll put my heart into enjoying the little things today. ♥

2

Pork

"Living high on the hog" is a saying often heard where I'm from. The cuts of meat higher up on a hog are the best and most expensive, which historically meant that poorer folks and those running low on resources tended to eat only lower cuts, or even scraps. So to live "high on the hog" means that one is living the good life. My grandparents often made the declaration that they were living high on the hog when they came to the table and saw a spread of crispy breaded pork chops, fresh creamed corn, and fluffy mashed potatoes. That meant they were indeed living well!

The recipes in this chapter are some of my dear favorites, and range from hams to chops, from ribs and roasts to bacon-topped breakfast pizza—and everything in between. These pork dishes are guaranteed to help you feel as if you're living high on the hog at your dinner table, too!

House Autry Pork Chops

SERVES 4

House Autry is a company known for their breading products. They make a delicious onion-flavored hush-puppy mix that my brother turned me on to. One day in passing, he said, "Let me tell you what you do if you want something good. Get you some of that House Autry's hush-puppy mix with onions, and get you some pork chops. . . ." It was love at first bite.

This is a very simple and fast way to cook delicious pork chops. I love the unique breading, which imparts the perfect amount of seasoning and gives the pork chops a nice crunchy coating. If you don't have this brand where you live, just look for another onion-flavored hush-puppy mix; many other companies make it. These pork chops are good served with pretty much any side, but I love them as a special Saturday morning breakfast with fluffy Cat Head Biscuits (page 220). I use thin-cut chops for breakfast and thick-cut ones for supper.

Vegetable oil

1 cup onion-flavored hush-puppy mix (I use House Autry brand but any will work fine)

4 boneless pork chops (each ¼ to ½ inch thick)

1 Pour the oil into a large skillet to a depth of ¼ inch and place it over medium-high heat. Line a plate with paper towels and set it aside.

2 Place the hush-puppy mix in a shallow bowl or plate. Dredge each pork chop through the mix, pressing each side gently so the mix adheres.

3 Reduce the heat under the skillet to medium and add the pork chops, making sure they don't touch (careful now—the oil may want to splatter). Cook the pork chops, turning once, until browned on both sides and no longer pink in the center, about 6 to 7 minutes for thin-cut pork chops, 8 to 10 minutes for thick. Transfer the cooked pork chops to the paper towel–lined plate to drain. Serve hot.

Crispy Breaded Pork Chops with Milk Gravy

SERVES 4

These pork chops—breaded in a delicious crunchy coating and served with a good coating of milk gravy and a scoop of MeMe's Loaded Mashed Potatoes (page 205)—make a fine meal if there ever was one. If you're looking to lighten up supper, just skip over this recipe. If you're looking for delicious comfort food, welcome home!

I love to make this with thick-cut, boneless pork chops because there is nothing like cutting through the deliciously crunchy breading to find a big juicy chop underneath!

Vegetable oil

2 large eggs

1 sleeve saltine crackers
   (about 35 crackers)

4 boneless pork chops
   (each about 1 inch thick)

1 recipe Milk Gravy (recipe follows),
   for serving

❶ Pour the oil into a large skillet to a depth of ¼ inch and place it over medium-high heat. Line a plate with paper towels and set it aside.

❷ Beat the eggs in a medium-size bowl. Crush the saltines into a shallow bowl or plate (I use a pie plate). Coat each pork chop by dipping it in the eggs, turning to coat both sides, and then in the cracker crumbs, pressing gently on each side so the crumbs stick. Transfer the coated pork chops to a plate.

❸ Reduce the heat under the skillet to medium and add the pork chops. Cook, turning once, until browned on both sides and no longer pink in the center, 7 to 8 minutes. Remove to the paper towel–lined plate to drain.

❹ Serve the pork chops with the gravy spooned over them.

Milk Gravy

MAKES 1½ CUPS

3 tablespoons bacon grease or
   butter (bacon grease is best)

¼ cup all-purpose flour

42

Crispy Breaded Pork Chops with Milk Gravy

½ teaspoon salt

¼ teaspoon ground black pepper

1½ cups milk, plus extra as needed

1 Place the bacon grease in a medium-size skillet over medium heat. Stir in the flour, salt, and pepper and cook, stirring constantly, until the flour begins to brown, 3 to 4 minutes.

2 Slowly pour in the milk, stirring constantly with a wire whisk to break up any lumps. Reduce the heat to low and continue cooking, stirring constantly, until the gravy thickens enough to coat the back of the spoon, about 5 minutes. If you prefer a thinner gravy, stir in more milk.

3 Serve over pork chops, mashed potatoes, biscuits, or anything else you can come up with!

Blackened Pork Chops

Blackened Pork Chops

SERVES 4

This recipe works just as well for chicken as it does for pork, but blackened chicken will take a backseat when you pat this spicy rub on a juicy, thick-cut, boneless pork chop. And don't worry—blackened doesn't mean burnt. This combination of herbs and seasonings darken to almost black as they cook and develop a flavor reminiscent of Tex-Mex. In this case "blackened" means it's just right!

Vegetable oil

½ cup (1 stick) butter, melted

1 teaspoon salt

1 teaspoon garlic powder

1 teaspoon ground black pepper

1 teaspoon onion powder

1 teaspoon ground cumin

1 teaspoon cayenne pepper

1 teaspoon paprika

4 boneless pork chops
(each ¾ to 1 inch thick)

1 Pour the oil into a large skillet to a depth of ¼ inch and place it over medium heat. Line a plate with paper towels and set it aside.

2 Place the melted butter in a pie plate or shallow bowl. Stir together all of the seasonings in a separate pie plate or shallow bowl.

3 Dip each pork chop in the butter, turning to coat both sides, then dredge it through the seasoning mixture, pressing each side gently so the seasoning adheres. Place the coated pork chop in the skillet and repeat with the remaining chops, making sure they don't touch.

4 Cook the pork chops until browned and crusty on the bottom, 3 to 4 minutes, then turn and cook them until no longer pink in the center, 4 to 5 minutes more. Remove them to the paper towel–lined plate to drain. Serve hot.

Coca-Cola Pork Chops

SERVES 4

This is a great last-minute pork chop recipe for those evenings when you just don't want to worry about what to make for supper. Rather than fretting over sauces and ingredients, I just grab a can of Coke from the fridge! These chops are flavorful and call for very few ingredients, and the dish comes together quickly. For fun, you can experiment with the type of carbonated beverage used. This recipe calls for Coca-Cola, obviously, but I like to use Dr Pepper for a little added sweetness, too.

These pork chops are excellent with rice—especially with the leftover sauce from the pan spooned over it.

1 tablespoon vegetable oil

4 pork chops (each about ½ inch thick)

1 cup Coca-Cola

1 cup ketchup

❶ Heat the oil in a large skillet over medium heat. Add the pork chops and cook, flipping once, until browned on both sides, 5 to 6 minutes.

❷ Stir together the ketchup and Coca-Cola in a small bowl and pour the sauce over the pork chops, turning the chops to coat. Bring the sauce just to a simmer, then reduce the heat to low and allow to cook until the pork chops are no longer pink in the center and the sauce has thickened, about 15 minutes.

❸ Serve the pork chops hot with the sauce spooned over them.

"You know, the best things in life belong to those who count their blessings—instead of comparing them."

—*Christy*

And They Think I Do It Because They're Hungry. . . .

I never understood how fast time flies until I became a parent. Now I have a teenager and I swear he was a baby just yesterday. My babies are growing up and both of them are going off each day and having little lives of their own. Some days I'm afraid if I blink, I'll miss it.

Thank goodness they come back home when I set the dinner table . . . a loving mama's secret weapon. ♥

Ricky's Favorite Pork Roast sc

SERVES 4 TO 6

This pork roast is so tender it falls off the bone and I have to spoon it out of the slow cooker to put it on a plate. It cuts easily with the slightest pressure of a fork and tastes every bit as good as you'd expect.

The carrots and cubed potatoes that cook with the roast make it a full meal—you don't need to serve much on the side. I just make some of my Easiest Ever Creamed Corn with Butter Sauce (page 184) the day before, then refrigerate it, and reheat it in the microwave for 1 to 2 minutes right before we sit down to supper.

1 pork roast (4 to 5 pounds)
1 pound carrots, cut into chunks
1 large onion, chopped
4 to 6 medium-size potatoes, unpeeled, scrubbed, and cubed
½ teaspoon kosher salt
½ teaspoon ground black pepper
1 recipe Cream of Mushroom Soup (page 282) or 1 can (10.5 ounces) condensed cream of mushroom soup

A Return to Sunday Dinners

Sunday has always been a special day where I'm from. For many of my ancestors, who worked from sunup until sundown, it was an added blessing to have a biblically ordered day of rest. Things slowed down, tea glasses got refilled again and again, and everyone enjoyed having company. Of course, to get folks to the table, you had to have food.

In the old days families lived closer to each other than they do now. These days, many of us (myself included) find ourselves hours or even days away from the family we grew up with, and so we're quick to banish Sunday dinners on the grounds that we don't have any family close by.

That was my attitude for years. I either excused it away with a bit of a pity party as I thought back to my Sundays growing up, and grieved over the fact that my kids would never have what I had. Or I put it off on my mother, *Well, Mama just doesn't do Sunday dinners anymore* . . . not realizing that the torch had been passed—I just hadn't thought to light it.

One day as I was pining for the good old days of Sunday dinners, it occurred to me that the only reason my children wouldn't have those memories was because of me. My mama had cooked those dinners, and I was the mama now. Maybe we don't have family close by, but we have the little family that lives within these four walls, and plenty of friends who like to eat. With all of my excuses gone, I set to making some Sunday dinner memories for my kids.

Now a lot of people think that in order to have a big meal, you have to set aside two hours just before the meal in order to prepare it. I do just the opposite. If I'm going to have people over, I prepare as much as possible ahead of time, certain dishes even days ahead of time. I seldom have more than one thing to prepare just before the meal and oftentimes find ways around that as well. Because, who are we kidding? I need that hour or two before company arrives to clean my house!

Here are some Sunday dinner menus to help inspire you to enjoy this special meal with your family. ♥

Sunday Dinner Menus

Sunday Dinner Ham / page 52
Big Fat Greek Taters / page 202
Blake's Green Beans / page 192
Ten-Minute Rolls / page 224
Mandarin Orange Freezer Pie / page 277

———

Ricky's Favorite Pork Roast / page 47
MeMe's Loaded Mashed Potatoes / page 205
Easiest Ever Creamed Corn with Butter Sauce / page 184
Cat Head Biscuits / page 220
Chocolate Sundae Cake / page 268

———

Beef Patties with Ketchup Gravy / page 10
Tomato Mozzarella Melts / page 197
Buttered Stewed Potatoes / page 204
Blake's Green Beans / page 192
Cheesy Garlic Biscuits / page 219
Buttermilk Peach Pie / page 247

———

Crispy Breaded Pork Chops with Milk Gravy / page 42
Mashed Potatoes / page 204
Roasted Asparagus / page 171
Cat Head Biscuits / page 220
Slow-Cooker Baked Apples / page 239

———

Chicken and Wild Rice Casserole / page 164
Candied Carrots / page 182
Squash Medley / page 196
Ten-Minute Rolls / page 224
Simple Fruit Crisp / page 233

1 If using a traditional oven, preheat it to 325°F.

2 Place the roast in a 6-quart slow cooker or a Dutch oven with a lid. Scatter the vegetables on top, add the salt and pepper, and pour the soup over all.

3 *If using a slow cooker:* Cover and seal the pot and cook until the roast is fork tender, 7 to 8 hours on low, 3 to 4 hours on high. *If using a Dutch oven:* Cover the pot and bake until the roast is fork tender, 1½ to 2 hours. Serve hot.

Tender Oven-Baked Baby Back Ribs

SERVES 3 TO 4

When I was younger, my dad used to spend hours outside making ribs on a hot grill or smoker, basting and fussing with them until they'd reached perfection. They sure were good.

Nowadays, my parents live an hour away. When a rib craving hits, I'm not about to stand over a hot grill for hours on end. Instead, I make them the easy way and am just as happy with the results.

There are countless methods for making ribs, and lots of folks will tell you that *their* way is the only right way. But as I see it, your kitchen means your rules. So I'm gonna show you how to cheat at ribs: no grill, no sweat, and fall-off-the-bone juicy results. Serve these with your favorite sides, such as Fast Italian Cucumber Salad (page 182) and Loaded Baked Potatoes (page 209).

1 rack pork baby back ribs
     (3 to 4 pounds), membrane
     removed (see Note)

1 recipe Barbecue Sauce in a Hurry
     (page 287) or 1 bottle (18 ounces)
     store-bought barbecue sauce

1 Preheat the oven to 300°F. Set out a large piece of heavy-duty aluminum foil (it should be about twice the size of the rack of ribs).

2 Place the entire rack of ribs in the center of the foil and brush it with half

Tender Oven-Baked
Baby Back Ribs

of the barbecue sauce, turning it to coat both sides. Wrap the ribs in the foil, seal well, and place them on a baking sheet.

3 Bake the ribs until very tender, about 2 hours. Remove them from the oven, carefully open the foil, and baste the top of the ribs with the remaining sauce. Return the ribs to the oven with the foil still open, and cook until the sauce is nice and thick, about 1 hour.

4 Cut the rib rack into sections of 2 to 3 ribs each and serve.

NOTE: If the butcher hasn't removed the membrane (that white "skin" on the back of the ribs), use a sharp knife to cut a hole in it, then use your hand to pull it away from the ribs; discard it.

> "If you can't see the bright side of life, polish the dull side."
> — *Unknown*

Sunday Dinner Ham

SERVES 10 TO 12

I buy ham whenever I find a good sale on it, and try to keep at least one in the freezer because it's such a versatile meat. Once it's cooked, it sets the stage for several meals.

Since the four of us can't possibly eat an entire ham ourselves, I slice up some of the leftovers and dice up the rest, storing both in the freezer in ziplock bags. Diced ham has countless uses in soups and casseroles, and the ham bone makes for a mean pot of pintos or Red Beans and Rice (page 56).

This is how my great-grandmother made her ham. The secret behind its yummy glaze is cooking it low and slow. You can serve the baked ham straightaway, or if you want to make it in advance and serve it later, you can cover it with foil to keep it warm while it sits on your stovetop. I suggest cutting it within a half hour of baking it—that's about as long as you'll be able to wait once you smell it!

Sunday Dinner Ham

1 smoked, ready-to-cook, bone-in
　　ham (about 8 pounds)
1 cup packed brown sugar
　　(light or dark, whatever you
　　have)
2 tablespoons Coca-Cola or other
　　soda (I like to use Diet Dr Pepper)
1 tablespoon yellow mustard

1 Preheat the oven to 350°F. Line a large rimmed baking sheet with aluminum foil.

2 Place the ham in the center of the pan.

3 Stir together the brown sugar, Coca-Cola, and mustard in a small bowl to make a glaze. Brush half of the glaze over the ham; set the rest aside.

4 Wrap the entire ham in foil and seal it well (this is to hold in all the wonderful juices). Bake for 2½ hours.

5 Remove the ham from the oven and carefully peel back the foil (but don't move the ham!). Brush the remaining glaze over the ham, return it to the oven, and bake, uncovered, until lightly browned, 30 minutes.

6 Allow the ham to rest at room temperature for 10 minutes, then slice and serve.

Sauerkraut and Weenies

SERVES 4

When I was little, we couldn't wait for supper each night. Mama always put together budget meals, not because she was trying to scale back on expenses, but because we barely had enough to feed us all. There are times when some families find themselves with half a pack of weenies in the fridge and need a little something to pull together for supper.

Nowadays, even when I can afford a more expensive meal, I still come back to this one. It is a prime example of what I call "poor folks food"—and like many such dishes, it's so very good!

This meal always takes me back to being a little girl with two ponytails, coming in from playing outdoors. I'd just barely slow down as I ran into the house and sat down at our table. Do you also remember flying through that front door when your mama called you for supper? Just as you hit the door you'd get a whiff of what was cooking and realize that you were starving.

I use two to four weenies here—or whatever I have on hand—but you can use more or less, or a different type of sausage altogether (Polish sausage or kielbasa works well). If you're vegetarian, just toss in some vegan hot dogs.

2 to 4 hot dogs or Polish sausages (kielbasa), sliced into small rounds

2 cups prepared sauerkraut, drained

Pinto beans and cornbread (such as No-Soak Dried Beans, page 191, and Buttermilk Cornbread, page 225), for serving (optional)

1 Place the hot dogs in a large skillet over medium to medium-high heat. Add the sauerkraut and cook, stirring often, until the hot dogs and sauerkraut brown slightly, 5 to 7 minutes.

2 Serve hot with the beans and cornbread, if you like.

"Your family is important. They left your home this morning and spread out to spend a day making new memories, acquiring knowledge, and growing up without you! Make it a priority to sit down to supper tonight with them and find out who they became today."

—*Christy*

Craving Beans SC

SERVES 4 TO 6 AS A MAIN DISH, 8 TO 10 AS A SIDE

Lots of traditional dishes came about because folks used to throw together whatever they had in their pantry. This is one such dish, but there is something a little different about it—once folks try it, they end up craving it. I told my friend Jyl about it one day over the phone and then sent her the recipe. She ended up making it four times that first week and took it to friends to try, who immediately started making it for their families, too.

This recipe works as a meal on its own, but it's also good as a side dish. One taste will have you craving it again!

1 can (15 ounces) kidney beans with their liquid

1 can (16 ounces) baked beans with their liquid (with or without pork)

1 can (15 ounces) butter beans, with their liquid

2 to 4 hot dogs, sliced into small rounds

1 medium-size onion, chopped

1 heaping tablespoon prepared mustard

½ cup ketchup

¾ cup brown sugar

½ teaspoon salt

½ teaspoon ground black pepper

1 Combine all of the ingredients in a 5- to 6-quart slow cooker or Dutch oven.

2 *If using a slow cooker:* Cover and seal the pot and cook until thick and bubbly, 7 to 8 hours on low, 3 to 4 hours on high. *If using a Dutch oven:* Cook over medium heat, stirring often, until the mixture begins to bubble. Reduce the heat to low and simmer, uncovered, until thick, about 30 minutes. Serve hot.

Red Beans and Rice sc
SERVES 4

This is a traditional "Monday" meal: In the old days, folks would cook a ham for Sunday dinner and use the leftovers (including the bone) to make a flavorful pot of spicy red beans to serve over rice. Since Monday was one of the busier workdays, women would leave this dish to simmer all day long while they got their chores done. I'm going to give you the more traditional method here and also a slow-cooker version (see Notes), because I know a lot of us aren't home to let pots simmer all day!

For the ham bone, you can use the leftovers from the Sunday Dinner Ham (page 52) or buy one from your butcher. Where I live, there are also specialty ham stores that sell the bones, which are loaded with bits of wonderfully flavored meat.

1 bag (16 ounces) dried small red beans (about 2 cups)

1 ham bone

1 small onion, chopped

1 teaspoon minced garlic

2 heaping teaspoons seasoned salt, such as Lawry's

1 teaspoon salt

1 teaspoon ground black pepper

⅛ teaspoon cayenne pepper or more to taste

1 dried bay leaf (optional)

1 cup sliced smoked sausage, such as kielbasa

4 cups hot cooked rice, for serving

1 Sort the beans, discarding any small stones, and place them in a large pot. Add water to cover and let them soak for 6 hours or overnight.

2 Drain and discard the soaking water and add fresh water to cover the beans to a depth of 2 inches. Add the ham bone, onion, garlic, seasoned salt, salt, black pepper, cayenne pepper, and bay leaf and bring to a boil over high heat. Reduce the heat to low and simmer until the beans are tender, 2 to 3 hours. (The longer you simmer the beans, the thicker and more flavorful their juices will be.)

3 About an hour before serving, remove the ham bone from the pot and take the ham off the bone. Return the ham to the pot and stir in the smoked sausage. Remove and discard the bay leaf, if using.

4 Serve the beans over the hot cooked rice.

NOTES: To make this in a slow cooker, place the sorted beans in the pot and add water to fill it three quarters full.

Add all of the ingredients except the sausage, cover and seal the pot, and cook until the beans are tender, 7 to 8 hours on low. Proceed with the recipe from step 3.

Dirty Rice

Dirty Rice

SERVES 4 TO 6

A few years ago my son had to plan a week's worth of meals in order to earn a badge in Scouts. I asked him to write down five supper ideas so we could shop for them together, and I really was expecting a week full of pizza. When he handed me his list and I saw this dirty rice at the very top, I knew it was going to be a yummy week after all!

This is great as a hearty meal, and the leftovers also make a fantastic side dish later in the week—although I've never managed to have leftovers unless I make a double batch!

1 tablespoon vegetable oil

1 rib celery, chopped

½ bell pepper, chopped

2 tablespoons chopped or minced garlic

1 small onion, chopped

4 tablespoons chopped fresh or 2 tablespoons dried parsley

1 pound pork breakfast sausage or ground beef (see Notes)

1 to 3 tablespoons Creole seasoning (see Notes)

4 to 5 cups cooked rice

❶ Heat the oil in a large skillet over medium heat. Add the celery, bell pepper, garlic, onion, parsley, and sausage and cook, stirring constantly and breaking up the meat, until the sausage is cooked through and the vegetables are tender, 10 to 12 minutes.

❷ Add the Creole seasoning and stir to combine. Stir in the rice and cook, stirring often, until it is heated through, 5 to 7 minutes.

❸ Serve the rice in bowls.

NOTES: If you use link sausage for this, remove the meat from the casing before cooking it.

The Creole seasoning adds spiciness to the dish. I adjust the amount based on my personal taste. Start on the low end and taste the dish after you stir in the rice; at that point you can add more seasoning if you like.

Easier Than "Meat and Three"

was raised in a traditional "meat and three" home. We had a meat, three vegetables, a bread, and usually a dessert. Every day. My mother was raised this way and her mother before her, so it really was just tradition being passed down (and a delicious tradition at that!).

We also had a family of five with at least two or three guests for supper every night. If you had tasted my mama's cooking, you would have wrangled an invite, too!

Unfortunately for my poor husband, when we got married I carried on the tradition. I'll never forget the night when my husband came home to our first dinner as a married couple. We lived in a tiny little trailer back then and our kitchen table was a small square one, the kind where there is usually just enough room for two but you can squeeze in four if you really need to.

Well, here he comes home and I have got that table loaded down just like Mama always did! The only problem is, I had cooked the exact same quantities I'd always seen Mama cook, too.

We ended up with dinner for seven and it was just the two of us. This went on for well over a week before I realized I had to get things under control and come up with a better plan.

While I was scaling back to cooking for two, I also decided to cook a little differently.

We just don't require as much food as our ancestors did—they were working in fields all day long, whereas my husband and I spend the majority of our workday sitting at a computer. It's a pretty big difference.

So it wasn't long before a typical meal in our home became "a meat and two," and then more often than not "a meat and one," with dessert making an appearance about once a week. Nowadays I tend to keep our meals simple when it's just the four of us. Most nights I serve an entrée, a vegetable, and a bread. These smaller meals are just the right size for my family.

I'm pretty sure most of us love the big meals with all the variety of dishes and colors, but it is important to evaluate your family and your lifestyle before planning out your meals. These days, when I want to make a meal like the ones I grew up on, with all the trimmings from start to finish, I just invite plenty of friends over to help us eat it!

Here are some menus to give you an idea of some of the simpler suppers I serve. I hope they inspire you.

Simple Weeknight Menus

Steak Tips over Rice / page 28
Roasted Brussels Sprouts / page 177

Ground Beef Stew / page 22
Cornbread Muffins / page 228

Always Tender Roast and
Vegetables / page 26
Ten-Minute Rolls / page 224

Smothered Steak / page 19
MeMe's Loaded Mashed
Potatoes / page 205

Janice's Stuffed Peppers / page 6
Easiest Ever Creamed Corn with Butter
Sauce / page 184

One-Skillet Chili "Bake" / page 32
Cornbread Muffins / page 228

Easy Stroganoff / page 18
Squash Medley / page 196

Baked Stuffed Pasta Shells / page 168
Ten-Minute Rolls / page 224

Tomato Mozzarella Melts / page 197
Breadsticks (from the bakery)
Meat Loaf with All the Trimmings /
page 12
Ten-Minute Rolls / page 224

Cornbread-Topped Chicken Potpie
/ page 160—a meal in one!

Flavorful Fried Chicken / page 83
Butter Dill New Potatoes / page 207
Roasted Brussels Sprouts / page 179

Spaghetti Lover's Soup / page 34
Fresh French bread (from the bakery)

Chicken Parmesan on the Fly /
page 84
Fast Italian Cucumber Salad /
page 182

Oven-Barbecued Chicken / page 87
Squash Medley / page 196

Shortcut Chicken Stew / page 93
Cornbread Muffins / page 228

Cheesy Chicken and Rice / page 101
Buttered Brussels Sprouts / page 177

Slow-Cooker Fiesta Chicken and Rice /
page 100
Cornbread Muffins / page 228

Catalina Chicken / page 87
Simple Skillet Vegetables / page 199

Shortcut Senate Bean Soup

SERVES 4

Senate Bean Soup is a big old tradition in D.C. and has been served in the Senate restaurant every day since the early 1900s.

The original Senate Bean Soup is famous for being flavorful, filling, and comforting. My shortcut version is all those things, too, but it's better suited to folks who want to cook their soup in an hour instead of all day long. My favorite trick to thicken soups and stews is to use instant mashed potato flakes. They thicken the broth in a flash without taking away from the flavor—and are a lot less work than thickening with flour.

4 chicken-flavored bouillon cubes

2½ cups finely diced or shredded ham

½ cup (1 stick) butter

3 ribs celery, chopped

1 medium-size onion, chopped

1 teaspoon minced garlic

4 cans (15 ounces each) navy beans, with their liquid

1 teaspoon salt

1 teaspoon ground black pepper

1 cup instant mashed potato flakes

1 Place the bouillon cubes and ham in a medium-size stockpot, add 6 cups water, and set over medium heat. Bring to a boil, then reduce the heat and simmer, uncovered, to produce a flavorful stock, 30 minutes.

2 Melt the butter in a small skillet over medium heat. Add the celery, onion, and garlic and sauté until lightly browned, 4 to 5 minutes.

3 Scrape the sautéed vegetables into the broth in the stockpot, add the beans, salt, and pepper, and return the soup to a boil.

4 Reduce the heat to low and simmer the soup, uncovered until thick, 20 to 30 minutes. Stir in the potato flakes and let simmer 5 minutes more. Serve hot.

Omelets Made Easy

SERVES 4

Back in my younger days, one of my favorite things to do with friends was head over to Shoney's on Wednesday nights for their weekly dinnertime breakfast buffet.

To a teenager this was pure bliss—*all of my favorite foods and I didn't have to get up early to enjoy them.* Of course there was never a shortage of volunteers to join our breakfast group, and our night out became a tradition I carried forward long after I got married. Gradually babies and schedules took precedence over omelets and strawberry-banana salad. I'm still a huge fan of breakfast for dinner, though, so I wanted to be sure and show you a supereasy way to make omelets. (And you can find the recipe for the Bananas in Red Stuff on page 281.)

Although this version is *my* favorite omelet, I hope you'll feel free to switch up the ingredients to make it your personal favorite, too.

Cooking spray

8 large eggs

1 cup shredded Cheddar cheese

½ cup milk

1 cup chopped ham

1 cup diced onion and bell pepper blend or ½ cup of each

Sour cream or shredded cheese, for serving (optional)

1 Preheat the oven to 350°F. Spray an 8-inch square baking dish with cooking spray.

2 Beat the eggs together in a large bowl. Add the cheese, milk, ham, and onion and pepper blend, and beat well until combined.

3 Pour the egg mixture into the prepared baking dish and bake until the omelet is set (it should not wiggle in the middle when you shake it a bit), about 40 minutes.

4 Cut the omelet into squares and serve warm with a dollop of sour cream, if you like, or a sprinkling of your favorite cheese.

Breakfast for Supper

Next time you feel like you're in a supper rut, pull out the breakfast plates and serve up your favorite morning dishes! Kids especially love breakfast for dinner, and parents love it, too, because it is usually one of the most economical meals to cook. At my house, we have breakfast *before* bed at least once a month.

Bacon Breakfast Pizza

SERVES 6 TO 8

My mother used to make this hearty breakfast pizza with canned biscuit dough when my brother was a teenager living at home. He loved it because it contains all of his breakfast favorites in one dish! He always seemed to be going out fishing early on Saturday mornings and then he'd come home shortly after breakfast with several hungry friends in tow. As he got older and lost his fondness for early mornings, Mama began making this for supper. Once canned crescent dough became available, she switched to using that since it is so much easier than pressing the biscuit dough into the pan.

You can easily adapt this recipe just by switching the toppings up a bit.

Cooking spray
8 slices bacon
1 pound bulk pork breakfast sausage
1 can (8 ounces) crescent roll dough
1 bag (16 ounces) frozen shredded
    hash browns (cubed are fine)
½ teaspoon salt
½ teaspoon ground black pepper
12 large eggs
1 cup shredded Cheddar cheese
Sautéed onions and mushrooms,
    for topping (optional)
Chopped fresh herbs, for topping
    (optional)

Bacon Breakfast Pizza

1 Preheat the oven to 350°F. Coat a 9- by 13-inch baking dish with cooking spray. Line a plate with paper towels.

2 Place the bacon in a large skillet over medium heat and cook, turning occasionally, until it is browned and crispy, 7 to 8 minutes. Remove it from the skillet to the paper towel–lined plate and set it aside. (Let the bacon grease cool slightly, then pour it into a heatproof container and reserve it for another use.)

3 Set the skillet over medium heat again. Add the sausage and cook, stirring with a wooden spoon to break up the meat, until no longer pink, 7 to 8 minutes. Drain and set aside.

4 Press the crescent roll dough into the bottom of the prepared baking dish, sealing any seams by pinching them together; the dough should extend up the side of the pan about half an inch.

5 Spread the hash browns over the dough and sprinkle with the salt and pepper.

6 Beat the eggs together in a large bowl and pour them over the hash browns, using a wooden spoon to spread them out evenly. Crumble the bacon over the eggs and sprinkle them with the sausage.

7 Bake until the eggs are set in the center, 30 to 35 minutes. Remove the baking dish from the oven, sprinkle the cheese over the top, and bake just until the cheese has melted, 2 to 3 minutes.

8 Top the pizza with the sautéed vegetables and fresh herbs, if using, then cut into squares and serve warm.

"Train a child in the way he should go, and when he is old he will not turn from it."

—Proverbs **22:6**

Save That Bacon Grease!

Southerners are known for our love of bacon grease. Since I've found that a lot of folks save their bacon grease without really knowing what to do with it, I've compiled a little information to make sure you're taking full advantage of your "liquid gold!"

HOW TO USE BACON GREASE

- **Substitute it for other oils** when sautéing and frying.
- **Use it to grease muffin tins** or cast-iron skillets.
- **Make milk gravy with it.** This flavorful gravy begins with a base of two tablespoons bacon grease. See page 42 for the recipe.
- **Put it in cornbread.** Add a tablespoon or so to the batter for extra flavor.
- **Season dried beans.** Traditional Southern beans are seasoned with a ham bone or bits of ham. If you find yourself without either, just add two or three tablespoons of bacon grease to the cooking water and the beans will taste just as good.
- **Add it to vegetables.** Stirring in just a tablespoon or so of bacon grease goes a long way as a natural flavor enhancer.
- **Flavor wilted greens.** Fry up some bacon and set it aside. Pour a little bit of the hot grease over fresh dark greens and then top them with crumbled bacon for a wilted salad like we had in the old days.
- **Fry up some eggs.**

HOW TO STORE BACON GREASE

Allow hot bacon grease to cool slightly before pouring it into a heatproof container. It is important to have one specific container just for bacon grease and to make sure not to put any other type of grease in it. Many people strain theirs but I don't. I enjoy all those little yummy bits of bacon.

Bacon grease is traditionally stored on the stovetop or next to the stove, but nowadays we don't use it nearly as often as folks used to, so it is best to store it in the refrigerator. If left on the counter indefinitely, bacon grease will go rancid; in the refrigerator, it will last for months (and it'll keep for a lifetime in the freezer).

3

Chicken

One of my favorite things to do as a child was gather eggs from the chickens at my grandparents' farm in Toney, Alabama. However, I was terrified of getting pecked! That's when it helps to have a younger sister who is easily talked into anything. I'd send Patti into the henhouse to get the hens riled up and away from their nests. Then I'd slip in and we'd both gather the eggs into a basket. No matter how many times we did it, finding each egg felt like discovering a special treasure.

I long for the day when I live in a place where I can raise chickens of my own. Many cities are allowing folks to do this now. Families are discovering the joy of having their own mini-farms as more and more kids get to go on treasure hunts for eggs like my sister and I used to do. For the rest of us limited by zoning restrictions, there are usually local farms to purchase eggs and poultry from, but fortunately grocery stores have their abundance, too!

As more and more families turn to chicken as their entrée of choice these days, I hope you'll enjoy the variety of recipes that I've compiled in this chapter.

"Rotisserie" Chicken and Potatoes SC

SERVES 4

This is a wonderfully easy recipe to throw together in your slow cooker—the chicken will end up tasting like a freshly made, juicy rotisserie bird from your local deli. I season mine lightly, but you can go heavier on flavor using whatever herbs and spices you like. Either way, it is delightful served with a green vegetable and rolls.

Placing the potatoes under the chicken allows the bird to cook above the juices rather than in them so that it browns nicely while the rich broth adds depth to the red potatoes beneath. Make sure you get small red potatoes, about golf ball size, because larger ones will hold the chicken up too high and the slow-cooker lid won't fit.

Once you have served the chicken and potatoes, save the broth: Allow it to cool and pour it into ice cube trays to freeze and use later.

6 to 8 small red potatoes, unpeeled and scrubbed

1 whole chicken (4 to 5 pounds), neck and giblets removed

2 tablespoons seasoned salt (such as Lawry's), lemon pepper, or dried Italian seasoning

1 Place the potatoes in a 6-quart slow cooker and set the chicken on top (be sure that the top of the chicken sits below the rim of the pot). Sprinkle the chicken liberally with the seasoned salt.

2 Cover and seal the pot and cook until the chicken is tender, 7 to 8 hours on low, 3 to 4 hours on high.

3 Remove the chicken to a cutting board and carve the meat. Transfer the meat and potatoes to a platter and serve hot.

Italian Chicken and Potatoes SC

SERVES 4

Sometimes we forget that we have staples already in our pantries that can make an everyday dish a sensation for the senses. This recipe serves up chicken and vegetables with a juicy pop of flavor. I always keep Italian dressing in my refrigerator because it is so versatile. This recipe is easily modified for pork chops or bone-in chicken breasts.

2 pounds boneless, skinless chicken breasts

4 to 6 medium red potatoes, unpeeled, scrubbed, and cut into large chunks

1 tablespoon dry Italian seasoning

1 can (14.5 ounces) chicken broth

½ cup Italian salad dressing

1 If using a traditional oven, preheat it to 325°F.

2 Place the chicken in the bottom of a 6-quart slow cooker or a 5-quart Dutch oven. Add the potatoes and sprinkle with the Italian seasoning. Pour the chicken broth and the Italian dressing over everything.

3 *If using a slow cooker:* Cover and seal the pot and cook until the chicken is cooked through, 7 to 8 hours on low, 3 to 4 hours on high. *If using a Dutch oven:* Cover and bake until the chicken is cooked through, 2 hours. Serve hot.

Old-Fashioned Sticky Chicken

SERVES 4

This is an old-timey recipe that has seen many variations throughout the years. It has a very distinct flavor and once you get a taste of it, nothing else will do! This chicken definitely lives up to its name of being sticky, but it is oh-so-good. There will be plenty of sauce leftover to spoon on top of the hot cooked rice (or try mashed potatoes, page 204) if that's what you'd fancy.

Cooking spray

1 cup ketchup

1 cup honey

1 cup brown sugar

½ cup light soy sauce

½ teaspoon garlic powder

8 to 12 chicken legs with skin (3 pounds total)

1 cup uncooked white rice

1 Preheat the oven to 350°F. Coat a Dutch oven or 9- by 13-inch baking dish with cooking spray.

Old-Fashioned Sticky Chicken

No Bones About It

I'm often asked if boneless, skinless chicken breasts will work in my Sticky Chicken recipe. Technically, they will, but you'll have an entirely different outcome. The boneless, skinless pieces will cook in the sauce and taste great, but there won't be any sticky coating on the outside even if you baste them. This recipe really needs bone-in, skin-on chicken to work. If you'd like to make it with skinless you can, but it just won't be *sticky* chicken.

2 Combine the ketchup, honey, brown sugar, soy sauce, and garlic powder in a medium-size saucepan over medium heat and cook, stirring constantly, until it comes just to a boil and the brown sugar has dissolved, 3 to 4 minutes. Remove from the heat.

3 Arrange the chicken legs in the prepared baking dish. Pour the sauce over the chicken, turning the pieces with tongs to coat them.

4 Place the baking dish in the oven, uncovered, and bake until cooked through, 90 minutes, turning the legs halfway through the cooking time.

5 Meanwhile, cook the rice according to package directions.

6 Place the rice on a platter and arrange the chicken legs on top. Spoon the sauce over all and serve.

Teriyaki Chicken and Brown Rice
SERVES 4

For those who love the twang of teriyaki in their takeout, this dish is sure to strike a note on the supper table. This dish tastes amazingly just like the restaurant version. Teriyaki chicken and brown rice is a quick and delicious dish to make and takes no longer than it would to go out for it. So, you are able to save yourself a trip and have more time to spend with your family.

4½ cups hot water

2 cups uncooked brown rice

1 teaspoon salt

1 tablespoon vegetable oil

1 pound boneless, skinless chicken breasts, cut into bite-size pieces

2 cups frozen broccoli florets

1 cup matchstick carrots, sliced yellow squash, sliced zucchini, and/or sliced mushrooms

½ teaspoon garlic powder

⅓ cup teriyaki sauce

1 Place the hot water in a medium-size saucepan over medium-high heat. Rinse the rice in a colander and add the rice and the salt to the water. Bring it just to a boil, then reduce the heat to low. Cover the pot and allow the rice to simmer until all of the water is absorbed, 20 minutes.

2 Meanwhile, heat the oil in a large skillet over medium-high heat. Add the chicken and cook, stirring frequently, until it is cooked through, 5 to 7 minutes.

Add the vegetables, garlic powder, and teriyaki sauce to the skillet. Reduce the heat to medium and cook, stirring often, until the vegetables are tender, about 10 minutes.

3 Stir in the cooked rice and serve hot.

"Speak more gently. Hug more tightly. Notice the sky rather than just scurrying about beneath it. Fill your heart with gratitude instead of anxiety. Live each day as if it were your last.

"One day, you'll be right."

—*Christy*

Slow Cookers Aren't Just for Wintertime

Most people consider slow cookers to be for fall and winter comfort food, but I love my slow cooker in the summertime. There is nothing like having supper ready on a day when it's a hundred-plus degrees outside without having to turn on your oven or stove. It sure does keep your kitchen a whole lot cooler!

Slow-Cooker Coke Chicken (SC)

SERVES 4

This is one of my all-time favorite things to eat, but first I have to warn you, it's going to be ugly. The chicken will be so tender that it will fall off the bone as you take it out of the slow cooker—and it really *must* be a whole chicken. I've made this with boneless, skinless breasts and even pork chops, and while they are good, the result is definitely not the same. This chicken will have been bubbling and marinating in the delicious sauce inside out and outside in all day long. The results are just magnificent.

In most of my recipes, I'll tell you to take it and make it your own, but with this one, I'd really like for you to try it exactly as it is. It's excellent served with corn on the cob, rolls, and green beans.

1 whole chicken (4 to 5 pounds),
   neck and giblets removed
1 medium-size onion, quartered
1 lemon, quartered
1 recipe Barbecue Sauce in a Hurry
   (page 287) or 1 bottle
   (18 ounces) store-bought
   barbecue sauce
1 can (12 ounces) Coca-Cola

1 If using a traditional oven, preheat it to 325°F.

2 Place the chicken in a 4- to 6-quart slow cooker or a 5-quart Dutch oven with a lid and add the onion and the lemon quarters. Pour the barbecue sauce and the Coke over all.

3 *If using a slow cooker:* Cover and cook until the chicken is falling apart, 7 to 8 hours on low, 3 to 4 hours on high. *If using a Dutch oven:* Cover and bake until the chicken is falling apart, 2 hours.

4 Carefully transfer the chicken to a platter and serve hot.

Grilled Chicken Tenders Without the Grill

SERVES 4

I'm not at all against grilling, I love pretty much anything cooked on an open flame! I just don't love standing over the burning coals outdoors in the heat and I seldom have the time to grill our supper. As a result, I've come up with several substitute recipes like this that taste or look like they've been grilled but without the hassle. These chicken tenders are absolutely bursting with flavor and once they're coated in the thickened marinade, it's hard to believe they were made on the stovetop!

2 pounds boneless, skinless chicken breasts, cut into strips

1 cup store-bought zesty Italian dressing

2 teaspoons lime juice

3 teaspoons honey

1 Place the chicken breasts in a gallon-size ziplock bag. In a small bowl, stir together the Italian dressing, lime juice, and honey. Pour the dressing mixture over the chicken, seal the bag, and let marinate in the refrigerator for at least 1 hour or overnight.

2 When ready to cook, heat a large skillet over medium heat. Place the chicken and marinade in the skillet and cook, turning the chicken every 10 minutes, until the liquid evaporates and the remaining marinade becomes thick and caramelized, about 30 minutes.

3 Rub each piece of chicken on the bottom of the pan to coat it in the marinade and serve.

Are You Already Living the Dream?

I have a firmly held belief that the most important lessons in life are learned in kindergarten. For this reason (and many others), when my five-year-old speaks, I listen. Often she'll say something that has me stifling a giggle, but other times she'll speak something truly profound and in her innocence has no idea that she has just opened her mama's eyes to wisdom once again.

One day we were sitting in the living room together and Katy Rose was watching *The Swan Princess* while I worked on my laptop. The movie came to a part where the "evil guy" (as my daughter calls him) was trying to keep the Swan Princess prisoner. Katy Rose watched for a few moments before turning to me in absolute frustration.

"You see that, Mama? See that stuff right there? That is why I've decided I don't want to be a princess when I grow up anymore—because you have to deal with that evil stuff." She huffed and looked back for a moment, clearly disappointed in the downside of her now former dream before adding, "So here is what I'm going to do. If I have kids, I'll just be a mama. If I don't have kids, I'm just going to live with you forever, okay?"

"Okay, baby, that works for me."

Bless her heart, at five years old she just really felt compelled to have her entire life plotted out, and realizing there was a downside to royalty threw her for a loop.

I don't reckon a lot of us think on the downside of our dreams and that is a good thing. The upside of things is infinitely more inviting and hopeful. What struck me most, though, about Katy Rose's two fallback dreams was that *both of them revolve around family.*

With that in mind, how many of us are living the dream right now? You may look at starring in a movie as "the dream," but I packed two lunches this morning and watched two beautiful little blond heads bob to the car as they headed off to school. There may be a big reserved room for someone in a fancy restaurant where the patrons all dress in formal attire, but tonight I'm going to sit down to dinner

with my husband and kids at an old oak dinner table *and I doubt a single one of us will even be wearing shoes.*

When I lay my head down tonight, at some point after the sun sets, I won't be in a luxury suite, but I will be in our warm house, safely sheltered with a peacefully sleeping family and a big old dog snoring at the foot of my bed.

And when I wake up tomorrow, I'll have a big grin on my face and a song in my heart.

Because I'm living the dream. ♥

A Note About Rice Sticks

Rice sticks are sometimes referred to as rice vermicelli or rice noodles. They're long, wiry noodles made of rice, not to be confused or replaced with traditional pasta noodles that we may be more familiar with. Straight out of the package, they are tough and even a little difficult to break, but when you drop them into hot oil they almost instantly become featherlight, airy, and crisp. I love to sprinkle a little salt on them immediately after removing them from the oil—we just can't resist nibbling on a few while I make these lettuce wraps.

Chicken Lettuce Wraps

SERVES 4 TO 6

I've developed a raging addiction to these things. You see, Ricky and I don't get to go out much. We've actually been out twice without the kids in the past four or five years. What we do instead is pick a night each week and eat a very light supper; after we send the kids to bed, one of us (he usually draws the short straw here) goes to get takeout for our supper.

A Chinese restaurant is very near us and chicken lettuce wraps are one of their signature dishes. This is one of those things that didn't sound too appealing to

me at first, but my mother kept insisting that I try them. Once I did, I was hooked. Shelling out the money for them on a regular basis got old quick, so I developed my own recipe. Now I make them frequently for my family, and there is never a bite left!

About ¾ cup vegetable oil

1½ pounds boneless, skinless chicken breasts, cut into bite-size pieces, or about 3 cups cubed cooked chicken or turkey

3 tablespoons soy sauce

2 tablespoons light or dark brown sugar

1 cup button mushrooms, finely diced

1 can (8 ounces) water chestnuts, drained and finely diced

3 scallions, finely chopped

½ package (3 ounces) rice sticks

1 head iceberg lettuce, cored, washed, and leaves separated

1 If using raw chicken, heat 3 tablespoons of the oil in a large skillet over medium heat. Add the chicken and cook, stirring every minute or so, until it is cooked through, about 5 minutes. Remove the chicken from the heat, let it cool, and finely dice it. (If using cooked chicken, no need to heat it—simply finely dice it.)

2 Place the soy sauce and brown sugar in a small bowl and stir well to combine. Add the sauce mixture to the skillet along with the chicken, mushrooms, water chestnuts, and scallions; stir to coat well with the sauce. Cook, stirring, over medium heat until the mixture is just heated through, 3 to 5 minutes. Remove from heat.

3 Meanwhile, pour the remaining oil to a depth of 1 to 2 inches in a small saucepan and place it over medium heat until it is hot, 2 to 3 minutes. Line a plate with paper towels.

4 Break off a handful of rice sticks, drop them into the hot oil, and cook until they puff up, 4 to 5 seconds. Immediately remove the puffed noodles from the pot with a slotted spoon and place them on the paper towel–lined plate to drain. Repeat with the remaining noodles.

5 Set out the lettuce leaves in a single layer. Divide the chicken mixture among them and top each with some of the cooked rice sticks.

6 Eat the wraps folded up as you would a taco. Enjoy!

> "I long to accomplish a great and noble task, but it is my chief duty to accomplish small tasks as if they were great and noble."
> —*Helen Keller*

Spicy Fried Chicken

SERVES 4 TO 6

For those who like their chicken with a hint of spice, here is a great way to prepare it. From a glance at the recipe, you would think it would be very fiery, but it really just ends up with a bit of a zing at the end. If you prefer a spicier bird, be sure to use the full two tablespoons of cayenne pepper.

¾ cup all-purpose flour

1½ to 2 tablespoons cayenne pepper

1 teaspoon salt

¼ teaspoon ground black pepper

2 large eggs

2 pounds boneless, skinless chicken breasts or tenders (see Note, page 84)

Vegetable oil, for frying

1 In a shallow bowl, combine the flour, cayenne pepper, salt, and black pepper.

2 Crack the eggs into a separate shallow bowl and beat them with a fork.

3 Line a plate with paper towels and set it aside. Dip each piece of chicken in the beaten eggs and then dredge it in the flour mixture and set it aside on a separate plate.

4 *If using a large skillet:* Fill it with oil to a depth of ¼ inch and place it over medium-high heat. When the oil is hot (a pinch of flour will sizzle and brown when dropped in), add the chicken. Working in batches and being careful not to overcrowd the skillet, cook, turning once, until the chicken is cooked through and the outside is golden and crispy, about 15 minutes. Transfer the cooked chicken to the lined plate to drain. *If using a deep fryer:* Fill it with oil according to the manufacturer's instructions and heat it until the thermometer registers 375°F. Working in batches and being careful not to overcrowd the fryer, carefully add the chicken and cook until golden, 10 to 15 minutes. Transfer the cooked chicken to the lined plate to drain.

5 Serve the chicken hot.

Spicy Fried Chicken
WITH FAST ITALIAN CUCUMBER SALAD
(PAGE 182)

Mealtime Conversation Starters

Sometimes it is hard to get our kids to open up, and if eating together as a family isn't already a habit, it can feel awkward when we suddenly begin. Here is a fun list of open-ended questions to toss out there that just might get your kids talking! Be sure to give them time to fill in the gaps in conversation whenever they are willing.

- You know, families are so alike but sometimes they're so different, too. Who do you think you're most like in the family and why?

- Who are you most unlike in our family? How is this a fun thing?

- Out of all of the trips we've taken, which has been your favorite and why?

- What was the funniest thing you remember learning in school?

- Is there somewhere in the world you dream of visiting?

- What do you think you want to do when you grow up? (Parents: Tell your kids some of the things you used to want to be when you were their age.)

- Tell me one thing you learned today.

I also like to ask questions that inspire optimism. Here are a few of my favorites:

- What was the best thing about today?

- How did you make someone's day better today?

- What are you most looking forward to tomorrow?

- What is something you really admire in one of your friends?

- Which teacher do you look up to the most? What is it about that teacher that you admire?

- If you could do one thing to make the world a better place, what would it be?

Supper or Dinner?

Where I'm from, supper is the meal you eat on weeknights and dinner is served on Sundays and special occasions such as holidays and family gatherings. Dinner is usually a little more elaborate and supper is more casual. Of course, I'm of the belief that there is no definitive answer here, whatever you were raised calling it is the right one. Regardless of what it's called where you're from, it sure is good to come home to! ♥

Flavorful Fried Chicken

SERVES 4 TO 6

There are countless ways to prepare fried chicken, and chicken fingers seem to be universally loved by young and old. Although all manner of recipes try to perfect that fried taste in the oven, including Granny Jordan's, which I'll share with you on page 85, sometimes you're better off going with the original or none at all.

So when you find yourself craving the real stuff, I suggest frying the chicken and serving it with raw vegetable sticks as a side and fresh fruit for dessert, to lighten up the meal. However, my mother says it's best served with mashed potatoes and fried corn!

This is how my friend Jyl makes her fried chicken and she has a reputation for making the best around. It is a great basic to have in your arsenal, with a good all-around flavor.

1 cup all-purpose flour

1 package (1 ounce) dry ranch
   dressing mix

2 large eggs

2 pounds boneless, skinless chicken
   breasts or tenders (see Note)

Vegetable oil

1 Stir together the flour and ranch dressing mix in a shallow bowl.

2 Crack the eggs into a separate shallow bowl and beat them with a fork.

3 Line a plate with paper towels and set it aside. Dip each piece of chicken in the eggs to coat, then dredge it in the flour mixture, and set it aside on a separate plate.

4 *If using a large skillet:* Fill it with oil to a depth of ¼ inch and place it over medium-high heat. When the oil is hot (a bread crumb will sizzle and brown when dropped in), add the chicken. Working in batches and being careful not to overcrowd the skillet, cook, turning once, until it is cooked through and the outside is golden and crispy, about 15 minutes. Transfer the cooked chicken to the lined plate to drain. *If using a deep fryer:* Fill it

with oil according to the manufacturer's instructions and heat it until the thermometer registers 375°F. Working in batches and being careful not to overcrowd the fryer, carefully add the chicken and cook until golden, 10 to 15 minutes. Transfer the cooked chicken to the lined plate to drain.

5 Serve the chicken hot.

NOTE: To make chicken tenders, cut a boneless, skinless chicken breast into 3 to 4 strips with kitchen shears. Each pound of chicken will yield about 8 chicken tenders. I generally allow 3 to 4 chicken strips per adult, and 2 per child.

Lemon Pepper Chicken

You might not think of lemon pepper seasoning when it comes to frying chicken, but it adds a surprising burst of flavor and is one of my favorite ways to make it. Simply replace the ranch dressing mix with 2 tablespoons lemon pepper in step 1.

Chicken Parmesan on the Fly

This recipe is easily adapted to make a simple chicken Parmesan that can be assembled in less than fifteen minutes. Serve it over cooked spaghetti with marinara sauce (use mine on page 284 or your favorite store-bought version), and top with grated Parmesan or fresh mozzarella. (I usually have mozzarella but seldom have Parmesan. We're probably one of the few families whose "chicken Parmesan" is actually "chicken mozzarella," but I'm all about adapting to your circumstances, or in this case, your refrigerator.)

Granny's Oven-Fried Chicken

SERVES 4 TO 6

Until I found this recipe in Granny Jordan's collection, I'd never been too impressed with oven-fried chicken. It never seemed to be as flavorful as the deep-fried version. This method changes all of that! By dipping the chicken in Italian dressing before dredging it in a well-seasoned bread crumb mixture, this comes out every bit as flavorful as its fried counterpart. This is fancy enough to serve for lunch after church with rolls and whatever vegetables are in season.

Cooking spray

½ cup panko bread crumbs

⅓ cup grated Parmesan cheese

1 tablespoon dried parsley flakes

¼ teaspoon garlic salt

¼ teaspoon ground black pepper

½ cup Italian dressing

3 to 4 pounds boneless, skinless chicken breasts

1 Preheat the oven to 350°F. Lightly coat a 9- by 13-inch baking dish with cooking spray and set it aside.

2 In a shallow bowl or pie plate, stir together the bread crumbs, cheese, parsley flakes, garlic salt, and pepper. Pour the Italian dressing into a separate shallow bowl.

3 Dip each chicken breast into the salad dressing to coat both sides, then dredge it in the bread crumb mixture and transfer it to a plate.

4 Place the chicken breasts in the prepared baking dish and bake until they are cooked through, 30 to 40 minutes.

5 Arrange the chicken on a platter, stand back, and wait on the compliments!

That's Just What You're Supposed to Do

My mother takes three of my nephews to school each morning. Over the past few years she's gathered some interesting tales from those fifteen-minute car rides with three young boys. It's amazing how much can occur in such a short span and how easy it is to see into a kid's world based on what he talks about at the start of his day.

Recently, Mama read an ad in her local paper saying that the school needed volunteer crossing guards at certain spots near the campus. She mentioned in an offhand way to my nephew Austin that if she didn't keep her youngest granddaughter during the day, she'd take that job just to help out.

Austin looked at her and remarked, "Grandmama, you just like to help people, don't you?"

Mama thought about it a minute and said, "Well, Austin, that's just what you're supposed to do. Whenever you get a chance you are always supposed to help out other people, and there is always something you can do to help."

Mama is right about helping people, but I think she also understands how good it makes us feel when we step up and help out. Just think about it: The last time you opened a door for someone, didn't you perk up just a little bit yourself? Each time we reach out and help someone else, even

in a small way, it boosts our heart just a little bit higher in our chest and makes our next smile come just a little bit easier.

So many folks are trying to change the world in broad strokes these days and that is certainly commendable. But I think most significant changes take place on a smaller scale—by helping a kid cross the street, opening the door for someone, or just looking around and offering a smile to someone who needs it. It helps us feel better, but as the wisdom of our elders teaches us, "That's just what you're supposed to do." ♥

Catalina Chicken ⓢⓒ

SERVES 4

Tired of the same old chicken? Try this for a twist! Boneless, skinless breasts cook all day in a rich and flavorful marinade of Catalina dressing and onion soup mix. This dish will take you to the islands with its fresh, sweet-and-tangy flavor.

1 bottle (8 ounces) Catalina salad dressing

1 package (1 ounce) dried onion soup mix

3 pounds boneless, skinless chicken breasts

❶ If using a traditional oven, preheat it to 325°F.

❷ Place the salad dressing and soup mix in a small bowl and stir until well blended.

❸ Place the chicken breasts in the bottom of a 4- to 6-quart slow cooker or a 5-quart Dutch oven. Pour the dressing mixture over the chicken.

❹ *If using a slow cooker:* Cover and seal the pot and cook until the chicken is tender, 7 hours on low, 3 hours on high. *If using a Dutch oven:* Cover and bake until the chicken is tender, 2 hours.

❺ Serve the chicken hot.

Oven-Barbecued Chicken

SERVES 4

This is a wonderfully simple entrée to pair with whatever side you're craving. Returning the chicken to the oven to bake at a higher temperature thickens the sauce, which forms a delicious smoky-sweet coating. This no-fuss preparation also works great for pork chops.

Cooking spray

3 pounds boneless, skinless chicken breasts

1 recipe Barbecue Sauce in a Hurry (page 287) or 1 bottle (18 ounces) store-bought barbecue sauce

1 Preheat the oven to 350°F. Coat a 9- by 13-inch baking dish with cooking spray.

2 Place the chicken breasts in the prepared baking dish. Pour half of the barbecue sauce over the chicken, using a brush or the back of a spoon to spread it evenly.

3 Cover the baking dish tightly with aluminum foil and bake until the chicken is cooked through and tender, 30 minutes.

4 Take the dish out of the oven and discard the foil. Increase the oven temperature to 400°F. Carefully drain off and discard the liquid and brush the chicken with the remaining barbecue sauce.

5 Return the chicken to the oven and bake until the sauce is thickened, 5 to 10 minutes more. Serve hot.

Chinese Chicken Salad

SERVES 6 TO 8 AS A MAIN COURSE

This recipe keeps in the fridge really well. I often make a double batch on the weekend and eat it for lunch for three or four days. Make it ahead so that it has time to chill for at least a couple of hours before serving. You may have had another version of this popular salad before—mine's a supereasy twist on the classic.

1½ pounds boneless, skinless chicken breasts

2 packages (3 ounces each) chicken-flavor ramen noodles, with seasoning packets

1 cup sliced almonds

½ cup vegetable oil

⅓ cup rice vinegar

¾ cup sugar

1 teaspoon salt

1 teaspoon ground black pepper

5 cups shredded coleslaw mix

1 package (16 ounces) matchstick carrots (about 2 cups)

3 to 4 scallions, sliced

Chinese Chicken Salad

1 Preheat the oven to 350°F.

2 Place the chicken breasts in a medium-size stockpot and add water to cover. Bring to a boil over medium-high heat and cook until the chicken is cooked through, about 20 minutes. Remove the chicken breasts with tongs and set them aside to cool.

3 Break up the ramen noodles and place them on a rimmed baking sheet, reserving the seasoning packets. Scatter the almonds over the ramen noodles and stir to combine. Place the pan in the oven and toast the ramen mixture until very lightly browned, about 10 minutes, stirring halfway through. Remove the pan from the oven and allow the mixture to cool completely, then transfer it to a large ziplock bag.

4 To make the dressing, place the contents of the seasoning packets, oil, rice vinegar, sugar, salt, and pepper in a quart-size mason jar. Seal the lid tightly and shake the jar vigorously until the mixture is well blended. Set the dressing aside.

5 Shred the chicken into bite-size pieces using two forks.

6 Place the coleslaw mix, carrots, scallions, and chicken in a very large bowl and stir to combine. Shake the dressing again, pour it over the salad, and stir to coat completely.

7 Refrigerate the salad, covered, for several hours or overnight, to allow the flavors to develop.

8 When you're ready to serve, assemble the salad on a platter and scatter the ramen mixture over the top.

NOTE: This makes a lot but lasts several days in the refrigerator. To ensure that the ramen mixture stays crunchy, keep it separate and add it just before eating the salad each time.

"BBQ Joint" Stew
SERVES 6 TO 8

At the first sign of chill in the air, BBQ joints around here start cranking out this delicious stew. Many people refer to it as Brunswick stew but *traditional*

Shopping Lists a Mile Long

One thing I hate is recipes that have an ingredients list that reads like an encyclopedia. Most folks, if they've worked hard all day, don't want to come home and have to read off twenty different ingredients in order to put supper on the table. In many places in this book, you'll notice a choice of homemade ingredients or store-bought convenience foods. Feel free to go with whichever option you prefer, but don't forget to make time to sit down with your family to enjoy the fruits of your labor!

Brunswick stew used to have rabbit or squirrel in it—most modern versions don't for obvious reasons. (I can't remember the last time I was invited to a squirrel hunt!) So, I call it "BBQ Joint" Stew to avoid the looks of fear that crop up from time to time when Brunswick is mentioned.

This stew is practical for BBQ joints because it helps them use up any leftover shredded pork and chicken that they may have. By mixing in their signature sauce and whatever vegetables they have on hand, they can turn out a flavorful, filling stew unlike any other.

This stew is excellent with a bit of hot sauce drizzled over each bowl. Leftovers freeze well for three months—just put them in ziplock bags or freezer containers.

1 whole chicken (about 4 pounds), neck and giblets removed

1 medium-size onion, chopped

1 recipe Barbecue Sauce in a Hurry (page 287) or 1 bottle (18 ounces) barbecue sauce

2 cans (15 ounces each) whole kernel corn, drained

1 to 2 cups frozen or canned baby lima beans, drained

5 medium-size potatoes, peeled and cubed

1 teaspoon salt

2 teaspoons ground black pepper

Saltine crackers, for serving

Hot sauce, for serving (optional)

1 Place the chicken in a stockpot and add water to cover. Add the onion and cook over medium heat until the chicken is cooked through and fall-apart tender, about 1 hour. Remove the chicken from the pot and set it aside to cool.

2 Add the barbecue sauce, corn, lima beans, potatoes, salt, and pepper to the pot and stir well to combine. Skin, debone, and shred the chicken (see page 162), and return it to the pot.

3 Bring the stew to a low boil and reduce the heat to a simmer, stirring often, until the vegetables are fully cooked, about 30 minutes. Serve hot, with the crackers and hot sauce, if you like.

Heather's White Chicken Chili

SERVES 4 TO 5

I love chili of all kinds, but this is a deliciously different take on the traditional tomato-based preparation and a great way to use leftover chicken. If you don't have leftover chicken and are in a crunch for time, just pick up a rotisserie bird from the deli on your way home. Don't be dismayed by what may look like a long list of ingredients—the prep for this recipe is really very quick.

1½ pounds boneless, skinless chicken breasts, cut into bite-size pieces, or diced leftover rotisserie chicken

1 tablespoon vegetable oil

1 cup chopped onion

2 cups chicken broth

1 can (4 ounces) chopped green chile peppers

½ teaspoon salt or to taste

1 teaspoon garlic powder

1 teaspoon ground cumin

½ teaspoon dried oregano

½ teaspoon dried cilantro leaves

⅛ teaspoon crushed red pepper

2 cans (15 ounces each) great northern or cannellini beans (or other medium-size white beans), drained and rinsed

Shredded Pepper Jack cheese, for serving

1 Place the chicken in a medium-size stockpot and add water to cover to a depth of 1 inch. Place over medium-high heat and bring just to a boil. Reduce the heat to medium and simmer until the chicken is cooked through, about 20 minutes.

2 Heat the oil in a medium-size stockpot over medium-high heat. Add the onion and sauté until it is translucent and tender, about 5 minutes.

3 Add the chicken broth, green chile peppers, salt, garlic powder, cumin, oregano, cilantro, and crushed red pepper. Reduce the heat to low and simmer, stirring from time to time, until the chili is heated through, 15 minutes.

4 Stir in the beans and simmer, 10 minutes more.

5 Serve the chili hot in bowls, topping each with the cheese.

Shortcut Chicken Stew

SERVES 4 TO 6

This stew is great for those days when you really want a hearty bowl of warmth, but you don't want to spend two hours working on it. Prep can be done in less than ten minutes. The remainder of the time you're just allowing the stew to simmer so the flavors develop.

2 cans (14.5 ounces each) chicken broth

1 large onion, chopped

6 medium-size russet potatoes, peeled and diced, or 1 package (1 pound) frozen cubed hash brown potatoes

1 rotisserie chicken, skinned, deboned, and shredded

1 can (29 ounces) crushed tomatoes

2 cups frozen corn or 1 can (15 ounces) whole kernel corn, drained

2 teaspoons salt

1 teaspoon ground black pepper

1 tablespoon butter

2 tablespoons sugar

1 Place a 5-quart Dutch oven over medium-high heat. Add the chicken broth and onion and bring to a boil. Reduce the heat to medium and cook until the onion is translucent, about 10 minutes.

2 Add the potatoes, chicken, tomatoes, corn, salt, and pepper. Bring just to a boil, then reduce the heat and allow the mixture to simmer, uncovered, until the potatoes are tender, 30 minutes. Stir in the butter and sugar just before serving.

Chicken Tortilla Soup

SERVES 4 TO 6

Don't let this long ingredients list fool you into thinking this recipe is complicated. Just trust me—the first line of the directions reads, "Combine all of the ingredients. . . ."

Yup. That's my kind of recipe. Bursting with flavor and easy as can be. I like to serve this with loads of cheese on top. And it keeps well, too—whip up a batch a day or two before a get-together to make your party prep easier!

1 can (14 ounces) chicken broth or 2 bouillon cubes dissolved in 1½ cups water

1 can (29 ounces) crushed tomatoes

1 can (11 ounces) red enchilada sauce

1 can (4 ounces) chopped green chiles

1 teaspoon chili powder

1 teaspoon ground cumin

1 teaspoon dried cilantro leaves

1 heaping teaspoon minced garlic or 1 clove garlic, minced

2 to 3 cups cooked, shredded chicken (or more, if you'd like)

2 cups frozen corn or 2 cans (15 ounces each) whole kernel corn, drained

1 small onion, chopped

Salt and ground black pepper to taste

4 to 6 corn tortillas (6 inches each)

Shredded cheese, sour cream, guacamole, salsa, and/or chopped scallions, for serving

Chicken Tortilla Soup

1 Combine all of the ingredients except for the tortillas and toppings with 2 cups of water in a large stockpot. Place it over medium-high heat and bring it just to a boil. Reduce the heat to medium and simmer until the soup is heated through, 30 minutes.

2 Using a pizza cutter or kitchen shears, cut each tortilla into thin strips. Place the strips in the pot and cook 10 minutes more.

3 Serve the soup in bowls with the desired toppings on the side.

Creamy Chicken Skillet

SERVES 4

I could eat this every day of my life and be happy as a lark. It's one of those meals that just makes your stomach feel good when you eat it, so I hope you'll try it soon. My son was feeling under the weather when I made it one day, and I took him a plate and said, "Here, baby, just try to eat this." He saw what it was and said, "Don't you worry one bit, Ma, I'll *sure* be eating all of that!" Apparently, it is also a miracle cure!

1 package (16 ounces) egg noodles

1 tablespoon vegetable oil

2 to 3 pounds boneless, skinless chicken breasts

1 recipe Homemade Cream of Chicken Soup (page 282) or 1 can (10.5 ounces) condensed cream of chicken soup plus ½ cup milk

1 packet (1 ounce) dry ranch dressing mix

1 cup chopped broccoli (see Note)

1 cup sliced yellow squash or zucchini (see Note)

2 carrots, thinly sliced (see Note)

1 Bring a large pot of salted water to a boil, add the egg noodles, and cook according to package directions. Drain the noodles and set them aside.

2 Heat the oil in a large skillet over medium heat. Add the chicken and cook, turning as needed, until browned on both sides, 5 to 7 minutes.

The Way to Begin a Meal

Just as the way you begin your day sets the tone for the rest of your waking hours, so the way you begin your meal sets the tone for both the meal and those enjoying it. That is why I always like to begin a meal with gratitude.

Giving thanks before a meal is common across many cultures and within many different faiths. For my ancestors, having food on the table each night was not a given. It was something that was hoped for and worked toward, but definitely not a given. It is important to me, personally, to draw my children's attention to the fact that there are still many families in the world for whom this is the case.

Setting your kids and family up to have a grateful heart before a meal bleeds into every area of their life. In just a few seconds or a couple of minutes each day, we are teaching them to hit pause on demands and schedules. We are helping them take a moment to experience the joy and peace of contemplating all that we have to be grateful for. Doing this one simple thing alters a person's thinking patterns and can easily change the course of his or her entire life.

So before your family and friends dig into the feast you've prepared, take a moment to help everyone catch a collective breath. Give thanks. For the food, for the hands that prepared it, and, most important, for the people around the table. ♥

3 Add the soup and ranch dressing mix to the skillet. Stir well and turn the chicken to coat it. Bring the liquid to a boil, then reduce the heat to medium and let simmer. Cover the skillet and simmer until the chicken is cooked through, about 10 minutes.

4 Uncover the skillet and stir in the broccoli, yellow squash, and carrots. Continue cooking until the vegetables are tender, about 10 minutes more.

5 Place the egg noodles on a platter and spoon the chicken and vegetables over the top. Serve hot.

NOTE: You may substitute a 16-ounce bag of frozen mixed vegetables, or an equivalent amount of the vegetables of your choice.

Chicken Fried Rice

SERVES 4

I just about lived on this chicken fried rice while writing this book. Most weeks I'd make a big batch of it for lunch on Monday and then ration it out over the next few days. When you're writing about food, you really want food! With this filling variety of flavors, this recipe can easily satisfy just about any craving. As with all of my recipes, feel free to customize it with whatever vegetables your family prefers and make it your own!

2 tablespoons vegetable oil

3 cups cooked rice, preferably brown

1 carrot, cut into ¼-inch slices or 1 cup matchstick carrots

1½ cups thinly sliced bell pepper (see Note)

½ cup diced onion (see Note)

1 cup fresh or frozen chopped broccoli

2 tablespoons low-sodium soy sauce

½ teaspoon ground black pepper

½ teaspoon garlic powder

2 large eggs, beaten

1 to 2 cups cubed cooked chicken

1 Heat the oil in a large skillet over medium heat for 2 to 3 minutes. Add the rice and cook, stirring constantly, until it is heated through, about 5 minutes.

2 Add the carrot, bell pepper, onion, broccoli, soy sauce, black pepper, and garlic powder and stir to combine. Continue to cook over medium heat, stirring constantly, until the vegetables are tender, about 10 minutes. Remove the rice mixture from the skillet and set it aside.

3 Pour the eggs into the skillet (no need to wash it) and cook, stirring often, until they are scrambled to your liking. Add the rice and vegetable mixture back into the skillet and stir well to combine. Add the chicken and cook until it is heated through, 3 to 4 minutes. Serve hot.

NOTE: In place of the bell pepper and onion, I often use a 12-ounce bag of frozen peppers-and-onions blend. This saves time and money and allows me to keep them on hand at all times. I have also used frozen mixed vegetables with great results.

"Being actively grateful causes others to pause and do a double take, not only at you but at their own lives. When we say, 'I am grateful for this . . .' and 'I am grateful for that . . .' folks think, 'Well, maybe instead of complaining, I should be grateful for those things, too,' and next thing you know, you've started a wonderful cycle!"

—*Christy*

Slow-Cooker Fiesta Chicken and Rice (SC)

SERVES 4

My kids love this dish because they get to select their own toppings, and I love it because it's easy to make ahead and reheat later. It is so good you will think you are sitting in a small cantina in Mexico.

Cooking spray (optional)

1 recipe Cream of Chicken Soup (page 282) or 1 can (10.5 ounces) condensed cream of chicken soup (fat-free works just fine here)

1 can (15 ounces) whole kernel corn, drained

1 can (15 ounces) black beans, drained and rinsed

1 cup salsa

1 packet (1.25 ounces) taco seasoning mix

3 pounds boneless, skinless chicken breasts

1 teaspoon salt

2 cups uncooked rice

Shredded Cheddar or Pepper Jack cheese, sour cream, guacamole, and/or salsa, for serving

1 If using a traditional oven, preheat it to 350°F and coat a 9- by 13-inch baking dish with cooking spray.

2 Pour the soup into a medium-size mixing bowl. Add the corn, black beans, salsa, and taco seasoning mix and stir to combine.

3 Place the chicken breasts in a 6-quart slow cooker or the prepared baking dish. Pour the soup mixture over the chicken.

4 *If using a slow cooker:* Cover and seal the pot and cook until the chicken is cooked through and tender, 7 to 8 hours on low, 3 to 4 hours on high. *If using a baking dish:* Cover the dish tightly with aluminum foil. Bake until the chicken is cooked through and tender, 30 minutes.

5 Thirty minutes before serving, fill a large saucepan with 4 cups of water. Add the salt and bring to a boil over medium-high heat. Add the rice to the pot and reduce the heat to low. Cover and cook, simmering until all the water is absorbed, 20 minutes.

6 Add the cooked rice to the chicken and stir to combine. Serve the chicken and rice with your favorite toppings.

"I discovered a long time ago that I wasn't superhuman. Sure, it was disappointing at first, but in the end it has made my life so much easier.

"Ease up on yourself today. You're only one person."

—*Christy*

Cheesy Chicken and Rice sc

SERVES 4

Warm rice, the sweetness of corn, all combined with juicy chicken and tangy, ooey-gooey cheese. This is one of those meals you just wanna eat in your pajamas at the end of a long day!

Cooking spray (optional)

3 pounds boneless, skinless chicken breasts, cut into strips (see Note, page 84)

1 large sweet onion, such as Vidalia, chopped

1 recipe Cream of Chicken Soup (page 282) or 1 can (10.5 ounces) condensed cream of chicken soup

1 box (8 ounces) Zatarain's Yellow Rice mix (see Note)

1 can (15 ounces) whole kernel corn, drained

1 cup shredded Cheddar cheese

1 If using a traditional oven, preheat it to 350°F. Spray a 9- by 13-inch baking dish with cooking spray.

Going North

Mama used to say, "If Christy gets it in her head to do something, she's gonna do it or die." Of course, nobody knows me like my mother does and I have to admit that she is right on that one.

I don't mean to be that way and it surely causes me far too much strife on any given day. I've lost a great deal of joy over the years simply because I get an idea in my head, and it ends up controlling me instead of me controlling it.

That was pretty much what happened on a beautiful spring weekend recently, which led to an epiphany . . . which led to this story.

Again, it was springtime, and I decided this was the year I was finally going to find those planters I wanted for my front porch. *I decided.* That was where this whole thing went south.

My husband needed some parts for our lawn mower, so we loaded up the family and headed off to the store. I just knew they'd have the planters I wanted, too.

The boys went to look for the parts while my daughter and I headed toward the garden section, both of us excited to get planters and flowers. Katy Rose and I looked and didn't see anything even close to what we were looking for . . . *so we looked again.* I had them pictured so vividly in my mind

that I just knew they had to have them. Still no luck. So we circled again . . . nothing.

I decided to go pick out flowers and then come back, feeling that once I had the flowers I wanted, the planters would have somehow appeared. Of course, I had decided that I *needed* periwinkles. Wouldn't you know it, not a periwinkle was in sight. *So we went back to where the planters were and circled again . . .*

This is where my husband found us about half an hour later. We headed out, although I was feeling slightly agitated, and I had him swing by a nearby garden store— they didn't have what I wanted, either.

We went home and had lunch. I did several online searches for what I was looking for, finding the exact thing, but at prices far above what I was able to pay. We did some housework and yard work before I decided to set off again, this time on my own to make it quicker to search from store to store. Three stores later, I could feel the anxiety welling up inside me. I was pretty frustrated, I was a little mad, and I was very disappointed.

Mostly though, that stubborn streak of determination had me running around in circles. It was so steadfast and strong in its hold on me that my chances of finding anything that could make me happy were disappearing pretty fast.

As I stood there with a growing knot of agitation, I mulled over where else I could go in hopes of finding what I was looking for. I came up with a mental list of five more stores, ten miles in this direction, fifteen in that … *and then I wondered how much larger that anxiety was gonna grow with each store.*

A quote came into my head that my friend Deb had recently posted on her Facebook page: "You have circled this mountain long enough. Go North" (Deut. 2:3). At that moment, it hit me. I was fighting a battle that simply was not worth fighting.

How often do we do that? How often do we wake up in the middle of a perfectly good life and decide to create a little stress for ourselves? We spend days, months, years, and sometimes lifetimes circling mountains that we built up in the middle of an otherwise green meadow. Negative attitudes, unnecessary drama, things that for whatever reason we decide to circle around and around instead of enjoying the good things.

The rest of my family was home on this beautiful sunny day, out playing in the yard and enjoying each other's company. There I was out on my own: circling a mountain, stepping away from a joyful day in my life to go on an anxiety-filled quest for something as silly as planters.

With the realization that I had circled this mountain for no real reason other than to be circling it, I went north, or in my case, *home.* I went back to my sunny green yard with the kids riding their bikes in the driveway.

There won't be any perfect rectangular planters filled with flowers on my porch this year. I'm no longer going to look for them, even if you tell me they are right down the road. But there also won't be a day or more of my life wasted seeking them out as if they were going to provide some type of fulfillment.

Life moves quickly. Every second, little joy-filled moments are floating through the air like the bubbles my children play with on the lawn. They're waiting to be plucked and experienced and every second we circle our seemingly important mountains, they are drifting right on by.

Sometimes we have to stop circling and go north. Go home. ♥

2 Place the chicken in a 6-quart slow cooker or the prepared baking dish. Sprinkle the chopped onion over the chicken and spoon the soup over everything.

3 *If using a slow cooker:* Cover and seal the pot and cook until the chicken is cooked through and tender, 7 to 8 hours on low, 3 to 4 hours on high. *If using a baking dish:* Cover the dish tightly with aluminum foil and bake until the chicken is tender and cooked through, 30 minutes.

4 Meanwhile, prepare the rice according to the package directions.

5 A few minutes before serving, add the cooked rice, corn, and cheese to the chicken mixture and stir well to combine. Serve hot.

NOTE: This yellow rice mix has Creole seasonings in it. If you'd like to substitute another brand, look for one that is already seasoned with your favorite flavors (saffron works well) rather than plain yellow rice.

Cashew Chicken Teriyaki SC

SERVES 4

This is another one of my recipes that duplicates our favorite takeout. Feel free to make your own variations: Substitute water chestnuts or peanuts for the cashews, or any fresh or frozen vegetable for the sugar snap peas. I like my cashews a little soft, so I add them at the beginning of the recipe. If you prefer yours crunchy, add them at the end.

> 2 pounds boneless, skinless chicken breasts
> 1 cup low-sodium teriyaki sauce
> 1 cup cashews
> 2 cups fresh or frozen sugar snap peas, thawed if frozen
> 2 cups hot cooked rice, for serving

1 If using a traditional oven, preheat it to 325°F.

2 Place the chicken in a 6-quart slow cooker or a 5-quart Dutch oven. Add the teriyaki sauce. If you prefer the cashews tender, add them to the pot now.

3 *If using a slow cooker:* Cover and seal the pot and cook until the chicken is tender and cooked through, 7 to 8 hours on low, 3 to 4 hours on high. *If using a Dutch oven:* Cover the pot and bake until the chicken is tender and cooked through, 2 hours.

4 Thirty minutes before the cooking time is finished, stir in the sugar snap peas and the cashews (if you did not add them earlier).

5 Spoon the chicken, veggies, and sauce over the hot cooked rice and enjoy!

Chicken Fettuccine

SERVES 4

Sometimes certain meals call for a little extra care. This chicken fettuccine is slightly more involved than most of the recipes in this cookbook but I think it's worth it. A rich cream sauce coats freshly cooked noodles with succulent chunks of chicken and a delightful crunch of pecans that have been sautéed in butter. This is a meal perfect for a special occasion.

Many thanks to Aimee Gibbs, who shared this recipe with Southern Plate. It is from her mother, Deb, who makes it for every birthday and big event in their family. It's no surprise they often have company to dinner!

FOR THE NOODLES AND CHICKEN

1 package (10 ounces) fettuccine

¼ cup (½ stick) butter

1 pound boneless, skinless chicken breasts, cut into bite-size cubes

¾ cup chopped pecans

1 cup sliced mushrooms

3 scallions, chopped

½ teaspoon salt

¼ teaspoon ground black pepper

½ teaspoon garlic powder

FOR THE SAUCE

½ cup (1 stick) butter

1 egg yolk

⅔ cup half-and-half

2 tablespoons dried parsley flakes

½ cup grated Parmesan cheese

¼ teaspoon salt

¼ teaspoon ground black pepper

¼ teaspoon garlic powder

Chicken Fettuccine

1 Bring a large pot of salted water to a boil, add the fettuccine, and cook according to package directions. Drain the pasta and set it aside in a large bowl.

2 Make the chicken: Melt the ¼ cup butter in a large skillet over medium heat. Add the chicken and sauté until it is cooked through, 5 to 7 minutes. Remove the chicken from the skillet and set it aside.

3 In the same skillet, add the pecans, mushrooms, scallions, the ½ teaspoon salt, ¼ teaspoon pepper, and ½ teaspoon garlic powder and sauté until the mixture

is heated through and the mushrooms are tender, 5 to 8 minutes.

4 Return the chicken to the skillet and stir well to combine. Cover the skillet and set it aside.

5 Make the sauce: Place all of the sauce ingredients in a medium saucepan over low heat, and cook, stirring constantly, until the sauce is just thickened, about 10 minutes. Pour the sauce over the chicken mixture and stir well.

6 Spoon the sauce and chicken over the cooked fettuccine, toss to combine, and serve.

4

Seafood

You'll probably notice right off that this chapter is the shortest in the book. There is a simple reason for that: I don't eat seafood. My reason is also pretty simple: My mother didn't eat seafood. Why didn't my mother eat seafood? Well, her mother didn't eat seafood. This goes back generations and it all boils down to one commonsense explanation: Cultures have their food traditions, and they're based on what was grown and raised locally.

My ancestors were mountain people. They didn't live in a place where seafood was available, so they just never ate it. Nowadays our world has shrunk to a point where once-regional foods are attainable across the country, but that happened a little too late for us—we already had our taste buds set on garden veggies and farm fare. I've tried all types of seafood, and I've had it prepared by some of the best chefs in the country—but I don't care for it because it isn't what I was raised on.

The wonderful thing about living in this day and age is that we have all manner of foods at the ready, and can choose what speaks to our heart. Since my heart doesn't speak seafood, I've collected some beloved recipes from dear friends and family to share with you instead.

Baked Tilapia

SERVES 4

Tilapia seems to be one of the most widely available and family-friendly types of fish in grocery stores these days. It has a mild taste that children love and it's also economical. If you don't live near a fish market, your best bet is to purchase frozen tilapia filets.

You can pull this meal together in no time flat, and whip up simple sides in the short time it takes the fish to cook. I suggest some hot rice and fresh Roasted Asparagus (page 171) or any of the vegetable recipes in this book.

    4 frozen tilapia filets (about 1 pound
        total), thawed
    ½ cup butter, melted
    1 teaspoon kosher salt
    ½ teaspoon ground black pepper
    1 tablespoon dried parsley flakes
    ½ teaspoon garlic powder

1 Preheat the oven to 350°F.

2 Place the tilapia filets in a single layer in a 9- by 13-inch baking dish. Pour the butter over the filets and flip them to coat. Sprinkle them evenly with the salt, pepper, parsley, and garlic powder.

3 Bake the fish until it flakes when cut into with a fork, 15 to 20 minutes. Remove from the oven and serve.

Heather's Lemon Parmesan Tilapia

SERVES 4 TO 6

Heather's husband is like me, he doesn't care for seafood. However, she makes this dish on a regular basis. She told me that every time she tells him they're having fish he groans, and then ends up eating two or three pieces once he gets home. He always says he doesn't like fish, but he loves this.

The baked fish ends up moist and flaky, and the Parmesan topping is lemony and flavorful. This would be a great starting point if you are dedicated to converting someone in your family to seafood.

Is "Fresh" Seafood Best?

Where I live, we still don't have access to truly fresh fish. Grocery store chains have displays of "fresh" fish, but at best, their stock has been there several days and the flavor has begun to deteriorate. If you're like me and don't live near a good fish market or in an area that has regular turnover of stock, frozen seafood is a great choice for quality and economy. To get the best quality, make sure the fish is shiny and rock solid, with no areas of freezer burn or ice crystals. (The fish should be stored below the frost line if it's in a freezer bin.) If you are unsure of the type of seafood to buy, the staff behind the seafood counter can answer any questions you may have about the taste of a particular product. And, if you decide to splurge on a fresh catch, be sure to talk to them first: They should know which fish is the freshest. A recent catch should have firm, shiny flesh that springs back when you press it. Be wary of discoloration, and any smells that are not clean and mild. The fish should not smell fishy! If you're buying a whole fish—often a great way to save money—the eyes should be clear, not glossy, and bulging a little bit.

Cooking spray (optional)

½ cup grated Parmesan cheese

¼ cup (½ stick) butter,
　at room temperature

3 tablespoons mayonnaise

2 tablespoons fresh lemon juice

¼ teaspoon dried basil

¼ teaspoon ground black pepper

⅛ teaspoon onion powder

⅛ teaspoon celery salt

6 to 8 tilapia filets (about 2 pounds)

1 Preheat the broiler on low with a rack placed on the top shelf. Coat a broiler pan with cooking spray or line a rimmed baking sheet with aluminum foil; set it aside.

2 Stir together the Parmesan cheese, butter, mayonnaise, and lemon juice in a small bowl. Stir in the basil, pepper, onion powder, and celery salt and mix until thoroughly combined. Set aside.

③ Arrange the filets in a single layer in the prepared pan and broil until lightly browned, 2 to 3 minutes. Flip the filets over and broil 2 to 3 minutes more, checking regularly to make sure they don't burn.

④ Remove the pan from the oven and brush the tops of the filets with the Parmesan cheese mixture. Return to the oven and broil until the topping is browned and the fish flakes easily with a fork, 2 minutes (be careful not to overcook the fish). Serve hot.

Mattie Lee's Salmon Patties

SERVES 4 TO 6

Mattie Lee was my friend Jyl's grandmother. She lived her life with grace and kindness, and was known never to have said a harsh word about anyone. Her heart was as warm as her kitchen, where she made these flavorful salmon patties. Her grandchildren always requested them whenever they came to visit.

1 can (14 ounces) salmon, with or without bones (see Note)
1 large egg
½ cup all-purpose flour
⅛ teaspoon ground black pepper
Vegetable oil, for frying
Lemon wedges, for serving

① Drain the salmon and dump it into a bowl (if it's not boneless, add the bones and all). Using a fork, break up any lumps and mash any soft bones down into the fish. Stir in the egg, flour, and pepper until combined. Form the mixture into four 3-inch patties or six 2-inch patties.

② Pour the oil to a depth of ¼ inch in a large skillet and place it over medium-high heat. Add the patties and cook, turning once, until browned on both sides, 3 to 4 minutes per side.

③ Serve hot with the lemon wedges alongside.

NOTE: The bones in canned salmon are soft, edible, and easily broken up with a fork. They're also an excellent source of calcium. If you prefer, though, you can purchase canned salmon without bones.

Fried Catfish

Fried Catfish

SERVES 4

Did I say I didn't eat seafood? Well, this is my recipe but my mother always says catfish doesn't count because it's "pond food, not seafood." I do love a good fish fry with crispy cornmeal-breaded catfish filets, finished off with Hush Puppies (page 230) and Vinegar Slaw (page 181).

Vegetable oil, for frying
1 cup cornmeal
½ teaspoon salt
½ teaspoon pepper
4 catfish filets (1 pound total)
Lemon wedges, vinegar, and/or store-bought tartar sauce, for serving

1 Pour the oil to a depth of ½ inch in a large skillet and place it over medium-high heat. Line a plate with paper towels and set it aside.

2 Place the cornmeal in a medium-size bowl and stir in the salt and pepper until combined.

3 Dredge the filets in the cornmeal mixture to coat on both sides.

4 Reduce the heat to medium. Place the filets in the skillet and cook, turning once, until browned on both sides, 5 to 6 minutes, then transfer them to the paper towel–lined plate to drain.

5 Serve the filets hot with the lemon wedges, vinegar, and/or tartar sauce.

"Today you are going to influence people. Your life, your behavior, your outlook, your attitude will be seen and even emulated by others. Your disposition will rub off on folks and the song in your heart will take root in their ears.

"Knowing this, how can we not do our best to make it a happy tune?"

—*Christy*

Erin's No-Fuss Shrimp Scampi

SERVES 4

My friend Erin loves to make this shrimp when the day has gotten away from her and she needs supper fast. The dish can be done, start to finish, in about 15 minutes!

1 package (10 ounces) fettuccine

1 pound peeled and deveined frozen medium to large shrimp

½ cup (1 stick) butter

1 tablespoon minced garlic

1 to 2 teaspoons lemon pepper

½ teaspoon kosher salt

2 tablespoons dried parsley flakes or ⅓ cup chopped fresh parsley

1 Bring a large pot of salted water to a boil over high heat. Add the fettuccine and cook according to package directions. Drain and return to the pot.

2 Meanwhile, place the shrimp in a colander, set it in the sink, and run cold water over it until the shrimp thaw slightly, 1 to 2 minutes. Set them aside.

3 Melt the butter in a large skillet over medium-high heat. Add the garlic and shrimp and cook, stirring until the shrimp turn pink, about 5 minutes. Add the lemon pepper, salt, and parsley, stir well, and remove from the heat. Pour the shrimp and sauce over the fettuccine, and toss to combine.

4 Transfer the fettuccine and shrimp to a platter and serve hot.

"Don't get so caught up in the scheduling, anxiety, and busyness of life today that you forget to take time to enjoy it! BREATHE. As Martha Foose, a fellow Southern cookbook author, once told me, 'Life is a marathon, not a race.'"

—*Christy*

Erin's No-Fuss Shrimp Scampi

West Indies Salad

SERVES 4

My aunt Sue has friends and family who live in Mobile, Alabama, where this salad is said to have been invented. Whenever she goes to visit, a dear friend or relative always has this salad waiting when she walks in the door. Sue says it's one of the most delicious welcomes you could ever hope to receive! She was kind enough to share the recipe with me and wanted me to assure you that sometimes the simplest recipes are the best.

    1 medium-size onion, diced
    1 pound fresh lump crabmeat
    Salt to taste
    Ground black pepper to taste
    ½ cup vegetable oil
        (Sue says not to use olive oil.)
    ⅓ cup cider vinegar
    ½ cup ice water
    1 head lettuce, washed, cored, and
        leaves separated, or crackers of
        your choice, for serving

1 Place half of the onion in a large bowl. Cover with the crabmeat and then sprinkle the remaining onion on top. Sprinkle salt and pepper over the mixture.

2 Stir together the oil, vinegar, and ice water in a small bowl. Pour it over the crabmeat mixture (do not stir it). Cover the bowl with plastic wrap and let marinate in the refrigerator for at least 2 hours, or overnight.

3 To serve, toss the salad lightly and arrange it on beds of lettuce or alongside your favorite crackers.

Patti's Seafood Salad

SERVES 4

My sister, Patti, often makes this salad for our holiday gatherings. She and my father are the only ones who eat it but between the two of them they practically lick the bowl clean! You see, Patti is the only one who takes after my

Your Choice for Today

Ever look at folks who always seem to be smiling and chipper and think, *Well, they must have an easier life than I have.* That's just not the case. I don't know a single human being who has made it to adulthood without their share of struggles and hard times. Everyone I know struggles each day, so don't discount happy or optimistic people as folks who just have it easy. Each of us has a choice to make when we wake up every morning. If you see someone smiling and making the best of their life, you know what choice they made. What is yours gonna be today? ♥

dad's side of the family as far as her love of seafood.

You can use real crabmeat but Patti usually chooses imitation to cut costs. You really can't tell the difference and it makes the dish more budget friendly.

1 pound imitation crabmeat
¼ cup chopped scallions
1 cup chopped celery
2 tablespoons low-fat mayonnaise
2 tablespoons nonfat plain yogurt
1 cup grated low-fat Cheddar cheese
¼ teaspoon paprika
1 tablespoon fresh lemon juice
Wheat crackers or toasted English
    muffins, for serving

1 Combine all of the ingredients except the crackers in a large bowl and stir until blended. Cover with plastic wrap and refrigerate for at least 2 hours, or overnight.

2 To serve, divide the salad onto the crackers and arrange on a platter.

You're Never Far from Home

Do you have those moments in your life that, no matter if they occurred twenty, thirty, or fifty years ago, can be called upon at a moment's notice and replayed in your mind as if they happened only yesterday?

I had one of those moments back when I was filming *Beat the Chefs,* a game show where home cooks compete with professionals to see whose version of a dish is best. We had a short break and I walked outside of the studio and looked up at the moon. I was on the tail end of a two-week filming session consisting of twelve-plus-hour days, working with some of the most wonderful people you could ever encounter. I'm blessed on many levels, but most important, I'm blessed because I have the wisdom to realize and see my blessings around me. That is a key factor that a lot of people miss. While I knew I was working with some special people and was living a dream of mine, it still did not stop me from missing my family something fierce.

I looked up at the moon and went back in time, a night just like that one, a moon just like the one I was seeing. My great-grandmother Lela had called me outside to join her in the driveway. "Come 'ere, Christy," she said. "I want you to look up at this moon." I stepped out onto the smooth cool concrete in my bare feet and looked up at her. Her face was weathered from a lifetime of hard work and caring for her family. There was that usual hint of a smile around the corners of her mouth and that little twinkle in her eyes that made you feel she knew something you didn't. Her countenance was made all the more beautiful by hair the color of the moon's glow and wrinkles from smiles dating back to 1902.

I followed her gaze up to the tilted crescent moon. "That's my favorite moon," she said. "When it's a-layin' on its back like that, it looks like it's restin'." Her lips curled up into a smile as she looked down to make sure I was looking up as she spoke. "Always did like to step out and look at the moon when it was like that."

Lela had lived a hard life, with years of working in the cotton fields and many times having to provide for her four kids on her own. Long hard days had given her strength that even advanced age couldn't take away, and here she was, looking up

and admiring the resting moon. I could just imagine how much it meant to her, when her back was nigh on breaking from picking cotton, to be able to find solace in knowing that even the moon got to rest sometimes.

The sky in Alabama is darker than it is in Los Angeles. The sky all those years ago was deep as pitch and the moon and stars were so bright they lit your path wherever you wanted to go, providing far more illumination than city streetlamps do. Lela was wearing her dark blue housecoat, just like the one of hers I have neatly folded and tucked away in a box

of treasures, which still holds the smell of her rose-scented lotion and Vita Moist face cream. She smiled up at the moon that night in a way that made me think she was stepping back to another moment, just like I do when I think of that night. In those moments, I find myself back under the carport with Lela, stepping to the edge to gaze up at the moon at her insistence that I do so.

I like it when it's resting like that, too, Lela. And thank you for giving me a little bit of home as I look at it again through your eyes. We're never as far from home as we think we are. ♥

5

Sandwiches

My family loves a good sandwich. Sometimes we eat them just because we're in the mood; other times, an occasion like tailgating or movie night demands a sandwich meal. Whatever your reason, sandwiches are always a quick and tasty solution for a day that is busier than most. They're also helpful to have on hand for those times when your kids might have to fend for themselves. When we were teenagers and our parents went out of town, my mother often made some ahead of time so my siblings and I wouldn't call with the age-old problem: "There is nothing here to eat."

You'll have all your bases covered with the sandwiches in this chapter. They are satisfying and delicious on their own, with your favorite sides, or simply served with chips and dips. And some can be made ahead and stored in the refrigerator, then quickly reheated in the microwave at a moment's notice.

Bama Steak and Cheese Sandwiches

MAKES 4 SANDWICHES

Philly folks are proud of their Philly steak and cheese with very good reason! So my shortcut version demanded a different name for those of us who need a quick, beefy, cheesy supper but don't have time to head to the Keystone State.

I keep things simple by picking up some roast beef from the deli counter. Our regional steak marinades, Dale's Steak Seasoning or Moore's Original Marinade, make the perfect sauce and really add a punch of flavor; I'm including my marinade recipe on page 284 in case neither is available in your area.

¼ cup (½ stick) butter

1 medium-size onion, chopped

1 bell pepper, stemmed, seeded, and chopped (optional)

4 tablespoons All-Purpose Marinade (page 284), Dale's Steak Seasoning, Moore's Original Marinade, or your favorite steak marinade

1 pound deli-sliced roast beef, chopped

1 to 2 cups shredded mozzarella cheese or cheese of your choice

4 soft deli rolls, halved

1 Melt the butter in a large skillet over medium heat. Add the onion, pepper, and 2 tablespoons of the marinade and sauté until the vegetables are tender, about 10 minutes.

2 Add the roast beef and the remaining marinade to the skillet and cook until the roast beef is warmed through, 5 minutes. Remove the skillet from the heat and sprinkle the mozzarella cheese over the beef mixture; let sit until the cheese has melted.

3 To serve, spoon some of the beef mixture onto the bottom half of each roll, then close up the sandwiches.

Two-Meals-in-One Beef Burritos sc

EACH MEAL SERVES 4

My family isn't big on leftovers, so when I have to repurpose a meal, I try to get creative. This is one of those great recipes that allows you to cook once and make two entirely different meals from a single effort. You make twice the meat you'll need for the burritos so you can use the second half tomorrow for barbecue sandwiches—or, if your family demands it, another round of burritos. If you've always had your burritos with ground beef, the shredded version here is sure to be a delightful switch!

1 chuck roast (4 to 5 pounds)

1 teaspoon kosher salt

½ teaspoon ground black pepper

1 recipe Basic Beef Gravy (page 285) or 1 jar (16 ounces) store-bought beef gravy

1 packet (1.25 ounces) taco seasoning mix

6 to 8 large flour tortillas or Maria's Flour Tortillas (page 230)

Shredded Cheddar or Pepper Jack cheese, sour cream, chopped tomatoes, chopped scallions, and/or avocado slices, for serving

❶ If using a traditional oven, preheat it to 350°F.

❷ Place the roast in a 6-quart slow cooker or 5-quart Dutch oven and sprinkle with the salt and pepper. Pour the beef gravy over the roast.

❸ *If using a slow cooker:* Cook until the roast is fall-apart tender, 8 hours on low, 4 hours on high. *If using a Dutch oven:* Cover and cook until the roast is fall-apart tender, 2½ to 3 hours.

❹ Remove the roast from the pot (if using an oven, leave it on), transfer it to a plate, and carefully discard the cooking liquid from the pot. When the roast has cooled slightly, use two forks to shred it. Reserve half the meat, covered and stored in the refrigerator for tomorrow's meal. Return the rest of the meat to the pot, add the taco seasoning and 2 cups of water, and stir to combine.

5 *If using a slow cooker:* Cover and seal the pot and cook on high until the mixture is heated through, 30 to 40 minutes. *If using a Dutch oven:* Cover and bake until the mixture is heated through, 30 minutes.

6 When the beef is almost done, place a large skillet over medium heat and in it warm each of the tortillas, turning once, about 1 minute per side. Remove the warm tortillas to a plate and cover with a clean kitchen towel.

7 Divide the beef mixture evenly among the warmed tortillas and serve with your favorite burrito accompaniments.

Barbecue Beef Sandwiches

Add 1 recipe Barbecue Sauce in a Hurry (page 287) or 1 bottle (18 ounces) store-bought barbecue sauce to the reserved beef and stir to combine. Place the beef in a medium-size saucepan over medium heat and cook until heated through, 10 minutes. Or heat it in a large bowl in the microwave on 100 percent power for 1 to 2 minutes. Serve the beef on hamburger buns.

Italian Beef Sandwiches ⓢⓒ

MAKES 8 SANDWICHES

These savory pulled-beef sandwiches—topped with peppers, onions, and mozzarella—are fun to take to a tailgating event. I make the meat ahead of time, and then transport it in my slow cooker along with the buns and shredded cheese.

But these aren't just for special sporting events—my husband loves to come home from work to these sandwiches for a hearty and fuss-free supper, too!

1 chuck roast (4 to 5 pounds)

1 recipe Basic Beef Gravy (page 285) or 1 jar (12 ounces) beef gravy

1 bottle (16 ounces) "zesty" Italian dressing

3 tablespoons vegetable oil

1 medium-size onion, chopped

1 bell pepper, stemmed, seeded, and chopped

8 kaiser rolls, halved

2 cups shredded mozzarella cheese, for serving

Italian Beef Sandwiches

1 If using a traditional oven, preheat it to 350°F.

2 Place the roast in a 4- or 6-quart slow cooker or a 5-quart Dutch oven and pour the beef gravy over it.

3 *If using a slow cooker:* Cover and seal the pot and cook until the roast is falling apart, 7 to 8 hours on low, 3 to 4 hours on high. *If using a Dutch oven:* Cover and bake until the roast is falling apart, 2½ hours.

4 Remove the roast from the pot (if using an oven, leave it on) and transfer it to a plate; discard the cooking juices. Use two forks to shred the meat, removing and discarding the fat. Return the meat to the pot, pour the Italian dressing over it, and stir to combine.

5 Heat the oil in a large skillet over medium-high heat. Add the onion and bell pepper and sauté until tender, about 5 minutes. Stir the vegetables into the beef mixture. Set the slow cooker to warm or the oven temperature to 200°F and let the beef mixture rest, covered, until you're ready to serve.

6 To serve, spoon the beef mixture onto the bottom half of each roll. Top the beef with the mozzarella, close up the sandwiches and serve.

Pizza Rolls

MAKES 12 SANDWICHES

When we were teenagers, our parents started getting out more by themselves and sometimes they'd even go away overnight on little trips. Mama always made two batches of these pizza rolls so we'd have quick heat-and-eat suppers. She was very sweet and thoughtful in doing so but I'm pretty sure she also did it so we wouldn't mess up her kitchen while she was gone.

It's easy to personalize this recipe by adding your favorite pizza toppings to the beef mixture. If you'd like to add onions, bell peppers, or another crunchy vegetable, simply cook them with the ground beef so they are tender.

You can serve these right away or refrigerate them, wrapped in plastic wrap, for three to four days. When you're ready to eat, remove the plastic wrap (see Note, page 138), place the pizza roll in a paper towel, and heat it in the microwave on 100 percent power for about 1 minute. If you have teenage boys, you might want to keep a stock of these handy!

I follow Mama's example and make these myself when I have to travel nowadays and I'm happy to report that they work like a charm—my kitchen is virtually untouched when I return!

> 2 pounds ground beef
> About 3 cups Quick Pizza Sauce (page 283) or store-bought pizza sauce
> 12 sub rolls (about 6 inches each)
> 2 cups shredded mozzarella cheese

1 Heat a large skillet over medium-high heat. Add the ground beef and cook until browned, about 10 minutes. Carefully drain and discard the grease.

2 Add the sauce to the beef in the skillet. Stir to combine and cook over medium heat until bubbly, about 10 minutes.

3 Use a sharp knife to split each sub roll lengthwise, cutting almost all the way

through. Open the rolls like a book and spoon the beef mixture into them, dividing the mixture evenly among the rolls. Sprinkle the mozzarella on top of the beef and close up the sandwiches. Serve warm.

Baked Stroganoff Sandwiches

MAKES 4 SANDWICHES

This is a basic baked sandwich recipe that can serve as a springboard for your creativity. Make it according to the recipe if you prefer to keep things simple. If you want to dress things up a bit, add sautéed onions and bell peppers, dried Italian seasoning, garlic powder, and any other toppings or seasonings you like before you fold up the dough. You can also use chicken in place of ground beef and add a can of diced green chiles to make a baked chicken sandwich with Mexican flair!

Have fun coming up with your own filling creations to really make this one your own. The possibilities are endless.

Cooking spray

1 pound ground beef or turkey

¼ teaspoon salt

⅛ teaspoon pepper

1 medium-size onion, chopped

1 cup chopped mushrooms
   (optional)

1 recipe Cream of Mushroom Soup
   (page 282) or 1 can (10.5 ounces)
   condensed cream of mushroom
   soup

¼ cup all-purpose flour

1 loaf frozen yeast bread dough,
   completely thawed

1 large egg, beaten

1 Lightly coat a baking sheet with cooking spray and set it aside.

2 Heat a large skillet over medium heat. Add the ground beef, sprinkle it with the salt and pepper, and cook, stirring to break up the beef, until it is fully browned, about 10 minutes. Add the onion and the mushrooms, if using, to the skillet and continue cooking until the onion is slightly translucent, 2 to 3 minutes more. Carefully drain off and discard the grease.

3 Transfer the beef mixture to a medium-size bowl, add the cream of mushroom soup, and stir to combine. Set aside.

4 Sprinkle the flour on a clean, flat surface and roll out the dough into a rectangle about 8 by 14 inches.

5 Spoon the beef filling lengthwise down the center of the dough, leaving about ½ inch of dough at the ends and on either side. Fold the sides of the dough over the filling as if wrapping a present and pinch the seam and the ends closed.

6 Place the dough, seam side down, on the baking sheet. Tear off a piece of plastic wrap large enough to cover the baking sheet and spray one side of it with oil to prevent it from sticking. Cover the filled dough with the plastic wrap, oiled side down. Set the baking sheet in a warm place and let the dough to rise until doubled in size, 1½ to 2 hours.

7 At least 1 hour into the dough's rising time, preheat the oven to 350°F.

8 Remove the plastic wrap (see Note, page 138) and brush the dough with the egg. Use a sharp knife to cut 4 to 6 angled slits, each about ¼ inch deep, widthwise along the top of the dough.

9 Bake the filled dough until the top is golden brown, 30 minutes. Allow it to cool for a few minutes, then slice it into 4 sandwiches and serve.

Big Juicy Burgers

MAKES 6 BURGERS

Growing up, I loved hamburger night at my house. Mama made thick, hearty burgers in a skillet and served them with big old French fries and plenty of ketchup on the side. I serve these to my children with fries, chips, or raw vegetables, whichever I happen to have on hand at the time. My favorite part of this recipe is that there is no need to fire up a grill or break a sweat!

The secret to these is browning them and then cooking them in a little water, which sizzles off and leaves the burgers nice and moist.

2 pounds ground beef or turkey

1 medium-size egg

1 package (1 ounce) dried onion
    soup mix

3 tablespoons vegetable oil
    (optional)

Sliced cheese of your choice,
    for serving (optional)

6 hamburger buns, for serving

Lettuce, tomatoes, pickles,
    mayonnaise, mustard, onions,
    and/or avocado (or anything else
    that interests you!), for serving
    (optional)

1 Place the ground beef, egg, and onion soup mix in a large bowl. Mix well with your hands. Mold the beef mixture into 6 donut-shaped patties each about ½ inch thick.

2 Heat a large skillet over medium heat, adding the oil if using very lean beef or turkey. Add the patties and cook, turning once, until browned, 3 to 5 minutes per side.

Big Juicy Burgers

3 Pour 1 cup of water into the skillet and continue cooking until the water has evaporated and the patties are cooked through, 15 to 20 minutes.

4 If desired, top each patty with a couple slices of cheese while still in the skillet. Remove the patties to a platter and serve alongside the buns and hamburger toppings.

Oven-Baked Sloppy Joes

MAKES 4 SANDWICHES

My feeling is that you can never have too many delicious sloppy joe recipes. After all, it is an all-American classic, right up there with apple pie! This recipe combines two of my favorites, fresh bread and sloppy joes. Because the meat is baked into the bread, these are wonderful for eating in front of the TV while the football game is on, since they are not as messy as regular sloppy joes. Give them a try and I think you will agree!

Cooking spray

2 pounds ground beef

1 teaspoon salt

¼ teaspoon ground black pepper

1 can (14.5 ounces) diced tomatoes, with their juice

1 cup ketchup

3 tablespoons sweet pickle relish

2 tablespoons Worcestershire sauce

1 tablespoon yellow mustard

¼ cup brown sugar

1 teaspoon minced garlic

¼ cup all-purpose flour

1 loaf frozen yeast bread dough, completely thawed

1 large egg, beaten

1 Lightly coat a baking sheet with cooking spray and set it aside.

2 Heat a large skillet over medium heat. Add the ground beef, sprinkle with the salt and pepper, and cook, stirring to break up the beef, until fully browned, about 10 minutes. Carefully drain off and discard the grease.

3 Add the tomatoes, ketchup, relish, Worcestershire sauce, mustard, brown sugar, and garlic to the skillet and stir to combine. Cook over medium heat until bubbly, 10 minutes. Reduce the heat to low and simmer, stirring from time to time until thickened, 10 minutes.

4 Meanwhile, sprinkle the flour on a clean, flat surface and roll out the dough into a rectangle about 8 by 14 inches.

5 Spoon the beef mixture lengthwise down the center of the dough, leaving about ½ inch of dough on either side. Fold the sides of the dough over the filling as if wrapping a present and pinch the seam and the ends closed.

6 Place the filled dough, seam side down, on the baking sheet. Tear off a piece of plastic wrap large enough to cover the baking sheet and spray one side of it with oil to prevent it from sticking to the bread. Cover the filled dough with the plastic wrap, oiled side down. Set the baking sheet in a warm place and let the dough rise until doubled in size, 1½ to 2 hours.

7 At least 1 hour into the dough's rising time, preheat the oven to 350°F.

8 Remove the plastic wrap (see Note, page 138) and brush the dough with the egg. Use a sharp knife to cut 4 to 6 angled slits, each about ¼ inch deep, widthwise along the top of the dough.

9 Bake the filled dough until the top is golden brown, 30 minutes. Allow it to cool for a few minutes, then slice it into 4 sandwiches and serve.

Not Your Average Joe Sloppy Joes

MAKES 8 SANDWICHES

The first time I made these, my husband took one bite and his eyes got really big. Then he took another bite, and his eyes got even bigger! After that, he practically inhaled the rest of the sandwiches. I've gotten the same reaction whenever I serve them to anyone, so watch your family for those bulging eyes and you'll know you've got a winner!

I like to make a double recipe of this and freeze the other half for a superquick meal on one of my busier days. Why cook just one meal when the same effort and time can produce two?

3 tablespoons vegetable oil
(optional)

2 pounds ground beef or turkey

1 medium-size sweet onion,
such as Vidalia, chopped

1 can (14.5 ounces) petite diced
tomatoes, with their juice

1 cup ketchup

2 tablespoons Worcestershire sauce

3 tablespoons sweet pickle relish

1 tablespoon prepared yellow
mustard

¼ cup brown sugar

1 teaspoon minced garlic

8 hamburger buns, for serving

1 cup shredded Cheddar cheese

1 Heat a large skillet over medium heat, adding the oil if using very lean beef or turkey. Add the ground beef and cook, stirring to break up the meat, until it is fully browned, about 10 minutes. Carefully drain off and discard the grease.

2 Add the onion, tomatoes, ketchup, Worcestershire sauce, relish, mustard, brown sugar, and garlic to the skillet and stir to combine. Cook over medium heat until just bubbly, 10 minutes. Reduce the heat to low and simmer, stirring from time to time, until thickened, 10 minutes.

3 Meanwhile, toast the hamburger buns.

4 Remove the skillet from the heat and stir the Cheddar cheese into the beef mixture. When the cheese has melted, divide the beef mixture among the toasted hamburger buns and serve hot.

Pulled Pork Sandwiches with Clear Barbecue Sauce SC

MAKES ENOUGH FOR 16 SANDWICHES

First of all, let me start this by stating that there is no such thing as bad barbecue! Whatever barbecue you have in your region, whatever barbecue is your favorite, whatever barbecue you think is the best in the world, I will stand up next to you and declare with my dying breath that you are absolutely right.

Pulled pork barbecue is pretty much heaven on a bun as far as I'm concerned. It seems every region has its own way of making it: Where I am from, the barbecue is smoked and juicy, served with a little bit of clear mild vinegar sauce poured over it, perhaps some of my White Barbecue Sauce (page 286), too.

In my husband's neck of the woods, it is served slathered in a thick layer of sweet red sauce, like the bottled barbecue sauce you buy in the stores. (I share a recipe for pulled pork barbecue like that on page 135.)

This recipe is for the juicy kind they make in barbecue joints where I grew up, but instead of smoking it (because I can think of a few things I'd rather do than stand over a fire for hours on end), I cook it overnight in a slow cooker. You can also make it in a Dutch oven—I've given you directions for that as well. The best part? This one recipe will yield enough barbecue for a few meals or one large gathering. It also freezes and reheats well (see Notes, page 135), which you'll appreciate on busy nights!

1 Boston butt pork roast
   (about 5 pounds)
1 tablespoon salt
1 teaspoon ground black pepper
1½ cups cider vinegar
2 tablespoons brown sugar
1 tablespoon hot sauce, such as
   Texas Pete's (see Notes)
1 teaspoon crushed red pepper
   flakes
16 sandwich buns, split in half,
   for serving

1 If using a traditional oven, preheat it to 325°F.

2 Place the roast in a 6-quart slow cooker or 5-quart Dutch oven with a lid, sprinkle it with the salt and pepper, and pour the cider vinegar over it.

3 *If using a slow cooker:* Cover and seal the pot and cook on low until the roast is fork tender, 12 hours (I cook mine overnight). *If using a Dutch oven:* Cover the pot and bake until the roast is fork tender, 3 to 4 hours.

4 Remove the roast to a cutting board and reserve 2 cups of the cooking liquid in a medium-size bowl. Shred the pork

Pulled Pork Sandwiches with Clear Barbecue Sauce

with two forks (this will be very easy) and return it to the pot.

5 To the reserved cooking liquid, add the brown sugar, hot sauce, and crushed pepper flakes, and stir well to combine.

6 Pour the sauce over the shredded pork and cover. Serve warm, dividing the pork evenly among the buns.

NOTES: This sauce is not spicy. If you prefer a spicier sauce, double the hot sauce and crushed red pepper flakes, according to your individual taste.

It's simple to freeze any leftovers: When the pork has cooled, divide it into meal-size portions and freeze them in ziplock bags (they will keep for up to 3 months). To reheat the pork, thaw it overnight in the refrigerator, then transfer it into a large bowl, cover, and heat it in a microwave until warmed through, 4 to 5 minutes, stirring halfway through.

Pulled Pork Sandwiches with Red Sauce sc

MAKES ABOUT 16 SANDWICHES

This is my husband's idea of pulled pork barbecue and it's awfully good. Although I grew up on barbecue with vinegar sauce (opposite), since we've been married we've managed to win each other over to both sides!

Like the Pulled Pork with Clear Barbecue Sauce (opposite), this one also freezes and reheats well; see the Notes at left.

1 Boston butt pork roast
   (about 5 pounds)
2 bottles (18 ounces each) "red"
   barbecue sauce or 2 recipes
   Barbecue Sauce in a Hurry
   (page 287)
16 hamburger buns, split in half,
   for serving
1 recipe Vinegar Slaw (page 181)
   or 4 cups store-bought coleslaw,
   for serving

1 If using a traditional oven, preheat it to 350°F.

2 Place the roast in a 5- to 6-quart slow cooker or Dutch oven with a lid and top it with half of the barbecue sauce.

3 *If using a slow cooker:* Cover and seal the pot and cook on low until the roast is fork tender, 12 hours or overnight. *If using a Dutch oven:* Cover the pot and bake until the roast is fork tender, 4 hours.

4 Carefully remove the roast to a cutting board to cool; discard the cooking juices. When the roast is cool enough to handle, shred it with two forks.

5 Return the pork to the pot, add the remaining barbecue sauce, and stir well to combine. Set the slow cooker to high and cook until heated through, 15 to 20 minutes (or place the pork back in the Dutch oven, set it over medium heat, and cook until heated through, 10 minutes).

6 Divide the pork among the buns, top with the vinegar slaw, close up the sandwiches, and serve.

Stuffed Pizza Sticks

SERVES 4

This is a great recipe for family movie nights, but you'll find it brings 'em running anytime it's served. When I first posted it on Southern Plate, my dad printed it off for my mother and asked if she'd make it the next day. Since then, he keeps printing it off and leaving it on the kitchen counter as a hint. Mama said she has to make it a few times a month or she knows that paper will show up again.

My family, God love them, hasn't got much of an adventurous streak when it comes to pizza toppings. I pretty much like everything except little fish and fruit on my pizza. They like: pepperoni. Yup, that's it. Pepperoni. So I suggest you use whatever pizza toppings your family likes to make this a custom recipe just for you. With just one batch or jar of pizza sauce, you'll have plenty left over for dipping.

Cooking spray
¼ cup all-purpose flour

1 loaf frozen yeast bread dough, thawed (I use Rhodes, which comes in packs of three)

1 recipe Quick Pizza Sauce (page 283) or 1 jar (15 ounces) store-bought pizza sauce

1 to 2 cups shredded mozzarella cheese

Black olives, pepperoni, sliced cooked meatballs, onions, green peppers, and/or crumbled cooked breakfast sausage, for topping (optional)

1 large egg, beaten

1 Lightly coat a 9- by 13-inch baking dish with cooking spray and set it aside.

2 Sprinkle flour on a clean, flat surface and roll out the dough into a ½-inch-thick rectangle. Let it rest for 5 minutes. After the dough has relaxed, roll it into a rectangle roughly 14 by 9 inches.

3 Envision the dough being divided lengthwise into three sections. Spread ½ cup of the sauce lengthwise over the middle section of the dough. Sprinkle the mozzarella cheese over the sauce, followed by the pizza toppings.

4 Using clean hands, dip your fingertips in water and wet the edges of the dough. Fold the first section over the meat mixture and then the third section over the first. Pinch the ends shut. Place the loaf, seam side down, in the prepared baking dish.

5 Lightly coat one side of a piece of plastic wrap with cooking spray and use it to cover the loaf. Set the baking dish in a warm place and let it rise until doubled in size, 1½ to 2 hours.

6 At least 1 hour into the dough's rising time, preheat the oven to 350°F.

7 Remove the plastic wrap (see Note) and brush the dough with the egg. Use a sharp knife to cut 4 to 6 angled slits, each about ¼ inch deep, widthwise along the top of the dough.

8 Bake the filled dough until the top is golden brown, 25 to 30 minutes. Allow it to cool for a few minutes, and then slice it into 1½-inch sticks.

9 Place the remaining sauce in a small bowl and warm it in the microwave, 20 to 30 seconds. Serve the pizza sticks with the sauce alongside for dipping.

NOTE: I added in "remove the plastic wrap" because when I was 14 years old, my mother didn't tell me that part when she asked me to put one of her lasagnas into the oven for our family's supper. She was pretty surprised at the smell when she came in the door and quickly realized that she needed to be *very* specific in her instructions!

"It's gonna be a beautiful day today. I haven't checked the weather, I don't know the temperature, but I know it's going to be beautiful. Because I just decided."

—*Christy*

Ham Salad

MAKES ABOUT 3 CUPS, ENOUGH FOR 6 TO 8 SANDWICHES

This is one of those old-fashioned recipes that uses up leftovers and scraps of ham to make something pretty, filling, and delicious.

There are as many ways to do ham salad as the day is long, so if you don't have your own recipe, feel free to take this one and customize it to your tastes or to what you have on hand. Don't have spicy brown mustard? Use a bit of yellow mustard and add a little more pepper if you like. Dislike mustard altogether? Then by all means just use mayonnaise. Go for it. Tweak it, mix it up, taste it, and make it your own.

Ham salad is excellent on sandwiches, on crackers, or in a bowl with dipping veggies.

2 cups chopped smoked or baked
     ham, cut up as finely as you like
     (I like mine coarsely chopped)
½ cup mayonnaise
¼ cup sweet pickle relish

1 teaspoon spicy brown mustard

Ground black pepper to taste
   (see Note)

2 hard-boiled eggs, chopped

Place the ham, mayonnaise, relish, mustard, and pepper in a large bowl. Stir with a spoon until well blended. Gently fold in the chopped eggs. Cover and refrigerate until ready to serve.

Ham salad will keep, covered, in the refrigerator for 3 or 4 days.

NOTE: I usually don't add salt to this because the ham is salty, but add it if you like!

Chicken Salad

MAKES ABOUT 3 CUPS, ENOUGH FOR 6 TO 8 SANDWICHES

My mother and I love to get together and chat over chicken salad sandwiches made just like this! There is nothing like some good chunky chicken salad in a soft bread roll. This recipe adds in the juicy sweetness of grapes, the crunch of pecans, and crisp apple. Feel free to adapt it to your own personal tastes—some folks don't like grapes, others prefer to leave the apple out.

Serve the chicken salad on a bed of lettuce leaves, or topped with lettuce and tomato in sandwiches.

1 small apple, unpeeled for color,
   cored and coarsely chopped
   (I like Red Delicious)

½ cup coarsely chopped seedless
   grapes

½ cup coarsely chopped pecans or
   almonds

1 cup chopped cooked chicken

½ cup mayonnaise

¼ teaspoon salt

¼ teaspoon ground black pepper

Combine the apple, grapes, and pecans in a large bowl. Add the chicken, mayonnaise, salt, and pepper and stir until combined.

The chicken salad will keep, covered, in the fridge for up to 4 days.

Your Life Through Rainbow-Colored Glasses

A few years ago I picked up a magazine and read an interesting article about the most amazing person—a woman who'd left her life in the big city to return home to Alabama and buy her own dairy. She began a stunningly successful venture that has earned countless accolades and awards.

The photo showed her walking in a field among goats. It was beautiful; just looking at it made my heart soar. Already well into the fourth decade of my life, *I wanted to be her when I grew up.*

I've often thought things like that, particularly when reading about life on a farm or when flipping through one of those pretty magazines that show women in aprons with contented smiles on their faces like they woke up in an early Judy Garland film.

As it turned out, the woman in this particular article and I have several friends in common. After a brief email introduction we found ourselves on the telephone talking kids and food—and I realized the woman walking among the goats was just like me in more ways than not.

I think we all have a tendency to look at the lives of others through rainbow-colored glasses, but you know what? I can assure you there is someone in this world who views you in a similar romanticized fashion.

So why do we tend to do this when observing others and not when looking at ourselves? I guess it's just easier when you're on the outside looking in. Our nature has us thinking *He or she has it all. Life must be grand.* And *Ours would be, too, if only we had X, Y, and Z.*

Experience and wisdom from the old folks has taught me that this is where the rubber meets the road for most of us in terms of whether or not we are going to achieve (or choose) happiness. *You see, at the end of the day, it's all about blooming where you're planted.*

Blooming where you're planted is about appreciating what you have and focusing on the positive.

Last year, when we moved to our new home, I felt a tremendous appreciation and gratitude toward not only the house itself but the land surrounding it as well.

Everything was green and lush, and to me it just looked magical.

Wildflowers sprang forth in little nooks and crannies like treasures presenting themselves to me. Ferns sprouted up randomly out of the yard as if they were checking up on us and just wanted to say "hi." Since I'd always longed for a hydrangea bush, imagine my delight at finding not one but *seven* blue hydrangea bushes flourishing in my new backyard, each producing my favorite color of hydrangea. I had found, in my mind and my heart, a utopia to raise my family in.

I wanted my new home to have a name and eventually settled on Bountiful, due to all of the bounty it had offered up to us as a family. I've often had folks email me when I speak so lovingly about Bountiful and ask me where it is. Since I view my home in a very romantic fashion, I tend to talk about it that way as well. From time to time I show photos from my yard on SouthernPlate.com and take care to frame them so I can better convey the beauty that I see. Over time, people have come to think of Bountiful as if it is some grand Southern estate, and in my mind it truly is. If you were to come visit Bountiful, though, you might be surprised to find that it rests right smack dab in the middle of an ever-crowded city and close enough to municipal buildings that every time there is a medical or police emergency our serenity is pierced with sirens and flashing lights.

But to me and to those who read my ramblings, Bountiful is how I see it. It is my home, my utopia, my own Southern estate. I don't sit around wishing for white columns on the front porch; instead I focus on the lush green grass and the gardens I plant with my kids. The strong and sturdy walls that protect us from the elements and the sunshine that beams into my window each morning.

The secret, too, is that *I decided to fall in love with my home and each day I decide to fall in love with my life.* I make it a point, whenever I put those rainbow-colored glasses on that we tend to view other people's lives with, to look into the mirror and be sure to give my own life more than just a passing glance.

Your life deserves no less. ♥

Chicken Patties

MAKES 5 TO 7 SANDWICHES

I love being able to recycle food into new dishes—mainly because I hate to waste food when I could provide one more delicious meal from it, and also because that is the way of my ancestors.

This is a great way to use leftover chicken. If you have leftover fried chicken, just take the skin off and shred it up! Leftover rotisserie chicken can also be used, as well as canned chicken. To really give this recipe a twist, substitute canned tuna or salmon for the chicken. I like these patties so much, though, that I usually cook chicken special just to make them.

1 sleeve saltine crackers
    (about 35 crackers)
2 cups chopped cooked chicken
¾ cup milk
2 large eggs
1 small onion, finely chopped
1 tablespoon poultry seasoning
¼ teaspoon salt
⅛ teaspoon ground black pepper
2 tablespoons vegetable oil

Hamburger buns, for serving
Mayonnaise, lettuce leaves, and
    sliced tomato, for serving

1 Put the crackers in a large ziplock bag, seal it, and finely crush them by hand or with a rolling pin.

2 Place the chicken in a large bowl, add the crushed crackers, and stir to combine.

3 Whisk together the milk, eggs, onion, poultry seasoning, salt, and pepper in a separate, small bowl. Pour the milk mixture over the chicken mixture and stir well to combine. Cover the bowl with a dish towel and allow the mixture to sit until it has moistened, 5 minutes.

4 Form the chicken mixture into 5 to 7 patties (each about ½ inch thick).

5 Place the oil in a large skillet and heat it over medium-high heat until hot, 2 to 3 minutes. (When the oil is hot enough, a small piece of cracker will sizzle when dropped into it.) Reduce the heat to medium.

6 Working in batches and being careful not to overcrowd the skillet, carefully add the chicken patties to the skillet and cook them, turning once, until well browned on both sides, 7 to 8 minutes.

7 Serve the chicken patties on their own or on buns, with the mayonnaise, lettuce, and tomato slices, if you like.

NOTE: These patties can be easily frozen after step 4. To reheat, start with step 5 and allow for a slightly longer cooking time when browning the patties in the skillet, about 15 minutes total.

Disconnect to Connect

Here is a bit of wisdom from me to you that has helped me keep my sanity:

- Facebook has a logout button.
- The TV can be turned off.
- Phones can power down.

When it feels like negativity is the only thing flowing through the wires, unplug from the constant connection.

Get outside. Take a walk. Look up at the trees and remember how small it all is in comparison.

I can assure you that this will lead to better mental, spiritual, and physical health. It will cause more smiles and decrease angst, and you'll breathe deeper than you have in years.

Now go have a *wonderful* life today! ♥

6

Casseroles

There is something heartwarming about serving a casserole for supper. It always brings back memories of a home-cooked meal at my mama's table with all the family gathered around. The beauty of serving casseroles is that while they taste like they have taken a long time to prepare, they are really one of the simplest meals to throw together. Usually casseroles contain everything needed for a meal except for bread—and a dessert if you really want to go over the top. The meat and vegetables are all cooked together into a wonderful concoction that everyone seems to love. I hope your family enjoys these casseroles as much as mine does!

Deep-Dish Pizza

SERVES 6 TO 8

Anyone with hungry men and teenage boys to feed, get ready for a home run with this one! Deep-dish pizza was often served in school cafeterias when my mother was a girl. I just love recipes from the lunch ladies back in the old days! Back then they used to get to the school long before it opened and make everything from scratch. Mama said the kids couldn't wait to see what was on the menu each day because everything was so good.

Don't let the long list of ingredients here deter you. This is a quick and easy recipe to throw together. One of the best things about it is how incredibly adaptable it is to whatever ingredients you have on hand. I've made it before with absolutely no cheese and it was still delicious!

When you remove this dish from the oven, the tender crust will be on top, with all of the yummy goodness bubbling beneath.

Cooking spray
2 pounds ground beef
1 medium-size onion, chopped
1 green bell pepper, stemmed, seeded, and chopped (optional)
Dash of ground black pepper
1½ tablespoons dried Italian seasoning
2 cups Quick Pizza Sauce (page 283) or 1 jar (15 ounces) store-bought pizza sauce
2 large eggs
1 cup whole milk
1 cup all-purpose flour
1 tablespoon vegetable oil
½ teaspoon salt
2 cups shredded mozzarella or Cheddar cheese
½ cup grated Parmesan cheese (you can substitute more mozzarella)

❶ Preheat the oven to 350°F. Coat a 9- by 13-inch baking dish with cooking spray.

❷ Heat a large skillet over medium heat. Place the ground beef in the skillet and cook until browned, using a wooden spoon to break up and stir the beef, about 10 minutes.

Deep-Dish Pizza

3 Add the onion and bell pepper, if using, and cook until the onion is translucent and the bell pepper is tender, 3 to 5 minutes. Carefully drain off and discard the grease.

4 Add the black pepper, Italian seasoning, and pizza sauce to the skillet and stir well to combine.

5 Place the eggs, milk, flour, vegetable oil, and salt in a large mixing bowl and stir to combine.

6 Sprinkle the mozzarella cheese over the bottom of the prepared baking dish and spread the beef mixture on top. Pour the egg mixture over the meat. Sprinkle the Parmesan cheese over all. Bake until the cheese is melted and the crust is golden, 30 minutes.

7 Cut the pizza into squares and use a spatula to serve.

Eggplant Parmesan

SERVES 4

Friends often give me eggplant during gardening season and I love to whip up this delicious vegetarian supper. Feel free to use the larger amount of sauce if you like, or go with less to keep it light and allow the eggplant's flavor to shine.

Cooking spray
1 recipe Fried Eggplant (page 187)
1 cup shredded mozzarella cheese
2 to 3 cups Simple Marinara Sauce
 (page 284) or store-bought
 marinara sauce
1 cup freshly grated Parmesan
 cheese

1 Preheat the oven to 350°F. Coat a 9- by 13-inch baking dish with cooking spray.

2 Place the fried eggplant slices in the baking dish and sprinkle the mozzarella cheese over them. Spread the sauce over the mozzarella and then evenly sprinkle the Parmesan cheese over the top.

3 Bake until the cheese is melted and the sauce is bubbly, 20 minutes. Serve hot.

Make Life an Adventure

Family Adventure Days began when my husband and I realized that while we and the kids were all at home together on the weekends, we weren't actually tuning in to each other as a family. Since the temptations of video games, TV, and the Internet were distracting us from each other, we decided to set aside one day each weekend to leave the house and have some family fun.

Most of the time, we try to make our adventure days inexpensive. This is easy to do since the whole premise is to spend time together, not spend money. Every now and then, though, we'll do something a little more extravagant, like head up to a cabin in the mountains.

I hope you'll consider taking a Family Adventure Day soon, and that it becomes a tradition you'll enjoy for years to come. Just be sure you declare it to be an "Adventure Day" because that sets it up to be fun in the kids' eyes right from the start. Here are some ideas to inspire you.

Be a tourist in your hometown. Even though I've lived in this town all of my life, we've still managed to find a few museums and attractions that we'd never been to!

Take a hike. We love to take short hikes when the weather is nice. It's a great way to escape being cooped up in the house, get some exercise, and have fun together the same time.

Go geocaching. Sometimes on our hikes we throw in a little geocaching as well. The activity is similar to going on a scavenger hunt but using your smartphone to help find the "treasure." There are caches hidden all over the world and some of them even have little prizes inside for the kids. (Find out more information at geocaching.com.)

Declare everyday activities adventures! Once, we were at a loss for what to do on our special day. Since we needed to get groceries, we told the kids we're going to make grocery shopping an adventure. It is amazing how much fun we had at the grocery store with everyone helping to plan what we'd cook. We even ate lunch in the deli. When we left, my daughter said, "That was the best Family Adventure Day ever," and my son replied with, "Yeah, it really was."

Remember, it's not about what you do, it's about the time you spend together!

Pizza Casserole

SERVES 8

I met Jen Hauler through my website and have had the joy of getting to know her through her comments and emails over the past few years. She is a sweet-hearted person who dearly loves her family, and she's one of the most memorable people I've ever known. When she sent me this recipe and told me how much her family loved it, I knew mine would feel the same way! I was doubly honored when she agreed to let me share it with you and your family, too.

Cooking spray

1 box (16 ounces) penne pasta

2 pounds ground beef

½ cup chopped onion

2 tablespoons seasoning salt,
 such as Lawry's

2 recipes Quick Pizza Sauce
 (page 283) or 2 jars
 (15 ounces each) store-bought
 pizza sauce (about 4 cups)

2 cups shredded mozzarella cheese

1 package (7 ounces) sliced
 pepperoni

1 Preheat the oven to 350°F. Lightly coat a 9- by 13-inch baking dish with cooking spray and set it aside.

2 Bring a large pot of salted water to a boil, add the penne, and cook according to package directions. Drain the pasta and set aside.

3 Heat a large skillet over medium-high heat. Place the ground beef, onion, and seasoning salt in the skillet and cook, using a wooden spoon to break up and stir the beef, until fully browned, about 10 minutes. Carefully drain off and discard the grease.

4 Transfer the beef mixture to a large bowl. Add the penne, pizza sauce, 1 cup of the cheese, and the pepperoni and stir well to combine. Pour the beef mixture into the prepared baking dish.

5 Sprinkle the remaining mozzarella over the beef mixture and bake until the cheese is melted and the sauce is bubbling, 20 minutes. Serve hot.

Stacey's Mexican Chicken Casserole

SERVES 4 TO 6

My friend Stacey Little loves to cook about as much as I do. We became friends through our blogs and I quickly adopted him and his wonderful family into my own. He shared this recipe with me and I just love how easy it is. The best part is that you don't even have to cook the rice before adding it; everything bakes together in the oven to produce a full and flavorful meal.

Cooking spray

4 cups chopped cooked chicken
  (about 2 pounds)

2 cups uncooked instant rice

1 recipe Cream of Chicken Soup
  (page 282) or 1 can (10.5 ounces)
  condensed cream of chicken soup

1 cup sour cream

½ cup diced onion

1 can (10 ounces) Ro*tel diced
  tomatoes and green chiles

¼ teaspoon ground cumin

½ teaspoon garlic powder

1½ cups chicken broth

8 ounces shredded Cheddar cheese

1 Preheat the oven to 350°F. Lightly coat a 9- by 13-inch baking dish with cooking spray.

2 Place the chicken, rice, soup, sour cream, onion, Ro*tel, cumin, garlic powder, chicken broth, and half of the cheese in a large bowl and stir well with a large spoon to combine.

3 Turn the mixture out into the prepared baking dish and top it with the remaining cheese. Bake until the casserole is hot and bubbly, 30 minutes. Serve hot.

"Hope is the warm
rays of sun stretching
up from the horizon
in all situations.
There is always hope."

—Christy

Finding the Perfect Casserole Dish

I have a collection of vintage Pyrex and Fire-King casserole dishes from the '50s through the '70s that I dearly love. I've collected these over the years at flea markets, online auction sites, and yard sales, though my favorites are the ones that were handed down to me by my mother and my husband's family.

I find that vintage casserole dishes have a charm and beauty that is not often seen in today's world of clear glass and stark white serving pieces. Baking something in a dish with pretty flowers painted on it just makes it more fun for me.

The durability of these dishes is superior to newer ones in many ways, but there are some things to look out for when shopping for vintage bakeware. Make sure there are no chips, as these suggest that the dish has been weakened and may not be safe to bake with. Cracks or obvious signs of damage are also telltale warnings.

Is it dishwasher safe? A good rule of thumb is if folks didn't have dishwashers when the dish was made, it isn't dishwasher safe. Many of the casseroles I have will do just fine in the dishwasher, but the harsh and abrasive cleaning cycle will ruin their luster and finish, even scratching the painted design on the dishes.

When it comes to price, I seldom pay more when buying a vintage baking dish than what I'd pay for a new one. I also want to feel sure I'm buying a quality piece that I'll use for years and years to come.

As far as pattern goes, pick out what appeals to you. What colors do you like? What patterns make you happy to look at? I once heard that you should only buy artwork that makes you feel happy when you see it and I think that guideline works beautifully when it comes to baking dishes, too.

King Ranch Casserole

SERVES 4 TO 6

This gooey, cheesy concoction is all spiced up with the best of seasonings. It has a wonderful Tex-Mex flavor that you just can't seem to get enough of! Make this classic a day (or two) ahead of time and store it in your fridge. Pop it in the oven just before supper and enjoy!

Cooking spray

2 tablespoons vegetable oil

1 onion, chopped

2 cups shredded cooked chicken
(see box, page 159)

2 recipes Cream of Chicken Soup
(page 282) or 2 cans
(10.5 ounces each) condensed
cream of chicken soup

1 can (4 ounces) diced green chiles

1 can (15 ounces) diced tomatoes,
drained

1 teaspoon chili powder

¼ teaspoon garlic powder

¼ teaspoon salt

¼ teaspoon ground black pepper

12 to 14 corn tortillas
(6 inches each)

2 cups shredded Cheddar cheese

1 Preheat the oven to 350°F. Coat a 9- by 13-inch baking dish with cooking spray.

2 Heat the oil in a large skillet over medium heat. Add the onion and sauté until lightly browned, 3 to 4 minutes. Add the chicken, soup, chiles, tomatoes, chili powder, garlic powder, salt, and pepper and cook, stirring, until the mixture is bubbly, 7 to 10 minutes.

3 Tear the tortillas into small pieces and layer half on the bottom of the prepared baking dish. Top with half of the chicken mixture, followed by half of the cheese. Repeat with the remaining tortilla pieces, chicken mixture, and cheese.

4 Bake the casserole until it is bubbly and lightly browned around the edges, 30 minutes. Allow the casserole to cool for 5 minutes before cutting it into squares and serving hot.

Mix-and-Match Casseroles

I created this chart to inspire you to develop your own casserole recipes. It is meant as a handy helper, giving you ideas and a mix-and-match formula for creating your own dishes. Simply choose an ingredient from each column in the amounts specified, follow the basic assembly and baking directions at the bottom of the page, and *poof!* Dinner!

STARCH 2 cups cooked (unless noted)	SAUCE 1 can or 10 ounces or 1 1/2 cups	VEGETABLES 2 cups	CHEESE 1 cup, shredded	MEAT 1 to 2 cups, cooked	SEASONINGS 1/4 to 1/2 teaspoon (choose one or more)	TOPPING 1 cup (optional)
Small-shape pasta (bow tie, small shell, macaroni, etc.)	Cream of chicken soup (regular, low-fat, or fat-free)	Frozen mixed vegetables	Cheddar cheese	Diced or shredded chicken	Salt	Crushed buttery crackers (such as Ritz) mixed with a cheese (1/2 cup each)
Rice (any kind, including saffron)	Cream of mushroom soup (regular, low-fat, or fat-free)	Frozen peas and carrots blend	Mozzarella cheese	Diced ham	Ground black pepper	Crushed corn flakes Chopped nuts
Frozen shredded potatoes (uncooked, thawed)	Cream of celery soup (regular, low-fat, or fat-free)	Frozen green beans	Reduced-fat Cheddar	Browned ground beef	Garlic powder	French fried onions (such as French's) mixed with a cheese (1/2 cup each)
Whole wheat pasta (small variety)	Cheese soup	Frozen corn	Reduced-fat mozzarella	Diced or shredded rotisserie chicken	Dried Italian seasoning	Crushed potato chips Crumbled bacon
Boxed scalloped potatoes (such as Betty Crocker)	Cheese sauce (such as Cheez Whiz)	Frozen chopped broccoli	Any other kind of cheese you like	Canned chicken	Onion powder	Crushed cheese-flavored crackers

TO MAKE YOUR CASSEROLE

❶ Preheat the oven to 350°F and lightly grease a 9- by 13-inch casserole dish.

❷ Cook the starch according to the package directions.

❸ Place the sauce of your choice in a small saucepan over low heat and stir in 1/2 cup milk (skim, low-fat, evaporated, or whole).

❹ Place the vegetables in a medium-size saucepan, cover with water, and bring just to a boil. Drain.

❺ Stir together the starch, sauce, vegetables, cheese, meat, and seasonings in a large bowl. Spoon the mixture into the prepared dish and bake until bubbly, 30 minutes.

❻ Add a topping, if desired, and bake an additional 5 minutes. Serve hot.

Ham Country Casserole

SERVES 4 TO 6

I never make just one of these—I always make at least three casseroles, bake one and freeze the other two (see page 163). Whenever I hear that someone is under the weather or just needs a night off from cooking, I thaw one out and bring it over to them. Casseroles like this have been taking care of folks as far back as I can remember.

2 cups small shell-shaped pasta

3 cups frozen mixed vegetables

Cooking spray

2 cups chopped cooked ham or chicken

1 recipe Cream of Chicken Soup (page 282) or 1 can (10.5 ounces) condensed cream of chicken soup

¼ cup milk

1 teaspoon ground black pepper

1 teaspoon garlic powder

½ teaspoon salt

2 cups shredded Cheddar cheese

1 can (2.8 ounces) French fried onions, such as French's

❶ Fill a medium stockpot with water and bring it to a boil over medium-high heat. Add the pasta and cook until tender, 8 to 10 minutes. Drain the pasta in a colander and set it aside.

❷ Refill the pasta pot with water and bring it to a boil again over medium-high heat. Add the frozen vegetables and cook until just tender, about 5 minutes. Remove them from the heat and drain them in a colander.

❸ Preheat the oven to 350°F. Coat a 9- by 13-inch baking dish with cooking spray.

❹ Combine the pasta, vegetables, ham, soup, milk, pepper, garlic powder, salt, 1 cup of the cheese, and half of the fried onions in a large bowl and stir well to combine. Spoon the mixture into the prepared baking dish.

❺ Bake the casserole, uncovered, for 25 minutes, then top with the remaining cheese and onions and bake until the cheese has melted, about 5 minutes more. Serve hot.

I'm All for Frozen Onions

I love to have frozen onions on hand. They work well in a pinch, especially if you don't use onion in your dishes often enough to keep fresh. Frozen onions are already diced and cook faster than fresh, so they are a great time-saver, too! You can use them pretty much anytime a recipe calls for diced onion.

Ham, Potato, and Cheese Casserole (SC)

SERVES 6 TO 8

This is a wonderful meal-in-one that can be served on its own or with a veggie side for supper. It is also great for breakfast with a nice warm muffin or French toast.

I love to make this when I have leftover ham, but I've also been known to grab some sliced deli ham from the grocery store when I get a hankering for it!

Cooking spray

1 bag (32 ounces) frozen shredded hash browns

1 large onion, diced

1 to 2 cups chopped ham

2 cups shredded Cheddar cheese

10 to 12 large eggs (see Note, following page)

1 cup milk

1 teaspoon salt

1 teaspoon ground black pepper

1 Preheat the oven to 325°F. Coat a 5-quart Dutch oven with cooking spray.

2 Place one third of the hash browns on the bottom of the pot and top with one third of the onion, then one third of the ham, and finally one third of the cheese. Repeat these layers two more times.

3 In a large bowl beat together the eggs, milk, salt, and pepper. Pour the egg mixture over the layers in the pot.

4 Bake, covered, until the eggs are set and potatoes are tender, 90 minutes. Serve hot.

How to Be a Positive Person

Here is my no-fail, tried-and-true way to be (or become) a positive person in TWO easy steps!

1. Think about the next thing that comes out of your mouth—make it positive.
2. Repeat step one. ♥

NOTE: Normally, I put a full dozen eggs into this recipe, but I specified 10 to 12 because unless you just went grocery shopping, you may not have a full dozen eggs sitting around. In those cases, use 1 or 2 fewer and it will turn out just fine!

Slow-Cooker Ham, Potato, and Cheese Casserole

Coat a 6-quart slow cooker with cooking spray. Layer the casserole in it as directed for the Dutch oven. Pour the egg mixture over the layers. Cover and seal the pot and cook on low until bubbly, 7 to 8 hours.

Taco Casserole

SERVES 4

Y'all are going to have to trust me on this recipe because the ingredients do look pretty odd. To be honest, if Mama had told me what was in it when she first started serving this a few decades ago, I would have been skeptical myself. But please do trust me because this is absolutely delicious. It has a tangy Mexican flavor that is wonderful. In fact, it is the one thing my sister-in-law and I both craved when we were carrying our children—it's that good.

The recipe is also very versatile: It can easily be doubled and baked in a 9- by

Taco Casserole

13-inch baking dish to serve eight. You can serve it with a few simple taco toppings or a full-fledged toppings bar—it's up to you!

¼ cup (½ stick) butter

½ cup milk

1 packet (1.25 ounces) taco seasoning mix

2 cups instant mashed potato flakes

1 pound ground beef

½ teaspoon kosher salt

¼ teaspoon ground black pepper

1 can (15 ounces) refried beans

½ cup barbecue sauce

Shredded Cheddar cheese, shredded lettuce, chopped fresh tomatoes, diced onions, sour cream, and/or your favorite taco toppings, for serving (optional)

1 Preheat the oven to 350°F.

2 Melt the butter in a small saucepan over medium heat. Add the milk and 2 tablespoons of the taco seasoning. Remove from the heat and stir in the mashed potato flakes. Press the mixture into the bottom and slightly up the sides of an ungreased 10-inch ovenproof pie plate.

3 Heat a large skillet over medium heat. Add the ground beef, sprinkle it with the salt and pepper, and cook, using a wooden spoon to break it into small, crumbled pieces, until fully browned, about 10 minutes. Carefully drain off and discard the grease. Add the refried beans, barbecue sauce, ¼ cup water, and the remaining taco seasoning to the skillet and cook, stirring until the mixture is bubbly, 10 minutes.

4 Turn the beef mixture out into the prepared crust. Bake, uncovered, until the casserole is bubbly, 30 to 35 minutes.

5 Cut the casserole into squares and serve with whatever taco toppings you enjoy.

Frozen Assets

Whenever I decide to make a casserole, I always buy enough extra ingredients to double the recipe. Then after all the ingredients are mixed, I divide it into two portions. One I put into my casserole dish to cook for supper and the other I place in a gallon-size ziplock freezer bag. I just squeeze out as much air as possible, then label the bag and freeze it flat. Once they're frozen, I stand the casseroles up in my freezer like books so they take up less space.

If the casserole calls for cheese or a topping of any kind, I like to go ahead and assemble that in its own quart-size bag and tape it to the casserole bag so that I know I'll have everything I need when the time comes to cook it. Mixing up two casseroles takes hardly any extra time since you already have all the ingredients out, but it is a lifesaver on the nights when you are running behind. Frozen casseroles will keep in the freezer for about three months.

If freezer space isn't a problem, you can freeze unbaked casseroles right in the baking dish. Simply line the baking dish with heavy duty aluminum foil, layer the casserole into it, cover tightly, and freeze. Once frozen, remove the foil-wrapped casserole from the dish and wrap the entire thing once more in foil; store the casserole in the freezer and return your now empty baking dish to its cabinet. When you're ready to thaw and bake the casserole, simply pull it from the freezer, remove the foil, and place it back in the dish it was frozen in.

When you plan to bake a frozen casserole, place it in the refrigerator the night before to thaw. Then put it in the casserole dish and bake according to the original directions.

Remember, the freezer is your friend.

Cornbread-Topped Chicken Potpie

SERVES 4 TO 6

This chicken potpie is unlike any other. With a homemade cream sauce and generous topping of cornbread, it is a comforting meal-in-one that can win over folks who may not care for more traditional chicken potpie recipes.

You can streamline this by preparing the filling the night before and storing it in a covered container in the refrigerator. Mix up the cornbread batter a half hour before supper, pour it on top of the filling, and bake—simple and so satisfying!

FOR THE FILLING

Cooking spray

1 package (14 ounces) frozen
   mixed vegetables

¼ cup (½ stick) butter

1 cup chicken broth or 1 chicken
   bouillon cube dissolved in
   1 cup water

½ teaspoon salt

¼ teaspoon ground black pepper

3 tablespoons all-purpose flour

2 cups heavy (whipping) cream

½ cup chopped onion

2 cups cubed cooked chicken

FOR THE CORNBREAD TOPPING

1 cup yellow or white cornmeal

1 cup all-purpose flour

2 tablespoons sugar

1 tablespoon baking powder

1 teaspoon salt

1 cup milk

¼ cup (½ stick) butter,
   melted and cooled

2 large eggs

1 cup shredded Cheddar cheese

1 can (15 ounces) corn, drained

1 Preheat the oven to 400°F. Coat a 9- by 13-inch baking dish with cooking spray.

2 Make the filling: Place the frozen vegetables in a large saucepan and add water. Bring to a boil over medium-high heat and cook until the vegetables are just tender, 5 to 10 minutes. Drain the vegetables and set them aside.

3 Melt the butter in a small saucepan over medium heat. Add the chopped

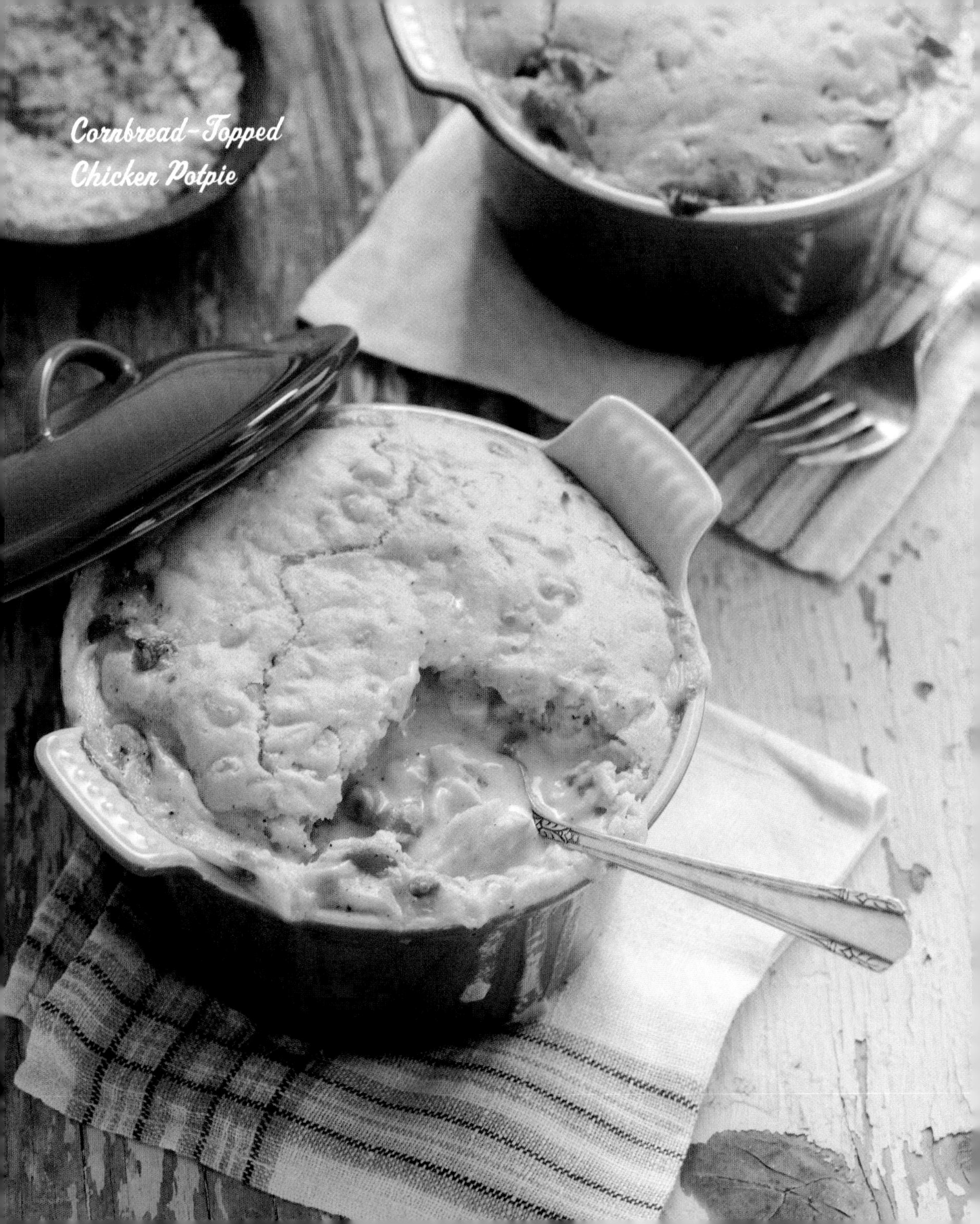
Cornbread-Topped
Chicken Potpie

onions and sauté until just barely tender, 2–3 minutes. Add the chicken broth, salt, pepper, and flour and stir until well combined. Add the cream and cook, stirring constantly, until the mixture has thickened, about 5 minutes. Remove from the heat and pour over the vegetables. Stir in the chicken.

4 Spoon the vegetable mixture into the bottom of the prepared baking dish and set it aside.

5 Make the cornbread topping: Place the cornmeal, flour, sugar, baking powder, and salt in a large bowl and stir to combine. Add the milk, melted butter, and eggs and stir until the mixture is smooth. Stir in the cheese and corn.

6 Spoon the cornbread mixture over the filling in the baking dish and spread it out to cover the filling. Bake until the cornbread is lightly browned on top, 20 minutes. Serve hot.

Microwave Chicken Tortilla Casserole

SERVES 2 TO 4

This is a recipe I make often in the summer because it doesn't heat up the house. It's a very flavorful casserole and leftovers heat up really well.

Folks are always surprised when they discover it was cooked in the microwave (see Note). I sometimes call it my "Mexican restaurant casserole" because it's so good, I feel like I ordered it off the menu at one of my favorite places to dine.

About 2 cups shredded cooked
   chicken (see box, opposite)
1 cup (8 ounces) sour cream
2 cups shredded Cheddar cheese
1 cup canned French fried onions,
   such as French's
1 can (4 ounces) chopped green chiles
1 packet (1.25 ounces) taco
   seasoning mix
3 tablespoons chopped fresh
   cilantro leaves
2 large flour tortillas or Maria's
   Flour Tortillas (page 230)

Quick Shredded Chicken Tip

Looking for a faster way to shred chicken? Here you go: Place boneless, skinless chicken breasts in a medium stockpot. Add water to cover them and bring just to a boil over medium-high heat. Reduce the heat to medium and simmer the chicken breasts until they're no longer pink in the center, about 20 minutes. Remove the chicken breasts from the water while they're still hot and place them in the bowl of a stand mixer fitted with the paddle attachment. Run the mixer on low for one minute and then turn up the speed to medium. Your chicken will be perfectly shredded in two to three minutes with no effort at all!

1 Place the chicken, sour cream, 1 cup of the cheese, ½ cup of the onions, the green chiles, taco seasoning, and cilantro in a large bowl and stir well to combine. Tear one tortilla into small pieces and add it to the bowl, stirring again until the pieces are well incorporated.

2 Line a 10-inch pie plate with the remaining tortilla and spoon the chicken mixture onto it. Place the casserole in the microwave oven and cook on 100 percent power until it is hot, 5 minutes.

3 Remove the casserole from the microwave and top it with the remaining cheese and onions, then heat on 100 percent power until the cheese is melted, 1 minute more. Enjoy!

NOTE: Microwave ovens vary widely in temperature, so you may need to alter the cooking time to suit your microwave. Since the chicken is fully cooked in this dish, there isn't a danger of undercooking it; you can just go with these guidelines and give or take a minute or so if you feel it needs it.

Chicken and Wild Rice Casserole

MAKES 6 GENEROUS SERVINGS

My mother was a stay-at-home mom most of our lives. When we became teenagers, though, she went back to school and got her real estate license. This was her first full-time career and she excelled at it. She still made supper a priority, though, and we continued to gather around the family table every night, many times thanks to a casserole such as this.

A few nights a week Mama would put together a casserole and put it in the refrigerator covered in foil. If she ever ran late, she'd just call me and have me put the casserole in the oven so it would be ready to eat when everyone got home.

Cooking spray

1 box (6 ounces) seasoned long-grain and wild rice mix, such as Uncle Ben's

2 cups shredded cooked chicken (see box, page 159)

1 recipe Cream of Mushroom Soup (page 282) or 1 can (10.5 ounces) condensed cream of mushroom soup

1 can (14 ounces) French-style green beans, drained

1 cup slivered almonds

1 cup sour cream (optional)

1 sleeve crackers (about 35), crushed (preferably buttery crackers such as Ritz)

¼ to ½ cup (½ to 1 stick) butter, melted

1 Preheat the oven to 350°F. Coat a 9-by 13-inch baking dish with cooking spray and set it aside.

2 Cook the rice according to the package directions and place it in a large bowl.

3 Add the chicken, soup, green beans, almonds, and sour cream, if using, and stir well until combined. Spoon the rice mixture into the prepared baking dish. Sprinkle the cracker crumbs over the top and drizzle with the melted butter.

4 Bake the casserole until hot and bubbly, 30 minutes. Serve hot.

Chicken and Wild Rice Casserole

Four-Cheese Macaroni and Cheese

MAKES 6 GENEROUS SERVINGS

This is one of my sister-in-law's recipes. She is possibly the only person I know who enjoys cooking more than I do! She likes to divide this into three mini casserole dishes and freeze them, reheating them in the oven for supper whenever the need for ooey-gooey mac and cheese arises.

Cooking spray

3 cups elbow macaroni, uncooked

¼ cup all-purpose flour

⅛ teaspoon ground black pepper

¼ teaspoon salt

2½ cups milk

6 ounces Velveeta cheese, cubed (¾ cup)

½ cup freshly grated Parmesan cheese

½ cup shredded Cheddar cheese

4 ounces cream cheese, cut into small cubes (½ cup)

1 Preheat the oven to 350°F. Coat a 9- by 13-inch baking dish with cooking spray.

2 Cook the macaroni in a large pot of boiling salted water according to package directions. Drain the macaroni and set it aside.

3 In a large saucepan over medium-low heat, combine the flour, pepper, salt, and ½ cup of the milk, stirring with a whisk until smooth. Stir in the remaining milk and continue stirring constantly until the mixture comes just to a boil. Remove from the heat.

4 Stir the Velveeta, Parmesan, Cheddar, and cream cheese into the hot mixture until melted. Add the macaroni and stir until well coated. Pour into the baking dish.

5 Bake the macaroni, uncovered, until hot and bubbly, 30 minutes. Serve warm.

A Light in the Darkness

Let's talk about that little light of yours . . . Whether you believe it or not, you've got one. Now, some people look at their light and say, "I'll shine mine on Fridays."

Others: "I'll shine mine when it's not raining."

". . . not windy."

". . . not cold."

". . . when I get a raise."

". . . work somewhere else."

". . . get more sleep."

Some people really just wanna wait until the sun is high and the temperature is warm. When the breeze is just right and weather is perfect.

Shining a light outside at high noon—now there's a concept. That's all well and good, but man, what I really appreciate are those lights that shine at midnight, in pitch black, when light is needed the most. Those folks who wake up and say, "Today is gonna be a long, tough day, so I'm gonna bring my A game and see if I can't make it a little easier for as many people as I can."

Someone who decides to shine their light in the darkness—now that's a light that makes a difference.

Which do you want to be: a light at high noon or a light at midnight? ♥

Slow-Cooker Macaroni and Cheese (sc)

SERVES 4 TO 6

This macaroni and cheese cooks a lot faster than most dishes do in the slow cooker, so you can put it on midday and still have it ready for suppertime. My friend Jyl shared the recipe with me a while back, and it has become a longtime family favorite.

This recipe can easily be doubled and cooked in a 6-quart slow cooker.

> 1 box (8 ounces) elbow macaroni
> 2 large eggs
> 1 can (5 ounces) evaporated milk
> 1½ cups whole milk
> ½ cup (1 stick) butter, melted and cooled
> 2½ cups shredded Cheddar cheese

❶ Fill a medium-size saucepan with 6 cups water and place over medium-high heat. Once it begins to boil, add the macaroni and cook, stirring occasionally, until the noodles are tender, 9 to 11 minutes. Drain the macaroni and place it in a 4-quart slow cooker.

❷ Beat the eggs together in a medium-size bowl. Add the evaporated milk, whole milk, butter, and cheese and stir together until well blended. Pour the milk mixture over the macaroni and stir to combine.

❸ Cover and seal the pot and cook on low until hot and bubbly, 3 to 4 hours. Serve hot.

Baked Stuffed Pasta Shells

SERVES 8

You can make these stuffed shells with or without meat, but my son and I really enjoy them with the sausage added in. This recipe makes enough to feed a crowd, or you can have half for supper one night and freeze the rest for future use (they freeze well and will keep for at least three months; see Note for reheating instructions).

> 1 teaspoon salt
> 1 box (12 ounces) jumbo pasta shells

1 pound Italian sausage (optional)

3 cups (24 ounces) ricotta cheese

4 cups shredded mozzarella

1 tablespoon dried Italian seasoning

2 large eggs, beaten

Double recipe of Simple Marinara
    Sauce (page 284) or 2 jars
    (24 ounces each) spaghetti sauce

1 Preheat the oven to 350°F.

2 Fill a medium-size stockpot three-quarters full with water and place it over medium-high heat. Add the salt and bring to a boil. Add the pasta shells and cook them until they're just tender, 8 to 10 minutes. Drain the shells in a colander and run cold water over them to stop the cooking process; set aside.

3 If using the sausage, heat a large skillet over medium-high heat. Remove the sausage from its casings, place it in the skillet, and cook, stirring to break up the meat, until it is cooked through and no longer pink, 8 to 10 minutes. Drain the sausage well, place it in a large bowl, and allow it to cool slightly.

4 Place the ricotta cheese, 2 cups of the mozzarella cheese, the Italian seasoning, and eggs in the bowl with the sausage (or in a separate large bowl if not using the sausage) and stir until well blended.

5 Spread half of the sauce in the bottom of two 9- by 13-inch baking dishes.

6 Carefully stuff each pasta shell with 2 tablespoons of the cheese mixture and divide among the prepared baking dishes, placing them on top of the sauce. Pour the remaining sauce over the shells.

7 If saving half of the recipe for later, tightly cover one dish with aluminum foil. Place 1 cup of the reserved mozzarella in a ziplock bag and tape the bag to the foil, then transfer the dish to the freezer.

8 Cover the remaining dish with foil and bake for 20 minutes. Remove the foil and sprinkle the remaining 1 cup of mozzarella cheese over the top. Return the dish to the oven and bake until the cheese is completely melted and the sauce is bubbling, 5 to 10 minutes. Serve hot.

NOTE: To cook the frozen stuffed shells, thaw them, still covered, overnight in the refrigerator and then proceed as directed in step 8.

7

Sides

When I was growing up, my mother always cooked a big supper with meat, several sides, bread, and usually a dessert. Nowadays, time usually doesn't permit me to cook such a large meal. Families are busy with jobs, school, extra-curricular activities, and other everyday demands. Still, just one side makes a meal seem more complete. That is why I have included lots of fast and simple dishes for you to make in just a few minutes while the rest of your meal cooks. While some of these recipes are not as labor intensive as sides were several years ago, they are equally as fulfilling.

I grow a small garden and love picking things fresh to prepare for supper, so I am partial to roasted fresh vegetables. I also like to keep it simple so the flavor of the vegetable is not covered up with complicated sauces. I am includ-ing lots of my recent favorites and some of our family's tried-and-true classics as well. I find that when I introduce my children to a new vegetable, they are so much more willing to try it if they are included in the preparation of the dish. Most of these are easy enough to prepare so that little ones can help make them. I hope your family enjoys cooking and eating these as much as mine has!

Roasted Asparagus

SERVES 4

It's funny how we grow up eating certain things and sometimes it never occurs to us that we are avoiding a vegetable because we simply have no idea what to do with it. Asparagus was that vegetable for me and my entire family for nearly forty years. All I knew about asparagus was that it was a favorite character in *VeggieTales* cartoons.

Last November, I was talking to my friend Jyl about our menu plans for Thanksgiving dinner and she mentioned that asparagus was her most requested dish. I responded, "Asparagus? What do you *do* with it?" "Oh, I roast it!" was her response.

Roast it, I did. I went and bought three bunches of it and put it in my fridge, waiting for the perfect meal to give it a try. Finally, one morning around 3:40 a.m. I got to wondering what it would taste like. I got up and roasted that stuff before the sun even came up.

Oh, have mercy, was it ever good! By the time my family got up and about, every bit of that asparagus was gone.

Guess what we had as part of our Thanksgiving dinner?

1 bunch asparagus

2 teaspoons olive oil

1 tablespoon lemon juice or juice from ½ lemon

2 teaspoons kosher salt

1 Preheat the oven to 425°F.

2 Gently bend each stalk of asparagus and snap the end off at the point where it gives when bent. Discard the ends and arrange the asparagus in a single layer on a rimmed baking sheet.

3 Drizzle the asparagus with the oil and lemon juice and sprinkle with the salt.

4 Roast the asparagus until tender and very lightly browned, about 20 minutes. Serve warm.

Simple Roasted Vegetables

Roasted vegetables are all the rage right now. I love them for their ease and flavor: There's minimal work to do before putting the veggies in the oven, and roasting brings out their natural sweetness while keeping their full-bodied flavor intact. By adding a drizzle of olive oil, some kosher salt, and a few simple herbs, you can create a unique side dish in no time flat using pretty much any vegetable that you have on hand.

It's fun to get creative with herbs and mix and match them. While fresh herbs are wonderful, dried are also very economical and what I use most often. I love using dill, parsley, and basil, but I'll put dried Italian seasoning on just about anything. It is the ketchup of dried herbs for me!

I also use plain old vegetable oil if I don't have olive oil handy, and melted butter makes a flavorful substitute as well.

Raw vegetables, such as sweet
   potatoes, bell peppers, onions,
   zucchini, and cauliflower,
   trimmed and cut into 1-inch
   chunks (see Notes)
Olive oil
Kosher salt to taste
Ground black pepper to taste
Herbs of your choice (optional;
   see Notes)

1 Preheat the oven to 425°F.

2 Place the vegetables in a large bowl. Drizzle them with a little oil, about 2 teaspoons per cup of vegetables, just enough to coat. Then sprinkle them with salt, pepper, and some herbs, if you'd like.

3 Spread the veggies out on a rimmed baking sheet and place them in the oven. After about 10 minutes, remove the veggies from the oven and flip them over with a spatula or stir them with a wooden spoon. Return them to the oven and roast until nicely browned and tender, another 10 to 20 minutes depending on the thickness and firmness of the vegetable (firm, dense vegetables like carrots and

Simple Roasted Vegetables

potatoes will take longer than softer ones like squash, peppers, and cauliflower).

NOTES: Usually I allow about 1 cup of vegetables per person.

Dried herbs are a little stronger than fresh. I usually use about 1 teaspoon dried herbs per cup of vegetables.

Broccoli with Cheese Sauce

SERVES 4

Many a child has been turned onto broccoli by eating it covered in a yummy cheese sauce. Lots of kids can be persuaded to try it if you call the florets "little trees." And once it has been sampled, this dish usually becomes a favorite. It's made with milk and cheese, the old-fashioned way, and it sure is good!

1 cup cold milk

1 tablespoon cornstarch

⅛ cup (¼ stick) butter

1 cup shredded Cheddar cheese

1½ teaspoons salt

¼ teaspoon ground black pepper

1 bag (16 ounces) fresh broccoli florets (about 2 heads broccoli)

1 Combine the milk and cornstarch in a small saucepan and stir together with a whisk. Place over medium heat and cook, stirring constantly, until just boiling. Reduce the temperature to low and stir in the butter until melted. Add the Cheddar cheese, ½ teaspoon of the salt, and the black pepper and stir constantly until the cheese has melted and the sauce is smooth and fully blended, 2 to 3 minutes. Cover and set aside.

2 Fill a medium-size saucepan three-quarters full with water and add the remaining teaspoon of salt. Heat over medium-high heat until it comes to a boil, then add the broccoli and boil until crisp tender, 4 to 5 minutes. Drain the broccoli and place it in a serving bowl.

3 Pour the cheese sauce over the broccoli and serve warm.

Broccoli Salad

SERVES 4 TO 6

A local deli used to prepare my favorite broccoli salad each morning and I loved to stop by there and buy a small container of it for a quick lunch. When they started selling premade salad in its place, which wasn't as good, I had to get creative and start making it myself!

Broccoli Salad

Refrigerator Salads

I love a nice refrigerator salad. They usually keep for several days (some up to a week) and can be made well ahead of time to serve as a quick side with your meal. Of course, they're wonderful additions to cookouts and summer parties, but I usually have at least one in the fridge year-round for those evenings when I have to throw supper together quicker than usual.

The Broccoli Salad here is one of my all-time favorites, but I've given you some other yummy options, too: Try the slaws on pages 181, the Shortcut Potato Salad (page 211), Classic Pasta Salad (page 213), Summer Corn Salad (page 184), and the tomato- and onion-studded Fast Italian Cucumber Salad (page 182).

1 head broccoli, florets and stalks chopped into bite-size pieces (4 to 5 cups)

½ to 1 cup raisins or dried cranberries

½ pound bacon, cooked and crumbled

1 medium-size red onion, chopped

1 cup sunflower seeds

1 cup mayonnaise

½ cup sugar

½ cup white vinegar

1 Place the broccoli in a large bowl. Add the raisins, bacon, onion, and sunflower seeds and toss to combine.

2 In a small bowl, stir together the mayonnaise, sugar, and vinegar until well combined. Pour the dressing over the broccoli mixture and stir to coat well. Store, covered, in the refrigerator, until ready to serve so that the dressing has time to chill and the flavors blend.

The broccoli salad will keep, covered, in the refrigerator for several days.

Roasted Brussels Sprouts

SERVES 4

We always called these "baby cabbages" growing up and my kids do the same thing now. Mama often made the Brussels sprouts in a butter sauce (see the following recipe), which I still love, but these roasted Brussels sprouts are equally delicious.

1 to 2 pounds Brussels sprouts

About 4 teaspoons olive oil

Kosher salt

1 Preheat the oven to 425°F.

2 Rinse the Brussels sprouts, trim and discard any tough stems, and cut each one in half through the stem end.

3 Arrange the Brussels sprouts on a rimmed baking sheet, drizzle with about 1 teaspoon of oil for every cup of vegetables, and stir to coat. Sprinkle with salt to taste.

4 Bake the Brussels sprouts, stirring once, until tender and lightly browned, 15 to 20 minutes.

Buttered Brussels Sprouts

SERVES 4

This is how my mother made Brussels sprouts when I was growing up. She usually used frozen sprouts since fresh were not often readily available then. Fresh work just as well and have a little more flavor. Either way, you can't go wrong.

1 pound frozen or fresh Brussels sprouts

¼ cup (½ stick) butter

½ teaspoon salt

¼ teaspoon ground black pepper

1 If using fresh Brussels sprouts, rinse them and trim and discard any tough stems. Place the Brussels sprouts in a medium-size saucepan and add water to cover by a depth of half an inch. Bring to a boil over medium heat, cover, and cook until tender, 10 to 15 minutes. Drain well and return the Brussels sprouts to the pan.

2 Add the butter, salt, and pepper and stir until the butter is melted and the Brussels sprouts are coated. Serve hot.

Picky Eater?
Get 'Em in the Kitchen!

I'm well acquainted with the trials of having picky eaters in the house but I've found that the more involved my children are in making a dish, the more likely they are to try it—and like it.

I usually start by taking them grocery shopping with me. I let them search for and pick out each item, even scanning the foods in the self-checkout lane. Once home, I get the kids in the kitchen and let them do as much of the prep work as possible.

If you try this, be sure and declare the dish "theirs" when you serve it, and credit their culinary skills when everyone talks about how delicious it is. You may just find your picky eaters asking for seconds. If your kids are persistently picky, though, at least you've still taught them how to make a recipe that they may serve to their own families someday!

Brady and Katy Rose love their fajitas—veggies and all!

Simple Boiled Cabbage

SERVES 4 TO 6

One of my grandmother's favorite meals is boiled cabbage and cornbread. Just the thought of the two dishes brings back memories of her childhood and sitting at the table with her brothers and sister. Cabbage was one of the first vegetables to be ready in the spring, so her family looked forward to it each year. It could be plucked just as they were growing tired of dried beans and were definitely ready for something "fresh from the garden."

One thing you should know about cabbage is that as it cooks, it greatly reduces in size, so plan on starting out with about twice the amount you would like to end up with. If you'd like to enjoy this as my grandmother does, make the Cornbread Muffins on page 228 and eat them alongside.

1 head cabbage, cored and chopped into large bite-size pieces
1 beef bouillon cube
1 teaspoon salt
½ teaspoon ground black pepper

1 Place the cabbage in a medium-size stockpot and add water to cover. Add the bouillon cube and cook, covered, over medium-high heat until just tender, about 30 minutes.

2 Drain the cabbage and place it in a bowl. Sprinkle with salt and pepper and stir well to mix. Serve hot.

"Food is the most primitive form of comfort."

— *Sheilah Graham*

Fried Cabbage

SERVES 4 TO 6

Don't let the "fried" part of this scare you off. There is a simple reason why so many of our Southern recipe titles start out with "fried" and I'm going to let you in on the secret. You see, where I live, we refer to a large skillet as a "frying pan." As a result, everything we cook in it usually gets labeled "fried," even if what we're really doing is sautéing. You ask any old-timers in the South what sounds better, fried cabbage or sautéed cabbage, and I know exactly which one they'll pick!

5 to 6 slices bacon
   (more or less if you like)
1 head green cabbage, cored and
   chopped
About 1 teaspoon salt
About ½ teaspoon ground black
   pepper

1 Line a plate with paper towels.

2 In a large skillet over medium-high heat, fry the bacon, turning once, until crisp, about 10 minutes. Transfer the cooked bacon to the paper towel–lined plate and carefully pour off all but 2 tablespoons of the bacon grease from the skillet (saving the rest for another use, see page 67).

3 Set the skillet over medium-high heat again, and add the cabbage, 1 teaspoon salt, and ½ teaspoon pepper. Crumble the cooked bacon on top. Cook, stirring constantly, until the cabbage is wilted, about 5 minutes. Reduce the heat to low, cover, and continue cooking until the cabbage is done to your desired tenderness, 5 to 10 minutes more. Add salt and pepper to taste and serve.

"I firmly believe that the positive folks in the world far outnumber the negative folks; it's just that negative folks cause such a ruckus they tend to get heard more. So I have a plan for us: Smile Louder!"

—*Christy*

Vinegar Slaw

SERVES 8 TO 10 AS A SANDWICH TOPPER,
6 TO 8 AS A SIDE DISH

As its name suggests, this is vinegar slaw—not to be confused with coleslaw. Instead of a mayonnaise-based dressing, this one has just vinegar and enough sugar to temper it. It doesn't taste sweet, though—it has just the right amount of tang.

We serve this atop Pulled Pork Sandwiches (pages 132 and 135) or as a refreshing side at a barbecue. It needs at least a few hours in the fridge before serving, so it's a great make-ahead dish. It'll keep, refrigerated, in a covered container for a couple of days, and only gets better (the dressing heightens in flavor over time).

½ head of cabbage, cored

1 cup white vinegar

1 cup sugar

1 teaspoon salt

½ teaspoon ground black pepper

Using a large knife or a food processor, very finely chop or shred the cabbage.

Place the cabbage in a large bowl and add the remaining ingredients. Stir well to mix, then cover and refrigerate for at least 3 hours or overnight before serving.

Pepper Slaw

SERVES 4 TO 6

This recipe comes from my sister-in-law, Tina. Her great-grandmother made this for family gatherings and it became a cherished recipe after she passed on. The spaghetti seems like an odd ingredient but it lends a wonderful texture to this coleslaw with a twist.

1 package (16 ounces) fresh coleslaw
   mix (about 2½ cups)

1 red bell pepper, stemmed, seeded,
   and chopped

1 green bell pepper, stemmed,
   seeded, and chopped

2 ounces cooked spaghetti
   (about 1 serving of spaghetti)

½ to ¾ cup mayonnaise

½ teaspoon salt

¼ teaspoon ground black pepper

Place all of the ingredients in a large bowl, beginning with the lesser amount of mayonnaise. Stir until well combined and add more mayonnaise to taste, if desired. Cover and refrigerate for several hours before serving.

Candied Baby Carrots

SERVES 4

These carrots have just a hint of honeyed sweetness but are not overly sweet. I use baby carrots, though you can take regular carrots and cut them into sticks or coins if you like.

You can also alter the sweetness of this recipe by adjusting the amount of honey. As always, I'm showing you how I do it but I hope you'll make it your own when you serve it at your table. Just remember, all recipes taste better if you make them for people you love.

2 pounds baby carrots
1 teaspoon salt

¼ cup dark or light brown sugar
¼ cup (½ stick) butter
¼ to ½ cup honey (depending on how sweet you like the carrots)

1 Place the carrots in large saucepan and add just enough water to cover them. Bring to a boil over medium heat, then reduce the heat to low, cover, and cook until the carrots are easily pierced with a fork, about 30 minutes.

2 Pour off half of the water and add the remaining ingredients. Cover again, turn the heat back up to medium, and bring it back to a boil. Reduce the heat to low once more and simmer until the sauce is heated through and the carrots are coated, 10 to 15 minutes.

Fast Italian Cucumber Salad

SERVES 4 TO 6

This is an ideal salad to serve with spaghetti or as a side at a picnic or family reunion. It's made with hardy vegetables instead of lettuce, so it keeps really well (which means you can make it far in advance if you need to). I usually snack on it throughout the day, too, because it is so effortless to make and keep on hand. Be sure you allow time for the flavors to develop before serving.

3 to 4 plum tomatoes or tomato variety of your choice, chopped (about 1½ cups)

1 large red onion, diced

2 large cucumbers, chopped

1 bottle (16 ounces) Italian dressing

Place all of the vegetables in a large bowl, add the entire bottle of dressing, and stir well to combine. Cover and refrigerate for several hours or up to 2 days before serving.

The Benefits of Being Stubborn

Yesterday on the radio I caught the tail end of someone talking about how a bad cup of coffee had ruined his day. Didn't take much, did it? We're gonna have things thrown at us. Like driving on an obstacle course, things will happen, but we just gotta keep driving around those cones and stay in control of the car. If a cup of coffee is all it takes to ruin our day, we never stood a chance to begin with. We just have to decide to have a great day each and every morning. We have to put our energy into giving the blessings more airtime than the complaints.

If someone should give me a cup of coffee at any point throughout my day, I'm just gonna be grateful for that cup of coffee regardless of how it tastes. Because I choose to be grateful—and I won't be easily swayed. I'm stubborn that way. ♥

Easiest Ever Creamed Corn with Butter Sauce

SERVES 6 TO 8

If your family members are fans of that frozen corn that comes in its own butter sauce, this will be your new go-to recipe. You can save a lot of money by just making it yourself at home. We actually like it better than the frozen butter sauce version!

½ cup (1 stick) butter

1 bag (32 ounces) frozen whole
   kernel corn

1 cup heavy (whipping) cream

1 tablespoon sugar

Salt

Ground black pepper

1 Melt the butter in a large skillet over medium heat. Add the corn and cook, stirring occasionally, until it is mostly thawed, about 3 minutes.

2 Stir in the cream and sugar, add salt and pepper to taste, and continue cooking, stirring constantly to prevent the cream from scorching, until the corn is cooked through and the sauce is thick, 10 to 15 minutes. Serve hot.

Summer Corn Salad

SERVES 4

Don't let the name fool you, this salad is delicious all year-round! I love it with CocaCola Pork Chops (page 46) or Grilled Chicken Tenders Without the Grill (page 75), and it's the perfect side for a barbecue. I also love it all on its own.

2 cans (15 ounces each) whole
   kernel corn, drained

2 medium-size tomatoes, cored
   and diced

1 bell pepper, stemmed, seeded, and
   diced

1 small onion, diced

1 cup Italian dressing (regular or
   zesty)

Combine all of the ingredients in a large bow and stir well to combine. Cover and refrigerate for several hours or up to 2 days before serving.

Summer Corn Salad

A Freezerful of Vegetables

Fresh vegetables would be my first choice at the market if they were always available and affordable, but since that isn't the case, frozen is the next best thing. I keep frozen vegetable blends and some of my favorite individual frozen veggies on hand so I can whip them up in no time flat using recipes like Basil Corn (recipe follows) and Simple Skillet Vegetables (page 199). With just a little butter and some seasoning to enhance the veggies' natural flavors, all I need is an entrée to create a satisfying meal.

Basil Corn

SERVES 4

I love this side dish because it's quick and easy and uses ingredients I usually have on hand. It's one of my standby recipes. My husband loves basil and corn, so this is one of his favorites, too.

> 1 package (28 ounces) frozen whole kernel corn
> ½ cup (1 stick) butter
> ½ to 1 tablespoon dried basil
> 1 tablespoon cornstarch
> ½ teaspoon salt
> 1 teaspoon sugar

1 Place the corn in a large pot and add water just to cover. Bring to a boil, then reduce the heat to low and cook until heated through and tender, 5 minutes. Remove the pot from the heat, drain the corn, and transfer it to a serving bowl.

2 Combine the butter, basil, cornstarch, salt, and sugar in a small saucepan over medium heat. Cook, stirring constantly, until the butter is completely melted and the mixture is well blended and bubbly.

3 Pour the butter mixture over the corn and stir well to coat. Serve warm.

Fried Eggplant

SERVES 4 TO 6

Eggplant is the vegetable gifted to me the most, with the exception of tomatoes. For some reason, folks just like to give me eggplant from their gardens. Not being one to waste, I'm quick to fry it up just like I would green tomatoes. If you are a fan of fried green tomatoes, you'll find that fried eggplant tastes surprisingly similar!

2 to 3 medium eggplants
    (about 2 pounds)
Salt
Vegetable oil, for frying
1 cup plain yellow or white cornmeal
1 teaspoon ground black pepper
Dash of ground cayenne pepper
    (optional)
1 cup buttermilk (see Note)
Ranch dressing, for serving
    (optional)

1 Rinse and slice the eggplant into ½ inch-thick slices. Lightly sprinkle salt on both sides of each slice and place the slices in a bowl. Cover the bowl with a dish towel and allow the eggplant to sit for 10 minutes to draw out the liquid. Line a plate with paper towels.

2 Meanwhile, pour the oil into a large skillet to a depth of ¼ inch and set it over medium heat.

3 Place the cornmeal, black pepper, 2 teaspoons of salt, and a dash of cayenne, if you like, in a medium-size bowl and stir to combine. Pour the buttermilk into a separate medium-size bowl.

4 Gently blot the eggplant slices on both sides with paper towel to remove any moisture. Dip each slice first in the buttermilk and then in the cornmeal, dredging to coat both sides.

5 Working in batches, cook the eggplant slices in the hot oil, turning once, until browned on both sides, about 5 minutes. Remove to the paper towel–lined plate.

6 Serve the eggplant hot, with ranch dressing to dip it in, if you like.

NOTE: If you don't have any buttermilk on hand, here's a great substitute: Add 1 tablespoon of white vinegar or lemon juice to 1 cup of whole milk. Stir and allow it to sit for 5 minutes before using.

A Trip to Remember

Last summer we took a four-day road trip to Kentucky. My husband and I had agonized for months over where we should go or what we should do for our summer vacation. I started up entire sections on my forum and Facebook just to get ideas.

We couldn't afford to fly four people anywhere and we didn't want to drive more than six hours from home, but the main thing is that *all four of us really wanted to do something we'd never done before*. Tired of brainstorming and not coming up with the ideal trip, my son chimed in, "You know, what if we just went all through Kentucky? We've never done that before. We could just go exploring."

My husband and I looked at each other and shrugged. Why not? For some reason, other than my occasional pilgrimage to the American Quilter's Society in Paducah, we've never done anything in Kentucky, even though it is awfully close. So we circled a few days on the calendar and we set off to Nowhere in Particular, Kentucky.

With our sole intent to connect with each other and just enjoy our family, and no agenda whatsoever, we ended up having a trip of a lifetime. We talked, we played little question games in the car, took turns deciding where we were going to eat and

stay, stopped off at a few national parks, and we laughed. We laughed a lot.

It was like a four-day decompression retreat from the stresses of the world around us. Four days where nothing mattered beyond the most important people in our lives. Am I sounding like a Hallmark movie yet? You know what? That's just what it felt like.

Each day was filled with little miracle moments beginning with the very first day, when the kids threw pennies in a fountain to make wishes. Katy Rose turned around to us and said, "You know what I wished for? I wished that Brady and I wouldn't fight so much."

Brady seemed to have a new awareness of his sister's adoration after that. The next morning as Katy Rose was standing at the window looking out, I saw Brady walk over to her and put his arm around her shoulder.

There were so many little moments like that I could detail the trip in its own book. But instead I'll just describe it like

Little Brady and Baby Katy Rose

my granddaddy did whenever he was awe-struck: "It sure was something."

When we got back home, I called our friend Jason, who had been taking care of our cats while we were away. When he asked how our trip went, I did my best to explain to him how four days in a car going nowhere in particular could be so meaningful (our "best" vacations up until this point had always involved princesses, a mouse, and various roller coasters). I told him, "I just can't explain it but this trip really changed things for us." On the way home I pulled up a card with the question "What was your best vacation ever and why?" One by one we took turns answering, and one by one it came out that this road trip to nowhere was the best vacation any of us had ever taken. No one could give a particular reason for it, but the look of joy and contentment on the faces of my family said it all.

I tried to convey this to Jason by saying, "I just don't know. There was something about this trip. I mean, technically it was nothing special but it ended up being—"

Jason interrupted me and said, "Sounds like it ended up being a trip that your kids are going to grow up and write about in their books."

I know he couldn't see me nod on the other end of the phone but that was all I could manage to do with the lump that had risen in my throat. Maybe he's right. Maybe this will be one of those memories my kids carry with them as an example of how much we all love each other. Maybe they will even write about it in a book someday. I bet their mama will beat 'em to it, though. ♥

Beefed-Up Baked Beans

SERVES 6 TO 8

These beans are a wonderful accompaniment to the ribs on page 50. They are also a tasty dish to take to a summertime get-together.

This is a very forgiving recipe, so feel free to use what you have on hand and modify it to suit your family's tastes. If you have some leftover pulled pork (see pages 132 and 135), you can certainly use that instead of the ground beef if you like. And I have used ketchup, yellow mustard, and even salsa in mine with good results.

Cooking spray
1 pound ground beef
1 can (28 ounces) or 2 cans
    (15 ounces each) baked beans,
    with their liquid
2 cans (15 ounces each) navy beans,
    with their liquid
1 small onion, chopped
1 cup Barbecue Sauce in a Hurry
    (page 287) or store-bought
    barbecue sauce

2 tablespoons Worcestershire sauce
2 tablespoons yellow mustard
½ teaspoon salt
¼ teaspoon ground black pepper
3 to 4 slices bacon

1 Preheat the oven to 350°F. Coat a 9-by 13-inch baking dish with cooking spray and set it aside.

2 Place the ground beef in a medium-size skillet over medium-high heat and cook, breaking up and stirring the meat with a wooden spoon, until it is cooked through, about 10 minutes. Drain and discard the fat.

3 In a large bowl, stir together all of the remaining ingredients except for the bacon. Spoon the mixture into the prepared baking dish and top with the bacon slices, laying them lengthwise across the pan.

4 Bake until the beans are bubbly, 45 to 60 minutes. Serve hot.

Creative Leftovers

Leftovers can be a huge help in the kitchen and I serve them far more often than my family realizes. Anytime you can cook once and get more than one meal out of it, you help both your time and your budget.

But if your family is like mine and doesn't care for leftovers, you may need to get creative. Here are a few tips I use when recycling my meals.

Don't serve leftovers the very next day. I always wait a day before serving a dish a second time. When I do this, no one minds and the dish seems fresh again.

Make it into something else. A random assortment of leftover vegetables can easily be turned into stew. Cooked hamburger rolls or hot dog buns become French toast. Cooked chicken can be shredded into soup, chili, or a salad. Get creative and you just might create a new favorite dish!

Don't serve them all at once. The secret to keeping my family in the dark, leftover-wise, is never duplicating a whole meal. So let's say I make a ham, green beans, and mashed potatoes on Sunday. On Monday, I'll serve a new entrée with just the green beans as a side. Tuesday, I'll serve the ham again with the mashed potatoes and a salad.

Freeze what freezes well. I love to dice up leftover ham and store it in my freezer for quick omelets. Soups and stews freeze well, as do casseroles. I store these in single servings for quick lunches throughout the week or a late-night supper if I need one.

No-Soak Dried Beans sc

SERVES 6 TO 8

I love cooking and serving dried beans. They're economical, simple, and a delicious slow-cooked side that reminds me of my childhood. My one problem with them, though, is that I often forget to presoak the beans! This recipe resolves that issue because there is no need. There is also no need to watch the pot to make sure it doesn't boil dry, because the slow cooker retains all of the moisture in the pot throughout the day.

- 1 bag (16 ounces) dried beans such as pinto, black, small red, navy, great northern, or black-eyed peas, picked over and rinsed
- 1 tablespoon sugar
- 1 tablespoon vegetable oil
- 2 ham hocks or leftover ham bone (see page 52)
- 1 tablespoon salt
- 1 teaspoon ground black pepper

1 Place the beans in a 5- or 6-quart slow cooker. Add the remaining ingredients and fill the slow cooker with water to within 1 inch of the top of the crock (you want to make sure there's enough space for the contents of the slow cooker to expand).

2 Cover and seal the pot and cook until the beans are tender, 8 to 9 hours on low, 4 to 5 hours on high. Serve hot.

Blake's Green Beans

SERVES 4

This is another recipe from my friend Heather, who says it's the only way her son Blake will eat green beans. She's been making these for him since he was just a boy. The tomatoes, bacon, and onion season the dish to perfection and make a truly irresistible green bean side dish. Even the little ones will like it, despite the fact that it's green! When I'm in a hurry I leave the bacon out and add a tablespoon of bacon grease instead.

- 3 to 5 slices bacon
- 1 small onion, chopped
- 1 can (29 ounces) green beans, drained
- 1 can (14.5 ounces) diced tomatoes, with their liquid
- ½ teaspoon salt (optional)
- ¼ teaspoon ground black pepper (optional)

1 Line a plate with paper towels.

2 Place the bacon in a large skillet over

Blake's Green Beans

Roasted Peppers and Tomatoes

medium-high heat and cook, flipping at least once, until cooked through and crispy, 5 to 7 minutes. Transfer the cooked bacon to the paper towel–lined plate and carefully pour off all but 2 tablespoons of the bacon grease from the skillet (saving the rest for another use, see page 67).

3 Add the onion to the bacon grease in the skillet and sauté until tender, 3 to 4 minutes. Stir in the green beans, tomatoes, and salt and pepper, if desired, and reduce the temperature to low. Crumble the bacon into the skillet, stir to combine, and simmer until heated through, 15 minutes. Serve hot.

Roasted Peppers and Tomatoes

SERVES 4

When roasting groups of vegetables, it's fun to put together your favorite flavors to make a signature combination. This recipe does that for me. The colors of your garden vegetables take center stage and make a lovely side dish. Just cut up the veggies into chunks and roast away! It's that easy!

This is excellent served as a side with pretty much anything, but I especially love it with beef dishes—the sweetness of the peppers and savory tang of the tomatoes really bring out the flavor of the meat.

2 large bell peppers, stemmed, seeded, and cut into ½-inch strips

2 large tomatoes, cored and cut into wedges

1 medium-size sweet onion, such as Vidalia, cut into wedges

3 teaspoons olive oil, plus extra as needed

2 teaspoons kosher salt

¼ teaspoon ground black pepper

1 Preheat the oven to 425°F.

2 Arrange the vegetables on a baking sheet and drizzle with the 3 teaspoons olive oil. Stir well to coat, adding more olive oil if needed. Sprinkle with the salt and pepper and roast, stirring halfway through, until tender and lightly browned on the edges, 20 minutes. Serve hot.

Sautéed Spinach

SERVES 4

This side dish can be made from start to finish in minutes, so I put it on the stove just as my daughter is setting the table. It will seem like you have a lot of greens but they cook down drastically. Six cups of raw leaves will yield about two cups once they're cooked. The greens are flavorful and delicious—and come together in a snap—every time!

1 tablespoon olive oil or butter

1 teaspoon minced garlic

6 cups fresh spinach leaves, well rinsed and drained

1 teaspoon lemon juice

½ teaspoon kosher salt

1 Heat the oil in a large skillet over medium-high heat. Add the garlic and sauté until lightly browned, 2 to 3 minutes. Add the spinach and cook, stirring constantly, until wilted but still bright green, 4 to 5 minutes.

2 Remove the spinach from the heat and stir in the lemon juice. Sprinkle with the salt and serve immediately.

Squash Medley

SERVES 4

This is a great side to serve with grilled meat and it also works well with Oven-Barbecued Chicken (pages 87–88) or anything else you're hankering for. The flavors are mild and fresh. You can add a bit more zing if you like by squeezing in some lemon juice and adding a light sprinkling (about half a teaspoon) of your favorite dried herbs.

2 yellow squash, sliced into ¼-inch-thick rounds

1 zucchini, sliced into ¼-inch-thick rounds

1 large sweet onion, such as Vidalia, cut into small wedges

About 3 tablespoons olive oil

2 teaspoons kosher salt

Dried herbs of your choice (optional)

1 Preheat the oven to 425°F.

2 Arrange the vegetables on a rimmed baking sheet and drizzle with the oil. Stir well to coat. Sprinkle with the salt and any herbs you may want to use.

❸ Bake, stirring once, until the vegetables are tender and lightly browned at the edges, 20 to 25 minutes. Serve hot.

Simple Squash

SERVES 4

When squash isn't in season, I buy bags of it frozen—it's of much better quality and a greater value than what's available in the produce aisle since it is picked and packaged at its very peak. When squash *is* in season, I usually have it growing in my garden for this recipe alone.

This dish is simple and easy to prepare, and, boy, is it delicious. I recommend using the bacon grease if you have it—it adds a subtle hint of smoke and salt.

3 to 4 cups sliced yellow squash (about 3 whole medium-size squash)

1 medium-size sweet onion, such as Vidalia, chopped

1 tablespoon bacon grease (optional)

Salt

Ground black pepper

❶ Place the squash and onion in a large skillet over medium-high heat. Add the bacon grease, if you like, and water just to cover the bottom of the skillet. Bring to a gentle boil, then reduce the heat to medium, cover, and simmer until the squash is tender and the onion is translucent, about 10 minutes.

❷ Strain the water out of the skillet, then add salt and pepper to taste. Serve warm.

Tomato Mozzarella Melts

SERVES 4

I make these often in peak tomato season, which for us is early May to late August, serving them as a side dish for supper or an entrée for my own lunch. I also enjoy them as an evening snack.

They're supereasy, fuss-free, and done in no time at all. Best yet, if you have a garden, chances are most of the ingredients are right outside your door!

This will serve as many as you allow tomatoes for. I usually allot two slices per person, but you can adjust the quantities based on how many you want to make.

2 to 3 large tomatoes, stemmed
    and thickly sliced (halve smaller
    tomatoes)
Salt (I prefer kosher salt here)
4 ounces fresh mozzarella, cut into
    ½-inch-thick slices
2 to 3 fresh basil leaves, torn,
    or 1 teaspoon dried basil

1 Preheat the broiler or set the oven to 500°F.

2 Place the tomatoes in a single layer on a rimmed baking sheet and sprinkle them with salt to taste. Broil or bake until tender, 3 to 5 minutes in the broiler, 5 to 7 minutes in the oven.

3 Remove the baking sheet and top the tomatoes with the mozzarella slices, sprinkle slices with the basil, and return to the heat until the cheese melts, 2 to 4 minutes. Serve warm.

"Feed someone today. Not their stomachs, but their hearts. Smile at people until they're full on bursting. Say something nice to the person who's obviously growing thin, starving for lack of kindness. Holding the door gives a morsel, happily taken in by those who need it, and a word of praise is a steak dinner with all the trimmings. We're all hungry today. But we each hold a tray of goodies just waiting to be handed out! Here's hoping today is a banquet for you!"

—*Christy*

Simple Skillet Vegetables

SERVES 4

On those nights when I have no idea what I'm going to make as a side, I usually reach for this recipe. It comes together especially quickly when I have a frozen vegetable blend tucked in my freezer, but sometimes I substitute three cups of fresh chopped vegetables instead. Either way, it makes a simple, tasty side that complements pretty much any entrée.

1 bag (24 ounces) frozen vegetable blend of your choice

¼ cup (½ stick) butter

1 tablespoon lemon juice

1 tablespoon dry ranch dressing mix, lemon pepper seasoning, or seasoning blend of your choice

Place the vegetables in a skillet over medium heat, add ½ cup water, and cook, covered, for 5 minutes. Stir, cover again, and cook until tender, 5 more minutes. Drain and discard the water, then stir in the butter, lemon juice, and ranch dressing mix and cook, uncovered, until the butter has melted and the sauce has heated through. Serve hot.

Simply Delicious Tomato Basil Soup

SERVES 2

Some days just beg for a bowl of creamy tomato soup and a grilled cheese sandwich at supper time. When you find yourself having one of those days, reach for this simple but flavorful recipe, which quickly dresses up store-bought soup and takes it to a whole new level.

1 can (10.5 ounces) condensed tomato soup

1 can (15 ounces) petite diced tomatoes, with their liquid

1 tablespoon store-bought pesto sauce

1¼ cups milk

Combine the condensed tomato soup, tomatoes, pesto sauce, and milk in a small

My Secret Soup Thickener: Instant Potato Flakes

I always have instant potato flakes in my pantry but never use them for their intended purpose! They are fabulous as a soup thickener. Just add half a cup to three to four cups of hot broth, stir, and let it sit for a few minutes so the flakes can "melt" into the liquid. If you'd like your broth thicker, add half a cup more. This is also a great way to have a creamier soup without the added fat of heavy cream.

I also use these handy little flakes in the crust for my mother's Taco Casserole (page 156). I suppose, in a pinch, you could actually make mashed potatoes with them, too!

saucepan over medium heat and cook, stirring constantly, until heated through and just barely bubbling, about 10 minutes. Enjoy!

My Favorite Potato Soup

MAKES 4 GENEROUS SERVINGS

I've gotten more compliments on this recipe than probably any other on SouthernPlate.com. It seems there are a lot of people who have been searching for the perfect potato soup recipe and this one hit a home run. Like any potato soup, though, this is easily customizable. You can use whole milk in place of the cream if you want to lighten it up, but my favorite shortcut is to use a 32-ounce bag of cubed Southern-style hash browns in place of the fresh potatoes. I just toss them in frozen and continue on as directed.

This soup is also great reheated. It can be stored, covered, in the refrigerator for up to four days and reheated before serving.

FOR THE SOUP

2 cans (16 ounces each) chicken broth (4 cups)

4 to 5 medium-size russet potatoes,
washed, peeled, and cubed
(2 to 2½ pounds)
1 medium-size onion, diced
About 1 cup chopped smoked ham
About ¼ teaspoon salt
About ⅛ teaspoon ground black
pepper, plus more to taste
1 cup instant potato flakes
1 cup shredded Cheddar cheese
1 cup heavy (whipping) cream

FOR THE TOPPINGS (OPTIONAL)

Chopped scallions
Crumbled cooked bacon
Shredded Cheddar cheese
Sour cream

1 Pour the broth into a Dutch oven and place over medium heat. Add the potatoes, onion, ham, ¼ teaspoon salt, and ⅛ teaspoon pepper. Bring the mixture to a boil, then reduce to a simmer. Cook, covered, until the potatoes are tender, 10 to 15 minutes.

2 Stir in the potato flakes, then add the cheese and cream and cook, stirring constantly, until the potato flakes have blended into the soup and the cheese has melted, about 5 minutes. Taste and add more salt and pepper, if desired.

3 Serve the soup immediately with the toppings of your choice.

Parmesan Oven Fries

SERVES 4 TO 6

This recipe came from my husband's granny Jordan, one of the best examples of grace and kindness you could ever hope to meet. They are a great side for any dish but I need to warn you that they are slightly addictive.

Cooking spray
3 medium-size russet potatoes
(about 1½ pounds), washed and
unpeeled
⅓ cup freshly grated Parmesan
cheese
¾ teaspoon garlic powder
¾ teaspoon salt
¾ teaspoon paprika
¼ cup (½ stick) butter, melted

1 Preheat the oven to 375°F. Lightly coat a rimmed baking sheet with cooking spray.

2 Cut each potato lengthwise into 8 spears. Combine the Parmesan cheese, garlic powder, salt, and paprika in a large, shallow bowl or pie plate. Dip the cut sides of the potato spears into the melted butter, then into the Parmesan mixture, dredging to coat.

3 Arrange the potatoes in a single layer on the prepared baking sheet and bake until they are tender and browned, 30 to 40 minutes. Serve hot.

Big Fat Greek Taters

SERVES 4

These potatoes get their name from the use of lemon juice and oregano, which make them divinely delicious! I'm really a meat-and-potatoes gal at heart, so this fuss-free side dish is one that I could happily eat several times a week. Fortunately, my family feels the same way. These have become popular with my nephews, too!

> 5 to 6 medium-size red potatoes (about 2 pounds), washed and unpeeled
> 2 to 3 teaspoons olive oil
> 1 to 2 tablespoons lemon juice
> 1 tablespoon dried oregano flakes
> 1 teaspoon kosher salt

1 Preheat the oven to 425°F.

2 Cut each potato lengthwise into 8 thick wedges and place in a single layer on a rimmed baking sheet. Drizzle with the olive oil and lemon juice, stir around a bit to coat, then sprinkle on the oregano and salt.

3 Bake, stirring halfway through, until tender and lightly browned at the edges, 30 minutes. Serve hot.

Big Fat Greek Taters

Butter Stewed Potatoes

SERVES 4

Stewed potatoes are supremely easy to whip up and make a filling side dish with fried pork chops or chicken, though they go with just about everything. The butter sauce soaks into the potatoes as they cool and makes them truly delectable. If you've never had these before, please try them as soon as possible!

6 to 8 medium-size russet potatoes (3 to 4 pounds), washed and peeled

½ cup (1 stick) butter

1 teaspoon salt

1 Cut each potato crosswise into ½-inch-thick slices and place them in a medium-size stockpot. Add water to cover the potatoes by a depth of 1 inch.

2 Place the pot over medium-high heat and bring just to a boil, then reduce the heat to medium and cook, covered, until the potatoes are tender, about 15 minutes. Drain the potatoes into a colander.

3 Return the potatoes to the pot and add the butter and salt. Stir gently, trying not to break up the potatoes, until the butter has melted. Serve warm.

Mashed Potatoes

SERVES 4 TO 6

This is a classic: mashed potatoes just like my grandmother makes. Evaporated milk is the key to their richness, but you can substitute whatever milk you have on hand.

I find that buying little cans of evaporated milk to keep in my pantry makes for the ultimate convenience should I forget and let the regular milk go bad in the refrigerator. Evaporated milk is also wonderful in macaroni and cheese (like the ones on page 166) and it works great in casseroles, too, if fresh milk isn't available.

7 to 8 medium-size potatoes
(3½ to 4 pounds), washed, peeled,
and cut into thick slices or large
cubes (any kind of potato can
be used but Yukon Golds are
wonderful!)

2 teaspoons salt

½ cup evaporated milk or whole
milk

½ cup (1 stick) butter, cut into
chunks

½ teaspoon ground black pepper

1 Place the potatoes in a medium-size stockpot, add water to cover by a depth of 1 inch, and add 1 teaspoon of the salt. Place the pot over medium-high heat and bring it to a boil, then reduce the heat to medium and boil gently until the potatoes are extremely tender, about 30 minutes.

2 Drain the potatoes well and add the remaining ingredients, including the remaining teaspoon of salt, to the pot. Mix with an electric hand mixer on medium speed until smooth and creamy. Serve warm.

MeMe's Loaded Mashed Potatoes

SERVES 4 TO 6

The trick to making these delicious potatoes is managing to have leftover mashed potatoes to begin with! I often make a double batch of regular Mashed Potatoes (previous) just for that reason.

You can crumble four or five strips of crisp-cooked bacon over the casserole when you add the cheese to make it doubly loaded. (Try keeping crumbled cooked bacon in a plastic bag in the freezer; it can be added directly to the casserole before you pop it in the oven.)

3 cups leftover mashed potatoes

½ cup sour cream

¼ cup finely diced scallions
(optional)

½ cup shredded Cheddar cheese

1 Preheat the oven to 350°F.

2 In a large bowl, stir together the potatoes, sour cream, and scallions, if using, to combine.

3 Spread the potato mixture into a 1½-quart casserole dish and bake for 20 minutes.

4 Remove the potatoes from the oven, top with the cheese, and bake until the cheese has melted, 5 minutes. Serve hot.

Potato Cakes

MAKES ABOUT 12 POTATO CAKES, SERVES 4

This was Mama Reed's recipe. She was my mother's grandmother and although I never got to know her personally, my mother has told me so many wonderful stories that I have always felt a close kinship to her, especially whenever I make one of her recipes.

Mama Reed worked hard all day long. She fed ten kids at every meal, every day, in addition to her husband and any men helping out on their farm. These potato cakes were served on huge heaping platters, with the kids often eating three or four each, so Mama Reed very likely made extra mashed potatoes just to have enough to stretch for a meal.

When my mother's parents got divorced, Mama Reed took my mother under her wing and had her help out with supper each night. My mother and her father would then eat there and Mama Reed would brag on what a good cook "Little Janice" was. Mama thought she was just being nice, but she realized in hindsight that Mama Reed wanted to make sure she knew how to cook so that she could pass on the recipes to her family. I sure am glad she did!

2 cups cold leftover Mashed
  Potatoes (page 204)

1 large egg

¼ cup all-purpose or self-rising
  flour

2 tablespoons finely diced onion
  (optional; see Note)

Vegetable oil

1 Place the mashed potatoes and egg in a medium-size bowl and mix with a fork until well blended. Add the flour and onion, if using, and mix well. The mixture will be very stiff.

2 Pour the oil into a large skillet to coat the bottom and heat it over medium heat. Line a plate with paper towels.

3 Working in batches, scoop out a heaping tablespoon of the potato mixture and carefully place it in the hot oil. Dip the back of the spoon into the oil and mash the potato mixture to flatten it to about ¼ inch thick. (Dipping the back of the spoon into the oil prevents the potatoes from sticking to it.) Continue adding spoonfuls of the mixture to the oil, being sure to leave enough space between them for flattening.

4 Fry the potato cakes until they are lightly browned on the bottom, 3 to 5 minutes. Flip them and lightly brown them on the other side, 2 to 3 minutes. Remove the potato cakes to the paper towel–lined plate to drain. Keep them warm while you continue frying the remaining potato mixture. Serve warm.

NOTE: The onion is optional in this recipe but if you do use it, make sure to dice it very fine so that it will cook in the short amount of time it takes for the cakes to brown.

Butter Dill New Potatoes

SERVES 4 TO 6

Dill is a beautiful complement to the garden-fresh flavor of new potatoes. Whenever I use new potatoes, I always leave the skin on for color and additional flavor. If you don't have new potatoes, just use whatever type you have for this.

About 3 pounds new potatoes, washed and quartered or cubed if large (5 to 6 cups)
½ cup (1 stick) butter
1 teaspoon salt or to taste
1 teaspoon dried dill

1 Place the potatoes in a large saucepan and add water to cover by a depth of 1 inch. Bring to a boil over medium heat and cook, covered, until the potatoes are fork tender, about 20 minutes. Drain and transfer to a large serving bowl.

2 Place the butter, salt, and dill in a small saucepan over medium-low heat and warm just until the butter has melted (or place it in a microwave-safe bowl and heat it on 100 percent power for 1 minute).

❸ Stir the butter sauce and pour it over the potatoes. Toss to coat well. Serve warm.

Roasted Sweet Potato Wedges

SERVES 4

If you're a devotee of sweet potato casserole, this may seem like a pretty big departure. But these spiced and sweet wedges have all the delicious flavors we enjoy so much in a casserole—no one will realize how lightened up they are!

2 medium-size sweet potatoes, washed and unpeeled
2 teaspoons olive oil
3 tablespoons dark brown sugar
1 teaspoon ground cinnamon
⅛ teaspoon salt
⅛ teaspoon ground black pepper

❶ Preheat the oven to 425°F.

❷ Carefully cut each potato lengthwise into about 6 wedges and place them in a single layer on a rimmed baking sheet.

Drizzle with the olive oil and stir to coat. Arrange the potatoes skin side down.

❸ Stir together the brown sugar, cinnamon, salt, and pepper in a small bowl and sprinkle half of the mixture over the potato wedges.

❹ Bake the potatoes, stirring them and sprinkling them with the remaining topping halfway through, until they are fork tender, 30 minutes. Serve hot.

Mashed Sweet Potatoes

SERVES 4 TO 6

When I was a girl we always scrambled to the kitchen when we found out Mama was making sweet potatoes. As she'd peel and slice them, if we stood around and asked nicely, she'd give each of us a raw slice to munch on. Oh, how I loved that wonderful crunch and flavor. Once they were cooked and sweetened just right, though, sweet potatoes rose to a whole new level. My brother, sister, and I always made sure that every bite was eaten!

> 4 medium-size sweet potatoes, washed, peeled, and cut into ½-inch chunks (about 6 cups)
> 3 tablespoons butter
> ¼ cup heavy (whipping) cream
> ¼ cup honey
> 1 teaspoon ground cinnamon

1 Place the potatoes in a medium stockpot and add water to cover by a depth of 1 inch.

2 Bring to a boil over medium-high heat, then reduce the heat to medium and cook until the potatoes are soft and tender, about 20 minutes. Drain the potatoes and transfer them to a large bowl.

3 Add the butter, cream, honey, and cinnamon to the potatoes and beat with an electric mixer at medium speed until well blended, light, and fluffy. Serve warm.

Loaded Baked Potatoes

MAKES 14 SERVINGS

Whenever I have company over for supper, I love to serve this go-to dish. It is a great way to round out the meal without taking too much additional prep time, since I make them up a few days ahead and keep them in the freezer. Then all I have to do is heat them up in the oven or, if I'm really pressed for time, the microwave.

To freeze these, simply place the baked, assembled loaded potatoes on a baking sheet and put them in the freezer for about an hour until they're partially frozen. Transfer the taters to a couple of large ziplock bags and store them in the freezer for up to three months. To reheat them, follow the directions in the Notes on the following page or pop them in a microwave at 100 percent heat for 1½ to 2 minutes.

Loaded Baked Potatoes

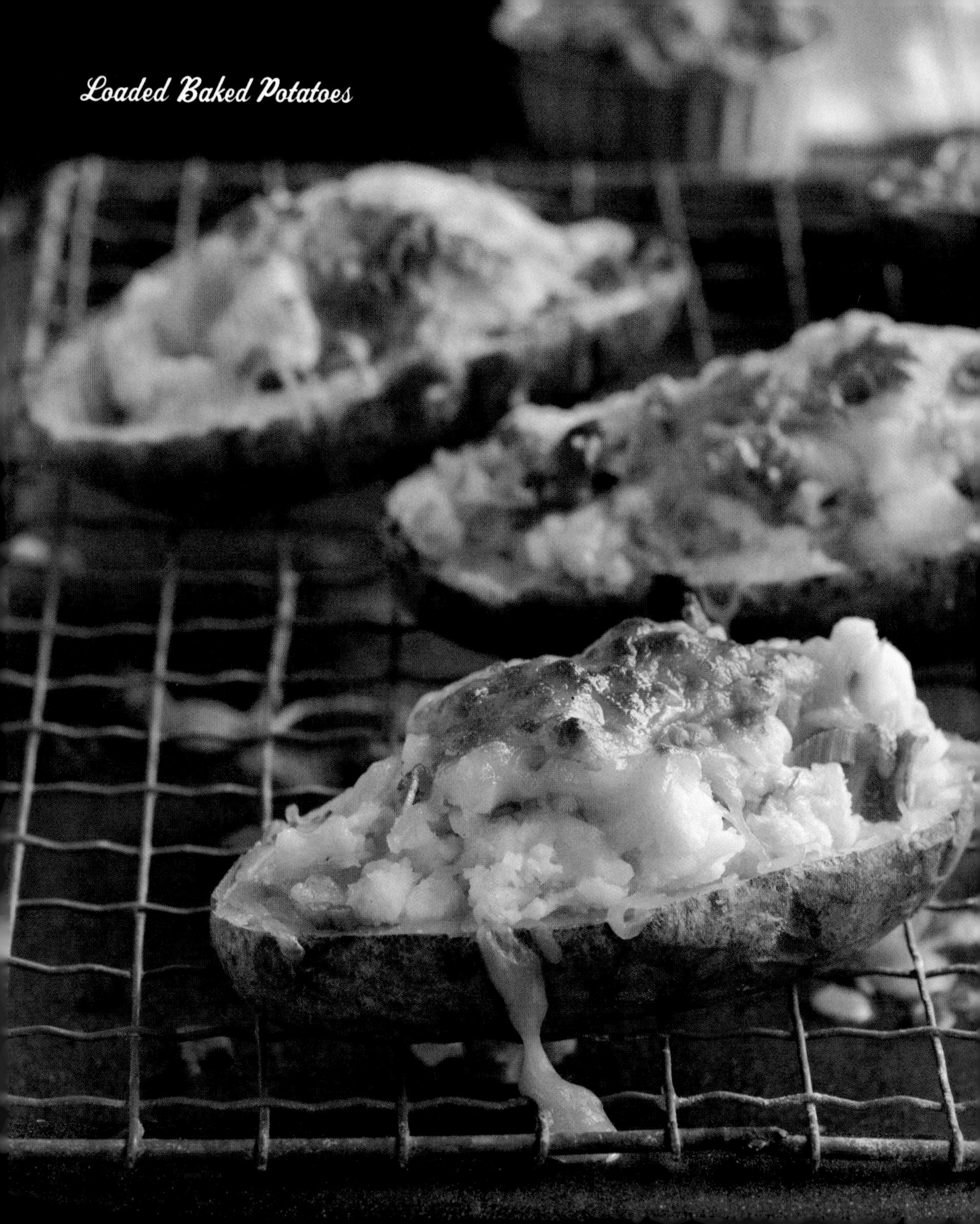

7 medium-size russet potatoes
(about 4 pounds), washed,
unpeeled, and pierced with a fork

3 tablespoons butter

½ cup sour cream

1½ cups shredded Cheddar cheese

½ teaspoon salt

¼ teaspoon ground black pepper

¼ teaspoon garlic powder

4 scallions, chopped

8 to 10 slices bacon, cooked and
chopped (see Notes)

1 Preheat the oven to 450°F.

2 Place the potatoes on a plate and microwave them on 100 percent power for 5 minutes. Transfer them to a baking sheet and bake until a fork pierces them easily, about 1 hour. Remove the potatoes from the oven and let them cool enough to handle; turn the oven down to 350°F.

3 Cut the potatoes in half lengthwise. Use a large spoon to scoop the pulp into a large bowl, leaving enough for the skins to retain their shape. Set the skins aside on a clean baking sheet.

4 Add the butter and sour cream to the potato pulp and mash together to combine well. Stir in 1 cup of the cheese, the salt, pepper, garlic powder, scallions, and bacon until well combined. Spoon the filling into the reserved potato skins.

5 Top the potatoes with the remaining ½ cup cheese and bake until they are heated through and the cheese has melted, 5 minutes. Serve hot.

NOTES: You can use 1 cup chopped ham or smoked pork chops in place of the bacon.

To reheat frozen potatoes, bake them for 30 minutes, then top them with the cheese and return them to the oven until the cheese has melted, 5 minutes more.

Shortcut Potato Salad

SERVES 6 TO 8

A few years back my mother asked me to create a recipe that would allow her to make a good potato salad in a hurry. It seems she has a lot of drop-in guests in the summertime and my dad usually fires up the grill to feed them, leaving Mama to come up with some quick sides.

I developed this recipe using the blend of flavors that we like best and relying on frozen cubed potatoes to significantly cut down on cooking time.

1 package (32 ounces) frozen Southern-style cubed hash browns

1 cup shredded Cheddar cheese

½ cup mayonnaise

2 tablespoons yellow mustard

⅓ cup sweet pickle relish

5 slices bacon, cooked and crumbled

3 hard-boiled eggs, chopped

Salt to taste

Ground black pepper to taste

1 Place the hash browns in a large pot and add water to cover. Bring to a boil over medium-high heat and cook until tender, 2 to 3 minutes. Drain the potatoes into a colander and transfer them to a large bowl.

2 Stir in the cheese, then add the mayonnaise, mustard, and relish and stir again. Add the bacon, eggs, salt, and

pepper and stir until well combined. Serve right away or refrigerate for up to 2 days—the potato salad only improves over time.

Seasoned Rice

MAKES 3 CUPS; SERVES 4 TO 6

The secret to making a savory white rice is cooking it in a rich liquid. This recipe produces a rice that is so full of flavor you can easily eat it on its own, but I serve it as a side most of the time!

1½ cups uncooked white or brown rice

3 tablespoons butter

1 small onion, chopped

2 cans (14 ounces each) beef or chicken broth

2 tablespoons dried parsley flakes

1 tablespoon dried basil

1 teaspoon salt

½ teaspoon ground black pepper

1 tablespoon Worcestershire sauce

1 Place the rice in a colander and rinse it well with cold water.

2 Melt the butter in a large saucepan over medium heat. Add the onion and sauté until it is translucent and lightly browned around the edges, about 5 minutes.

3 Add the broth, ½ cup of water, the parsley, basil, salt, pepper, Worcestershire sauce, and rice. Stir well and bring to a boil, then cover, reduce the heat to low, and simmer until the rice is tender and all the liquid has been absorbed, 15 minutes. Fluff with a fork and serve.

Classic Pasta Salad

SERVES 4 TO 6

A classic pasta salad can be made with pretty much anything, so look to this recipe as a guide and not a rule.

When cooking pasta for a pasta salad, cook it until it is just barely done and then drain it. Immediately run cold water over it to stop the cooking process. This will help your pasta keep its yummy al dente texture when it's dressed.

10 ounces short pasta,
   such as bow tie
½ to ¾ cup mayonnaise
1 tablespoon spicy brown mustard
   (yellow mustard works, too)
1 small onion, finely diced
⅓ cup sweet pickle relish
½ teaspoon salt
¼ teaspoon ground black pepper

1 Bring a large pot of salted water to a boil. Add the pasta and cook according to package directions until it is just tender (taste it occasionally—this may be 1 or 2 minutes less than called for on the package). Drain the pasta into a colander and immediately run it under cold water.

2 Stir together the remaining ingredients, using the lesser amount of mayonnaise, in a medium-size bowl. Add the pasta and mix well. Add more mayonnaise if needed. Cover and chill for at least 2 hours or up to 4 days. Stir before serving.

213

The Five People All Kids Need in Their Lives

As a mother, I realize that there will be a lot of things in my kids' lives that will be beyond their control. But I also know from personal experience that the most important things in their lives will be left entirely up to them.

They may not get to decide where they're going to live, how much money they are going to make, or perhaps even how educated they become. In fact, when they get out into the world there is a chance that a great many of the doors they want to open just might not open for them as they'd hoped. But the one thing they will have control over is the type of person they choose to be.

I've seen a lot of folks who don't realize that we each have the power when it comes to who we are. Without having ever set a standard for themselves or mapping out the type of person they want to be, they end up blowing willy-nilly in the wind, controlled by emotions and whims, with no framework or purpose.

I think one of the most important things I can do for my children is to take them aside while they're young and just come out and tell them, "You need to be coming up with a set of standards for your life. A set of rules you make for yourself that you will live by. You need to decide what kind of person you want to be and start working toward that goal now, while you're young."

Kids just don't get golden nuggets of wisdom like that nowadays, and in this crazy modern world, we need them more than ever.

My kids aren't going to have the role models in society like I had growing up. I had *Little House on the Prairie*, where Pa gently guided his children through life with a loving hand and a firm grasp on the importance of doing the right thing. My kids have reality television, with no Michael Landon in sight, and whoever causes the loudest public spectacle gets their own series. With that kind of contrast, it's more important than ever to stop beating around the bush and just say, "Look, kid, life is complicated, but if you listen, I'm going to show you how you navigate it."

I've spent a lot of time thinking over how I can provide the right influences in the lives of my children. I've come to the conclusion that there are five people that they really need in their lives, but it's up to me to make sure they know to be on the lookout for these folks. They begin with the founding father of America.

ALL KIDS NEED A GEORGE WASHINGTON.

It is often said that George Washington was offered the throne of the United States of America, that his fellow countrymen literally offered to make him King of the USA. He turned it down because he felt it was better for the people. There are some who say this didn't happen, some who swear it did. It takes just a small amount of study into the integrity and ethics with which George Washington lived his life to be able to see why such a noble action would be attributed to him. What an example of the type of person we should all strive to be!

When I was growing up, my George Washington was my dad. He worked three jobs so Mama could stay home because they both felt it was the right thing to do for us. He sacrificed by taking the high road in more ways than one. As a direct result of his choices, my brother, sister, and I are the only three grandkids in my father's family to graduate high school. We each went on to college as well. Our kids are now being raised with integrity and taught to value

Daddy, my George Washington

hard work and honor. Would my dad have turned down a kingdom if he felt it was in the best interest of the people? You better believe it, and I know that one day, if my kids find their George Washington, I'll be able to say the same thing about them.

ALL KIDS NEED SOMEONE WHO LOVES THEM UNCONDITIONALLY.

All kids need that one person who acts as if he or she had been waiting all day to see them and once that happens, that person's day is complete. That one person who loves them so strongly and fiercely that they feel as though they could do no wrong.

Obviously and for a multitude of good reasons, neither I nor my husband can be this person to our kids. We are meant to train them up, guide them, correct them, and teach them. Of course, we love them no matter what, but the very process of teaching them life's principles means they're better off with us being their parents, not their best friends.

My most important unconditional love came from my granddaddy. He made me feel like I was the center of his universe. He loved me so deeply and absolutely that I would have walked through fire in order to live up to his expectations. My kids are going to need someone like that when those tumultuous teenage years hit. There will naturally be times when they won't care what we—their parents—think, but that one other person can keep them towing the line when they most want to let it go.

All Kids Need a Mentor.

Kids need a role model—an example of walking the straight road on the path they want to take. If a boy is interested in football, he needs a Tim Tebow. My son, Brady, wants to be a computer programmer and we were very blessed to find a good-hearted older kid who happens to be a computer whiz and who is now taking time to work with Brady each week. He encourages him and shares his knowledge. He also sets an example of mentoring, something I hope Brady will do for someone else when he gets older.

My mentor was my mother. I didn't know what career I wanted to have but I knew I wanted to be good-hearted and kind, and to treat others with compassion and grace. I looked to Mama for an example of how to live that way.

My mentor and me, some years ago :)

All Kids Need Someone They Don't Want to Be When They Grow Up.

I know from personal experience that this is going to be every bit as important as having a mentor. Just like my kids need examples of the kinds of people they want to be, they're going to need examples of the kinds of people they don't want to become, too. These people will serve as motivation to stay on their chosen path, even in the midst of bumps and ruts.

For my kids, these are the people who seek the bad in every situation, who find constant fault with others, who complain constantly rather than opening their eyes to their blessings. These are the people who, when my son comes to me in exasperation as a result of their behavior, I can say, "You see how that made you feel? You see how they treat others? Don't be like them."

THE FIFTH PERSON ALL KIDS NEED IN THEIR LIVES IS YOU.

If you have a child in your life, whether it be a student, a niece, or a neighbor, the child was put there for a reason. Maybe you're the mentor or the George Washington. Maybe as the child's grandparent you're the one perfectly placed to offer that unconditional love. I hope you'll find out which role you were meant to fill and assume it with purpose, knowing that we'll never be able to measure the dividends of our time and investment in a child's life.

As my kids grow older, I want to remind them to be on the lookout for these people.

To shadow them whenever they can, to watch how they interact with the world. When the wise speak, I want them to be quiet and listen. No matter how exciting my kids' day was or what social activity is going on, I want them to know that when these folks speak they are speaking wisdom and history and knowledge that they won't ever get from a sale at the mall or a party at the popular kid's house.

I want to make sure they know that all of the *things* of youth fly by faster than they could ever imagine, that when these moments are gone, it's the truly meaningful experiences that remain as a solid foundation.

I want to make sure I tell them that when the day comes that you wake up and find you are suddenly an adult and you don't know how it happened or what to do next, these are the people you can call to mind.

To my dear Brady and Katy Rose: If you want to be an oak, don't spend your time searching through the weeds for the answers. You've got to stand among the oaks instead. Stand among them as long as you can and one day you'll look down and find saplings standing as close as they can to you. ♥

8

Breads

I don't always serve bread with my meals like my mother did when I was grow-ing up, but when I do, it just feels like that perfect finishing touch. The aroma of freshly baked bread is one of the best smells in the entire world. Whether you are making one of the varieties of biscuits or breads offered here or a tradi-tional cornbread, your family is sure to feel it is the ideal ending to a wonderful home-cooked meal. If you have been afraid of making bread in the past, give these recipes a shot. They are all manageable for even the novice baker and will give you satisfying results every time.

Cheesy Garlic Biscuits

MAKES ABOUT 12 BISCUITS

These classic biscuits can be found in many a restaurant bread basket, but I think they taste better than ever when made with my hearty oat baking mix and enjoyed at your own dinner table!

> 2 cups Hearty Oat Baking Mix (recipe follows) or store-bought biscuit baking mix
> ⅔ cup milk
> ½ cup shredded Cheddar cheese
> ⅛ cup (¼ stick) butter
> ¼ teaspoon garlic powder

1 Preheat the oven to 425°F.

2 Combine the baking mix, milk, and cheese in a large bowl and stir together until they form a well-blended dough.

3 Using ¼-cup measuring cup, drop the dough 2 inches apart onto an ungreased baking sheet.

4 Bake the biscuits until they're lightly browned on top, 8 to 10 minutes.

5 Melt the butter in a small saucepan over low heat (or in a microwave-safe dish in a microwave on 100 percent power for about 45 seconds). Stir in the garlic powder and brush the flavored butter over the hot biscuits. Serve warm.

Hearty Oat Baking Mix

MAKES 7 CUPS

This great homemade baking mix can be used for an assortment of recipes in addition to my Cheesy Garlic Biscuits (this page). I love it in 7UP Bread (page 222) and Hearty Lip-Smacking Pancakes (page 224), but I hope you'll have fun playing around and coming up with your own uses!

By using half oats and half flour in the mix, you add some great nutrient content, making it better for you than traditional store-bought mixes. Since this has fresh butter in it, I store it in the refrigerator in ziplock bags or a sealed container. A good way to know how long your mix will last is to check the expiration date on your butter. Once the mix is made up, I write that expiration date on the storage container or bags and then I know how long I have to use it up.

 3 cups all-purpose flour

 3 cups quick-cooking oats

 3 tablespoons baking powder

 1 tablespoon baking soda

 3 tablespoons sugar

 1 tablespoon salt

 1 cup (2 sticks) butter, at room
  temperature

1 In a large bowl, stir together all the dry ingredients until well combined.

2 Add the butter and mix thoroughly with a hand mixer until well incorporated and no longer lumpy.

3 Store in a sealed plastic container or ziplock bags in the refrigerator.

Cat Head Biscuits

MAKES 10 TO 12 BISCUITS

These drop biscuits are big and fluffy with a delicious, delicate crunch on the outside. The story goes that they got their name because when baked they are the color of a marmalade cat and are about the size of its head. The secret is baking them with a very light coating of vegetable oil that heats in the oven while you mix up the dough. You drop the dough—really more like a batter—onto the hot oiled baking sheet, spoon a little hot oil on top (or just give the biscuits a quick misting of cooking spray), and bake. No fuss, no muss, but lots of delicious bread!

These are especially good served with apple butter but are certainly tasty enough to eat on their own, too.

 2 to 4 tablespoons vegetable oil

 2 cups self-rising flour
  (see page 287)

 ½ cup vegetable shortening

 1 cup milk, plus a bit more if needed

Cat Head Biscuits

1 Preheat the oven to 425°F. Pour 2 tablespoons of the oil onto a large rimmed baking sheet and tilt it to cover the bottom with a very thin layer (add more if needed). Place the pan in the oven to heat.

2 Place the flour in a large bowl and cut in the shortening with a dinner fork until crumbly. Pour in the milk and stir until combined, adding a little more milk if needed (the dough will be wet and a little lumpy).

3 Carefully remove the hot pan from the oven and set it on a heatproof surface. Drop the dough by heaping tablespoonfuls onto the pan, leaving about 1 inch between each biscuit, then carefully spoon a bit of the hot oil from the pan over each one.

4 Bake the biscuits until lightly browned, 10 to 15 minutes. Serve warm.

Variation: You can bake this as a single loaf of bread. Although it takes a little longer to cook, there is not as much prep work as for biscuits. Use an 8- or 9-inch metal cake pan in place of the rimmed baking sheet and coat it with the lesser amount of oil. Pour the batter into the pan, coat it with cooking spray and bake until browned, 20 to 25 minutes. Let cool slightly, then cut into squares and serve.

7UP Bread
ABOUT 8 PIECES

My daughter especially loves this recipe because it calls for half a can of 7UP and she volunteers to take care of the rest! When made with my hearty oat baking mix, these bake up tender and fluffy, but you can substitute a store-bought baking mix if you prefer.

½ cup (1 stick) butter
2¼ cups Hearty Oat Baking Mix (page 219) or store-bought biscuit baking mix
½ cup sour cream
½ cup 7UP or other lemon-lime soda

1 Preheat the oven to 450°F.

2 Place the butter in an 8-inch square baking dish and put it in the oven to melt.

Starting Your Day Right

One of my favorite things to do is get up a little earlier than everyone else and creep into the kitchen to make that first cup of coffee. Then I go sit down in the sunroom and look out on the trees in the backyard. It is a little ritual that helps center me, kind of like taking a deep calming breath before the day begins.

I don't get to do that very often, though, because my Katy (who has informed us that from here on out she is to be called by her first *and* middle names, Katy Rose)—excuse me, my Katy *Rose*—is an even earlier riser than her mama. Some mornings I get my coffee made and get ready to head out into the sunroom when a little

curly-headed pixie pops into the kitchen. So I turn around and head to the recliner instead, where she curls up in my lap and lets me stroke her hair while we talk about our day.

And that's a pretty good way to start the day, too.

I have one rule in my house about mornings: I don't care how early you get up as long as you wake up happy. I don't think this is very difficult to do, either, so I'm pretty serious about enforcing it. When my kids emerge in the morning with sour faces, I make them go back into their rooms, turn around, and come back out again with a smile (surprisingly, it works!).

A positive attitude will bring you happiness every time, so why not start your day off with one? Even if you have to go back into your own bedroom and come out again! ♥

3 Meanwhile, combine the baking mix, sour cream, and 7UP in a large bowl and stir until it is well blended and forms a soft dough. Carefully remove the baking dish from the oven and spoon the dough over the melted butter in the dish.

4 Bake the bread until lightly browned on top, 12 to 15 minutes. Allow it to cool slightly, then cut it into squares and serve warm.

Ten-Minute Rolls

MAKES 6 ROLLS

I'm the world's worst about planning out an entire meal and not thinking about the bread until we're about ready to eat. That is where these rolls come in handy. If you work fast, you can have them ready start to finish in about ten minutes using ingredients you probably have on hand. The mayonnaise gives them a subtle flavor as sour cream would, acts as a shortening, and produces a tender crumb.

Cooking spray
1 cup self-rising flour (page 287)
2 tablespoons mayonnaise
½ cup whole milk
⅛ teaspoon salt

1 Preheat the oven to 425°F. Coat 6 cups of a muffin tin with cooking spray.

2 Combine the flour, mayonnaise, milk, and salt in a medium-size bowl and stir until well combined.

3 Divide the batter evenly among the prepared muffin tin cups. Bake until browned, 8 to 10 minutes. Allow the rolls to cool for 2 to 3 minutes before removing them from the pan. Serve warm.

Hearty Lip-Smacking Pancakes

MAKES ABOUT 8 PANCAKES

I love the texture of pancakes made with oat baking mix. They end up tasting like a cross between pancakes and French toast! My family loves these, too. I sometimes add a teaspoon of cinnamon to the batter while I'm mixing it up.

This recipe serves four people easily but can also be doubled if you have a larger family.

Cooking spray

2 cups Hearty Oat Baking Mix
(page 219) or store-bought
biscuit baking mix

1 cup milk

2 large eggs, beaten

Butter and maple syrup, for serving
(optional)

1 Coat a large skillet with cooking spray and place it over medium heat.

2 Combine the baking mix, milk, and eggs in a large bowl and stir with a wooden spoon until all ingredients are moistened. The mixture will be a little lumpy.

3 Working in batches, pour the batter onto the hot skillet ¼ to ½ cup at a time. Cook the pancakes until they are bubbly on top and dry around edges, 3 to 4 minutes. Flip and cook them until they are lightly browned on the other side, about 1 minute more.

4 Serve the pancakes warm with butter and syrup, if you like.

Buttermilk Cornbread

MAKES 10 PIECES

This is how my mother makes her cornbread. She always uses an iron skillet to give it a crispy outside, and her skillet is the one my great-grandmother gave her way back when. Our family has passed down iron skillets from one generation to the next.

I've eaten countless pieces of this cornbread in my lifetime. My favorite thing to do is get one of the "corner" pieces and slather it with butter while it's still steaming hot. Although oil is traditionally used in this recipe, I also like the flavor that butter provides. If you don't happen to own a cast-iron skillet, you can use an eight-inch square metal pan instead.

¼ cup vegetable oil or melted butter

1½ cups self-rising cornmeal mix

½ cup self-rising flour (page 287)

1 large egg

1¾ cups buttermilk

Butter, for serving

1 Preheat the oven to 400°F. Pour the oil into a 10-inch cast-iron skillet and place it in the oven while it preheats.

2 Stir together the cornmeal mix and flour in a medium-size bowl. Add the egg and buttermilk and mix with a wooden spoon until well combined and smooth.

3 Remove the skillet from the oven and carefully pour the hot oil into the batter while stirring, leaving enough oil in the skillet to cover the bottom. Stir the batter well until everything is combined.

4 Pour the batter back into the skillet and bake until the cornbread is light brown on top, 25 to 30 minutes. Immediately turn the cornbread out onto a plate. Cut it and serve. (It's great at any temperature.)

Ice Cream Rolls

MAKES 6 ROLLS

Yes, this really is bread made with melted ice cream. When my friend Jyl gave me the recipe I didn't think she was crazy, though, because I know her well enough to know that we're both a little on the loony side, but in those fun ways that have us making delicious rolls out of ice cream.

These are so quick to throw together with only two ingredients. The result is a very tender-crumbed roll (more like a biscuit) with a light sweetness and just a tiny hint of vanilla. They are absolutely delicious and may become your standby rolls for any occasion.

Cooking spray

1 cup self-rising flour (page 287)

1 cup melted vanilla ice cream

1 Preheat the oven to 350°F. Coat 6 cups of a muffin tin with cooking spray.

2 Stir together the flour and melted ice cream in a medium-size bowl until well combined.

Ice Cream Rolls

3 Divide the batter evenly among the prepared muffin tin cups. Bake until golden on top, 15 to 20 minutes. Allow the rolls to cool for 2 to 3 minutes before removing them from the pan. Serve warm.

Cornbread Muffins

MAKES 12 MUFFINS

This is a basic cornbread muffin recipe with juicy bits of corn and shreds of cheese throughout. It is a pleasant change from regular cornbread with little "surprises" inside. The sugar gives a hint of sweetness to the muffins, which are wonderful when slathered with butter while hot. This batter also serves as the crust for my Cornbread-Topped Chicken Potpie (page 160), and makes excellent hush puppies (see the variation that follows).

If you don't have a need for the full batch of muffins, don't let that stop you—these freeze well. Place the cooled muffins in a large ziplock bag and store them in the freezer for up to three months. To reheat a muffin, wrap it in a paper towel and microwave it on 100 percent power for about 45 seconds or until warm, or in a 350°F oven for about 5 to 10 minutes.

Cooking spray
1 cup yellow or white cornmeal
1 cup all-purpose flour
1 tablespoon baking powder
1 teaspoon salt
2 tablespoons sugar
2 large eggs
1 cup milk
¼ cup (½ stick) butter, melted
1 can (15 ounces) whole kernel corn, drained
1 cup shredded Cheddar cheese

1 Preheat the oven to 400°F. Coat a 12-cup muffin tin with cooking spray.

2 Combine the cornmeal, flour, baking powder, salt, and sugar in a medium-size bowl and stir. Add the eggs, milk, and melted butter and stir well until combined. Stir in the corn and cheese until incorporated.

3 Spoon the batter into the muffin tin cups and bake until golden on top, 15 to 20 minutes. Allow the muffins to cool

Cornbread Muffins

for 2 to 3 minutes before removing them from the muffin tin. Serve warm.

Hush Puppies

The cornbread batter (page 288) can be used for hush puppies, too. They are great served hot with fish, French fries, and slaw or your favorite seafood dish.

Just pour vegetable oil into a skillet or deep fryer (either works just as well) to a depth of 1½ to 2 inches; place the skillet over medium-high heat or heat the deep fryer to 375°F. When the oil is hot (a little bit of batter will sizzle up immediately when it's dropped in), cook the hush puppies in batches: Carefully drop in the batter by tablespoonfuls. (To get the batter for each hush puppy to slide easily off the spoon, keep a glass of water nearby and dip your spoon into it before each scoop.)

Fry, turning the hush puppies as needed until golden brown, 4 to 5 minutes per hush puppy.

Transfer the cooked hush puppies to a paper towel–lined plate to drain.

Maria's Flour Tortillas

MAKES ABOUT 18 TORTILLAS

On a trip out West a few years back, I was treated to my first homemade tortilla—and I would never be the same. After that trip I began to search high and low for the perfect tortilla recipe, so I considered it divine providence that this one literally showed up at my front door one day.

Last summer, my friend Tara's mother-in-law, Maria Maestes, came from New Mexico for a wonderful weeklong visit. We had them all over for supper one night, and two days later Maria dropped by with a package of freshly made tortillas for me. One bite and I knew I had finally found the perfect tortilla recipe! These are slightly thicker than store-bought flour tortillas and have a wonderfully different bite to them, just a little bit more chew. They're great when served with your favorite taco filling, but they're also irresistible with butter and cinnamon sugar.

Homemade tortillas are easier to make than you think! Special thanks to Maria for letting me share this recipe with you.

Making Do

I love using what I have on hand to prepare a meal, being able to make a meal for my family without having to take any last-minute trips to the grocery store. I think the best meals come out of that, just like the best lives come out of "using what you have on hand" to make your own happiness. ♥

---

5 cups all-purpose flour, plus extra
    as needed

1 tablespoon salt

2 teaspoons baking powder

⅓ cup vegetable oil

1½ cups warm water

1 Stir together the dry ingredients in a large bowl. Add the oil and warm water and stir until a sticky dough forms.

2 Lightly flour a work surface and your hands, dump out the dough, and use your hands to roll it into a ball, kneading just enough to help it hold together.

3 Pinch off golf ball–size portions of dough and roll each one into a small ball between your hands. Return all of the dough balls to the mixing bowl, cover it with plastic wrap, and allow the dough to rest for 5 minutes.

4 Meanwhile, heat a large skillet over medium-high heat and dust a rolling pin with flour.

5 Working in batches, roll out each ball into an 8-inch circle and place it in the skillet to lightly brown, flipping it once with a spatula, 10 to 15 seconds on each side. (Be careful because they burn fast!) Transfer the cooked tortillas to a plate and cover with a dish towel to keep them warm.

9

Desserts

At my house, dessert is a special treat that makes an appearance once or twice a week. Usually, it's one of the low-fuss recipes you'll find featured in this chapter. Some of these recipes are family favorites that have been passed down for generations and some have been shared by friends. I have also developed some, such as the Faux Pecan Pie (page 262), to fill a need for people who have nut allergies and to save money. I have tried to choose recipes that appeal to everyone and that are still delicious. This chapter includes everything from cookies to cobblers, puddings to pies, and delicious cakes for those special moments and people in our lives. I hope that you enjoy making these to round out meals at your dinner table.

Simple Fruit Crisp

SERVES 4 TO 6

This is my basic fruit crisp recipe, which can be adapted to use with any fruit. If you want to make it with large fruits such as apples or pears, core, peel, and dice them. I often use canned peaches, canned fried apples, and canned pears, too. This also works well with berries, which can be baked whole. We've made this crisp all my life and it's very versatile and very delicious.

2 cups drained canned fruit or
    fresh fruit (see headnote)
½ cup all-purpose or self-rising
    flour
¾ cup brown sugar
½ cup quick-cooking or
    old-fashioned oats
1 teaspoon ground cinnamon
½ cup (1 stick) butter,
    at room temperature
Ice cream, for serving (optional)

1 Preheat the oven to 350°F.

2 Place the fruit in an 8-inch square baking dish.

3 Combine the dry ingredients in a large bowl and stir them together. Cut in the butter with a dinner fork until the mixture is well blended and crumbly.

4 Sprinkle the flour mixture over the fruit and bake until the crisp is lightly browned on top and bubbly, 30 minutes. Serve hot with ice cream, if desired.

The crisp will keep for up to 3 days when stored, covered, in the fridge.

Candied Apples That You Eat with a Fork

Candied Apples That You Eat with a Fork

SERVES 4

As a girl, I found nothing more magical than a shiny red candied apple. My mother often surprised us with them when we got home from school. I'm afraid my teeth just can't manage them nowadays, though, so I use my friend Jyl's recipe for these yummy candied apples that you eat with a fork. All of the same flavors but no risk of needing a dental visit after the fact!

My mama's candied apple recipe appears in my first book, *Southern Plate*, if you'd like it. I still love to surprise my kids like she did—I just have these on hand for myself when I do! These are delicious hot or cold.

4 to 5 apples, cored, peeled, and roughly chopped (about 3 cups)

1 cup tiny cinnamon candies (such as Red Hots)

¼ cup (½ stick) butter

1 Place the apples in a large skillet. Pour the candies over them and add the butter.

2 Place over medium heat and cook, stirring often, until all the candies are melted. Reduce the heat to low, cover, and simmer until the apples are fork tender, about 10 minutes. Serve hot or cold.

Apple Doozie

SERVES 6 TO 8

I love those dessert pizzas served at pizza chain restaurants and so I developed my own recipe using a ready-made pizza crust and canned pie filling. When I was deciding what to name this recipe and thinking about how delicious it was, the name "apple doozie" came to mind. I think it describes how I feel about the wonderful aromas and flavor of this dish just fine! This comes together in no time at all—I have even made it two nights in a row for company because they liked it so much.

1 store-bought prebaked
   unseasoned pizza crust
1 can (21 ounces) apple pie filling
   (see Note)
½ cup all-purpose flour
½ cup quick-cooking oats
½ cup dark brown sugar
1 tablespoon ground cinnamon
¼ cup (½ stick) butter, at room
   temperature
About 1 cup confectioners' sugar
About 2 tablespoons milk
1 teaspoon pure vanilla extract

1 Preheat the oven to 350°F. Place the pizza crust on a baking sheet.

2 Empty the pie filling into a shallow bowl and cut it up a bit with a sharp knife. Spread it over the pizza crust, leaving a ½-inch space around the edge.

3 Combine the flour, oats, brown sugar, and cinnamon in a small bowl and stir to combine. Using a dinner fork, cut the butter into the mixture until it's crumbly. Sprinkle the flour mixture on top of the pie filling.

4 Bake until the top is lightly golden, 25 minutes.

5 While the pizza bakes, make the glaze: Place the confectioners' sugar, milk, and vanilla in a small bowl and stir until smooth. Add a little more milk if the mixture is too thick, more sugar if it is too thin.

6 Drizzle the glaze over the baked pizza with a spoon and serve warm.

NOTE: If you'd like to use fresh apples, core, peel, and chop about 4 apples (to make 2 to 3 cups). Melt 2 tablespoons of butter in a large skillet over medium heat, add the apples, and sauté until tender, about 10 minutes. Spread them onto the pizza crust and proceed with the rest of the recipe as written.

Apple Scoop Pie
SERVES 4 TO 6

This apple scoop pie offers an easy way to fill your house and tummy when you're longing for the smells and tastes of fall. Baked in a pie plate with no crust to contend with, apples mingle with juicy raisins and spices to provide the perfect dessert (or even a side dish!). My mother said that developing this recipe was one of my greatest accomplishments in life—I'm pretty sure that's a good thing!

This pie is also good served over ice cream, and leftovers keep well in the refrigerator, so you can stir them into oatmeal the next morning.

5 to 6 medium-size sweet crisp
   apples, such as Gala
1 cup pecan pieces
½ cup raisins
1 cup brown sugar
1 tablespoon ground cinnamon
1 teaspoon ground allspice

 Preheat the oven to 350°F.

❷ Core the apples and cut them into bite-size pieces (don't peel them). Place them in a large bowl, add the remaining ingredients, and stir until well combined.

❸ Pour the apple mixture into a deep-dish 10-inch pie plate, cover with aluminum foil, and bake for 20 minutes. Uncover and bake until the apples are tender, 10 to 15 minutes more. Serve warm.

"We can always be a little nicer. We can smile a little bigger and more often; instead of passing by folks on the street quietly we can greet them with a smile. We can be the bigger, nicer person to the persistent grump at work. In time, you'll be amazed at the people you can soften through the simplest kindnesses, but you'll be even more amazed to find that each little act removes another brick over a huge fountain of joy within you. Eventually, you'll have a geyser."

—*Christy*

Grandmama and the Baked Apples

Grandmama Lucy just loved baked apples. Of course we all do, but they were always such a treat for her. When she was growing up, it was a rare occasion to get them, and she often told us a story of the day she got one for dessert.

Grandmama and her family were share-cropping in a field at a nearby farm and had walked over there in the morning to work. It was customary that when you worked the field for a family, they provided a midday meal for you. Lunchtime rolled around and the workers were already cold and tired by the time they headed up to the main house. As they walked in the door, the smell of baked apples filled the air. Grandmama said, "Those apples smelled so good. I'll never forget that, never."

They all sat down to eat their meal but Grandmama said all she could think about were those apples. She sat there trying to eat but was hoping so bad the lady had made some for them. When they finished eating, the lady who owned the house came to the table with two big old pans of baked apples, an apple for everyone.

Grandmama said, "There was a lot of workers there so you know that woman must've put a good bit of time into coring

My beloved Grandmama Lucy

all those apples for us. But they sure were good! We didn't hardly ever get baked apples and we sure did enjoy those. They were the best things!"

I remember asking her, just a few years back, "Grandmama, why didn't y'all ever get baked apples?" Her answer was so obvious that you and I would likely never think of it, but it made perfect sense when she replied, "Because we didn't have an apple tree!" ♥

Slow-Cooker Baked Apples sc

SERVES 4 TO 5

This is a simple recipe, prepared like they did it in the old days where you just cored your apple, filled it with some good stuff, and baked away! The bonus is that you can start it in the morning and come home to that same smell my grandmama walked into all those years ago (see the box at left).

These are fantastic served with ice cream—my favorite is vanilla bean—and the leftovers are also great over oatmeal.

4 to 5 large baking apples
   (I like Granny Smith)
⅔ cup dark brown sugar
⅓ cup dried cranberries or raisins
1 tablespoon ground cinnamon
½ teaspoon ground allspice
¼ cup (½ stick) plus 1 tablespoon
   butter
Ice cream, for serving (optional)

1 If using a traditional oven, preheat it to 350°F.

2 Core the apples and peel a 1-inch strip from around the top of each one. Place the apples in a 6-quart slow cooker or a deep 8-inch square baking dish.

3 Combine the brown sugar, cranberries, cinnamon, and allspice in a small bowl and stir until well combined.

4 Stuff each apple with the filling, spooning it all the way to the top of each hole and pressing down with your finger to make room for more. Top each apple with a tablespoon of butter.

5 Pour ½ cup water into the pot or baking dish so it surrounds the apples. *If using a slow cooker:* Cover and seal the pot and cook until the apples are tender, 6 to 8 hours on low, or 3 to 4 hours on high. *If using the oven:* Bake the apples until they are tender, 30 to 45 minutes.

6 Serve the apples warm, on their own or with ice cream.

The apples will keep for up to 2 days when stored, covered, in the fridge.

Cranberry Crunch

SERVES 4 TO 6

Some recipes just get you talking about the old days, which is why we love them so much. This is one of those recipes that gets my mother to talking about her childhood. The school lunch ladies often made this around the holidays and she loved it so much that one of them gave her the recipe for it, which has led us to enjoy it for the past couple of generations. Nothing like an heirloom recipe to bring memories back to life, especially around the holidays. Which brings me to my point . . .

Cooking spray

1 cup oats (I use old-fashioned but
   quick-cooking will work, too)

½ cup all-purpose flour

1 cup brown sugar
   (I use dark but light is fine)

½ cup (1 stick) butter

1 can (16 ounces) whole berry
   cranberry sauce

Homemade Whipped Cream
   (page 281) or ice cream,
   for serving (optional)

1 Preheat the oven to 350°F. Coat a 9-inch pie plate or 8-inch square baking dish with cooking spray.

2 Combine the oats, flour, and brown sugar in a medium-size bowl and stir together until well blended. Cut the butter in with a dinner fork until the mixture is well blended and crumbly.

3 Pat half of the oat mixture into the prepared pie plate to form a crust. Spread the cranberry sauce over the crust and top with the remaining oat mixture.

4 Bake until the topping is lightly browned, 45 minutes to 1 hour. Serve warm or at room temperature—it's excellent with whipped cream or ice cream.

The cranberry crunch will keep for up to 2 days when stored, covered, at room temperature.

Cranberry Crunch

Pineapple Cobbler

SERVES 4 TO 6

Guntersville, Alabama, is one of the most beautiful lakeside towns I've ever seen. We love to go up there for the day with the kids, but every now and then we treat ourselves by staying a night in the Guntersville State Lodge. As I was writing this book, we had a little family getaway and were introduced to this amazing pineapple cobbler in the lodge's dining room. Kim Steger was the chef and home cook who developed it, and she was generous enough to share this recipe with me and give me permission to share it with you. I've already lost count of how many times I've made it.

FOR THE FILLING

Cooking spray
2 cans (20 ounces each) pineapple
  chunks in juice
½ cup (1 stick) butter
½ cup all-purpose flour
½ cup dark brown sugar

FOR THE TOPPING

2 cups Hearty Oat Baking Mix
  (page 219) or store-bought
  biscuit baking mix
1 cup brown sugar
1 cup milk

1 Preheat the oven to 400°F. Coat a 9- by 13-inch baking dish with cooking spray.

2 Make the filling: Pour the pineapple juice from the cans into a medium sauce-pan, reserving the pineapple chunks. Add the butter and flour and stir over medium heat with a wire whisk until well blended. Stir in the brown sugar and bring to a boil, stirring constantly, until the sauce has thickened, 7 to 10 minutes. Remove the sauce from the heat and stir in the pine-apple chunks. Pour the fruit mixture into the prepared baking dish.

3 Make the topping: Place the baking mix and brown sugar in a medium-size bowl and stir well until combined. Add the milk and stir until the batter is creamy and smooth. Pour it over the pineapple.

4 Bake the cobbler until it is set in the center and the topping is golden brown, 25 to 30 minutes. Serve warm.

Coconut Meringue Pie

SERVES 6

You often hear tales of pregnant women and their cravings, and I was no different with both of my children. With Brady, I wanted extra-sour lemonade and chicken noodle soup. With Katy Rose, all I wanted was this pie. Thing is, you can't go to the grocery store and buy this pie. Sure, they have coconut pies for sale in the freezer section but the only resemblance they bear to a true old-fashioned coconut pie is their name. This is one of those pies that, if you find yourself craving it, you're just gonna have to make it yourself.

But don't worry, it's easy to do and you probably have everything you need on hand except for the coconut.

FOR THE CRUST AND FILLING
1 store-bought 9-inch pie shell
⅓ cup all-purpose flour
½ cup sugar
½ teaspoon salt
½ cup (1 stick) butter, melted
½ cup milk

3 egg yolks (reserve whites for the meringue)
½ teaspoon pure vanilla extract
1 heaping cup sweetened flaked coconut, plus 2 tablespoons for garnish

FOR THE MERINGUE
3 large egg whites
¼ cup sugar

1 Preheat the oven to 325°F.

2 Bake the pie shell according to the package directions and let cool.

3 Stir together the flour, ½ cup sugar, salt, butter, milk, and egg yolks in a large saucepan over medium heat and cook, stirring constantly with a wire whisk, until thick, 4 to 5 minutes. Remove the custard from the heat and stir in the vanilla and 1 heaping cup coconut. Pour the custard into the baked pie shell.

4 Make the meringue: In a large, clean bowl, beat the egg whites with an electric mixer on high speed until foamy. Gradually add ¼ cup sugar and continue beating until stiff peaks form.

5 Spread the meringue on top of the custard, being careful to seal the layers together at the edges. Sprinkle the 2 tablespoons of coconut on top of the meringue.

6 Bake until the meringue is golden, 10 minutes. Allow to cool completely and refrigerate, uncovered, to chill until serving.

The pie will keep for up to 3 days when stored, covered, in the fridge.

Old-Fashioned Peanut Butter Pie

SERVES 6 TO 8

This is a favorite from the old days that you hardly see anymore, which is all the more reason to make it because it will wow your family! A wonderful peanut butter crumble is placed in the bottom of the piecrust, then covered with a warm custard that melts into it with perfection. Finish it off with a meringue and a classic is given new life!

FOR THE CRUST AND FILLING

1 store-bought 9-inch deep-dish pie shell
1 cup confectioners' sugar
½ cup peanut butter
(smooth or chunky)
3 large egg yolks
(reserve whites for the meringue)
2 cups milk
⅔ cup sugar
1 teaspoon pure vanilla extract
Dash of salt
4 tablespoons cornstarch

FOR THE MERINGUE

3 large egg whites
¼ cup sugar

1 Preheat the oven to 325°F.

2 Bake the pie shell according to the package directions and let cool.

3 Place the confectioners' sugar and peanut butter in a small bowl and cut together with a dinner fork until the mixture is crumbly. Place half of the peanut butter mixture in the baked pie shell, reserving the remainder.

Old-Fashioned
Peanut Butter Pie

Are You Who You Want to Be?

Are you who you want to be? I'm not talking about your job or your house, your salary or your college degree. Are YOU the person you wanna be?

Sometimes we get altered, mowed down by life and circumstances. It's human nature to let this change us. We can become bitter and tired, and lose that eagerness we once possessed. Complaining rather than doing what naturally comes next in the process. Happens to all of us. But is that where you want to live?

Then don't. The first step is that simple. Because, as it turns out, I checked the casting sheet of this production of life and that person you wanna be is *exactly* who we've been waiting for!

So this is your day to step back into those shoes. Put a smile on, roll away the stone—lights, camera, *action!* ♥

④ In a large saucepan, stir together the egg yolks, milk, ⅔ cup sugar, vanilla, salt, and cornstarch. Cook over medium to medium-low heat, stirring constantly, until thick, 4 to 5 minutes. Pour the custard into the pie shell.

⑤ Make the meringue: In a large, clean bowl, beat the egg whites with an electric mixer on high speed until foamy. Gradually add the ¼ cup sugar and continue beating until stiff peaks form.

⑥ Spread the meringue on top of the custard, being careful to seal the layers together at the edges. Sprinkle the remaining peanut butter crumbles on top of the meringue.

7 Bake until lightly browned, 30 minutes. Refrigerate, uncovered, for several hours to chill and allow the pie to set.

The pie will keep for up to 3 days when stored, covered, in the fridge.

Buttermilk Peach Pie

SERVES 8 TO 10

This old-fashioned buttermilk custard pie has juicy pieces of peach throughout and a hint of cinnamon in every bite.

It's as good hot as it is cold—and you can easily substitute 2 cups of your favorite berries for the peaches.

1 can (29 ounces) yellow cling
    peaches, drained
1 store-bought 9-inch deep-dish
    pie shell
2 heaping tablespoons all-purpose
    flour
1 cup sugar
3 large eggs
⅓ cup buttermilk
½ cup butter (1 stick), melted
1 teaspoon pure vanilla extract
½ teaspoon ground cinnamon

1 Preheat the oven to 350°F.

2 Place the peaches in the pie shell.

3 Place the remaining ingredients in a large bowl and mix well with a wire whisk until combined. Pour the buttermilk mixture over the peaches.

4 Place the pie on a baking sheet and bake until the middle is set and doesn't jiggle, 40 minutes.

5 Serve warm or, to serve cold, allow the pie to cool, cover, and refrigerate it for up to 3 days.

Lime Meringue Pie

SERVES 6

If you are a fan of lemon meringue pie, this lime meringue will be high on your beloved list as well. It's creamy with just the right amount of tang, and I like to bring it out for special occasions, or when I'm serving a lemon pie lover!

To save time, you can use a store-bought graham cracker crust instead of making the cookie crumb crust.

FOR THE CRUST

1 box (11 ounces) vanilla wafers, such as Nilla

3 tablespoons sugar

⅜ cup (¾ stick) butter, melted

FOR THE FILLING

1 can (14 to 15 ounces) sweetened condensed milk

½ cup fresh or bottled lime juice

2 large egg yolks (reserve the whites for the meringue)

FOR THE MERINGUE

3 large egg whites

¼ cup sugar

1 Preheat the oven to 325°F.

2 Make the crust: Finely crush half of the wafers (about 40) into a large bowl. Stir in the 3 tablespoons sugar and the ⅜ cup butter until well blended. Pat out the crust into a 9-inch pie plate.

3 Make the filling: Combine the sweetened condensed milk, lime juice, and egg yolks in a large bowl and beat with an electric mixer on medium speed until well blended. Pour the custard onto the crust.

4 Form a border around the sides of the pie by pressing some of the remaining vanilla wafers into the edge between the custard and the crust.

5 Make the meringue: In a large, clean bowl, beat the egg whites with an electric mixer on high speed until foamy. Gradually add the ¼ cup sugar and continue beating until stiff peaks form. Spread the meringue on top of the custard, being careful to seal the layers together at the edges.

6 Bake the pie until the top is golden, 15 minutes. Allow to cool completely and refrigerate, covered, for several hours to chill before serving.

The pie will keep for several days when stored, covered, in the fridge.

You're Never Too Old to Fly

I had to run some errands one afternoon and came home to find my husband washing his car and my daughter riding her bicycle in the driveway. She beamed from ear to ear as I got out of the car and she told me it was the first spring day of riding her bike. I put my groceries down and perched on a porch step as I watched her for a bit. It seems like yesterday, but it has been over thirty years since I was exactly where Katy Rose was.

Did you have a bicycle as a kid? I had a pink one with a banana-style seat and the words "Powder puff" written on it. It was beautiful, my pride and joy. I put a piece of masking tape running down the center of the seat as soon as I got it. I'd get on it and line up the zipper of my brother's hand-me-down jeans with that strip of tape to help me find my balance as I was teaching myself to ride.

Once I learned, man, I was off! I imagine some folks who didn't know any better might have thought I was just riding a bicycle as I wore trails into the roads in my neighborhood, but if you were ever in the seat of your own bicycle as a child you know the truth—I was flying!

Every morning I'd get up with the sun, get dressed as quickly as I could, and then head out for a day of peddling as fast as I could while the wind flew through my hair and I soared through the skies of Huntsville.

Oh, how I remember the joy of that first day when it was warm enough to ride your bike after the winter! I'd ride all day long only to wake up the next day with legs so sore I could hardly walk, but, by golly, I'd still get on that bike and within a day or two be back to flying again.

You know, so much of life is like that.

It starts out fun, then we realize it's hard, but we stick with it and pedal some more and eventually we'll be rewarded with some good flight time.

If we just stick with it.

And keep pedaling.

If it feels hard today, if you're a little sore from trying, don't give up.

Keep pedaling.

You'll fly soon.

Now let's park our bikes and go make a pie. ♥

Cinnamon Pudding Cobbler

SERVES 4 TO 6

This recipe is similar to my mother's chocolate cobbler, which I featured in my first book, except cinnamon lovers will flock to this one! The beauty of it is the simplicity of the ingredients and the fact that you don't even need an egg!

Cooking spray
1 cup self-rising flour (page 287)
¾ cup sugar
½ cup milk
2 tablespoons vegetable oil
1 teaspoon pure vanilla extract
1¾ teaspoons ground cinnamon
¾ cup brown sugar (preferably dark)
1¾ cups hot water
Ice cream, for serving (optional)

1 Preheat the oven to 350°F. Coat an 8-inch square baking pan with cooking spray.

2 In a large bowl, stir together the flour, sugar, milk, oil, vanilla, and 1 teaspoon of the cinnamon until a smooth batter forms. Spread the batter into the prepared pan.

3 Stir together the brown sugar and remaining cinnamon in a small bowl until well combined.

4 Sprinkle the brown sugar mixture over the batter. Very slowly pour the hot water over the batter.

5 Bake until the cobbler is set on top, 40 to 45 minutes. Remove from the oven and serve hot. It's excellent with ice cream.

Easy Tender Cookie Bars

MAKES 18 SMALL OR 9 LARGE BARS

These moist and buttery cookie bars are one of my most versatile recipes. When you start with this base recipe, the options are nearly endless: I suggest you

use it to make one of the irresistible variations that follows. Other pluses: It only
takes one bowl to make the dough and it's
mixed by hand.

Cooking spray
½ cup old-fashioned or quick-
  cooking oats
1 cup packed brown sugar
  (preferably dark)
2 cups Hearty Oat Baking Mix
  (page 219) or store-bought
  biscuit baking mix
1 large egg
½ cup (1 stick) butter, melted and
  cooled slightly
1 teaspoon pure vanilla extract
Add-ins of your choice
  (see the variations that follow)

1 Preheat the oven to 350°F. Coat an
8-inch square baking pan with cooking
spray.

2 Combine the oats, brown sugar,
baking mix, egg, butter, and vanilla in a
large bowl and stir until well blended. Stir
in any add-ins and pat the dough into the
prepared pan.

3 Bake the dough until it is set and
lightly browned on the top, 25 to 30 minutes. Let cool for 15 to 20 minutes, then
cut into 18 small or 9 large bars.

The bars will keep for several days
when stored at room temperature in a
sealed container.

M&M's Cookie Bars

Mix 1 cup semisweet chocolate chips into
the dough and top with ½ cup M&M's
candies before baking.

Oatmeal Raisin Scotchies

Mix 1 teaspoon ground cinnamon, 1 cup
raisins, and 1 cup butterscotch chips into
the dough.

Oatmeal Cranberry Bars

Mix 1 cup dried cranberries and ½ cup
chopped walnuts into the dough.

Pecan Bars

Mix 1 cup chopped pecans into the dough
and top with ½ cup pecan halves before
baking.

No-Bake Cafeteria Peanut Butter Bars

MAKES ABOUT 20 BARS

These peanut butter bars are an old school cafeteria recipe. They date from back when the lunch ladies would come in at the break of dawn and set to making the day's meals from scratch. These lunch ladies were our mothers away from home, always there to make sure we got enough to eat and to offer a kind smile and hug whenever we needed it—and, boy, was their food ever good!

Peanut butter treats were usually in abundance in those days since peanut butter was a government commodity, provided in large quantities to lunchrooms.

This is a great recipe that requires no baking and tastes the way a Reese's Peanut Butter Cup aspires to. I usually make the batter in the microwave, but I've given you stovetop directions (see Stovetop Variation), too.

½ cup (1 stick) butter
½ cup packed brown sugar
   (light or dark)
1 teaspoon pure vanilla extract
2 cups crunchy or smooth
   commercial peanut butter
2½ cups confectioners' sugar
2 cups semisweet chocolate chips

1 Place the butter, brown sugar, vanilla, peanut butter, and confectioners' sugar in a large microwave-safe bowl. Microwave on 100 percent power until the butter and peanut butter have melted, 1 to 2 minutes.

2 Use a large spoon to stir the butter mixture until it forms a ball of dough that pulls away from the side of the bowl. Pat the dough into an ungreased 9- by 13-inch baking pan.

3 Pour the chocolate chips into another microwave-safe bowl and microwave on 100 percent power in 30-second intervals, stirring after each, until completely melted. Spoon the melted chocolate over the peanut butter mixture and spread it evenly with a rubber spatula.

4 Allow the peanut butter bars to cool completely at room temperature until the chocolate hardens, 30 to 45 minutes, or place them in the refrigerator, uncovered, for about 15 minutes. Cut into 20 squares.

The bars will keep for several days when stored at room temperature in a sealed container.

Stovetop Variatiion: In step 1, place the butter, brown sugar, vanilla, peanut butter, and confectioners' sugar in a medium saucepan over medium-low heat. Heat, stirring occasionally, until the butter and peanut butter have melted, 4 to 5 minutes. Proceed with step 2 as directed. In step 3, melt the chocolate chips in a small saucepan over medium-low heat, stirring occasionally. Complete the recipe as written.

Granny's Five-in-One Bars

MAKES 20 BARS

These bars are incredibly easy to throw together and are a home run whenever I make them. The recipe was passed down to me by my husband's Granny Jordan, who was known for her cooking. You can adapt the recipe to your own tastes by leaving out the coconut, switching up the nuts, or using chocolate chips in place of the butterscotch morsels.

½ cup (1 stick) butter, melted
1½ cups graham cracker crumbs
 (from about 8 sheets crackers)
1 cup sweetened flaked coconut
1 cup chopped pecans, walnuts, or
 peanuts
1 cup butterscotch morsels
1 can (14 ounces) sweetened
 condensed milk

1 Preheat the oven to 350°F.

2 In a medium-size bowl, stir together the butter and graham cracker crumbs until combined. Press this mixture into the bottom of a 9- by 13-inch baking pan with your hands to form a crust. Sprinkle the coconut, nuts, and butterscotch morsels over the crust and pour the sweetened condensed milk over the top.

3 Bake until set, 30 minutes. Allow to cool before cutting into 20 bars.

The bars will keep for several days when stored at room temperature in a sealed container.

They Told Him He Was Dying, So He Showed Them How to Live

My granddaddy is someone I try not to talk about much in public because he will always be a very tender subject to me. In the grand scheme of things, though, Granddaddy was no different from the rest of my family: someone with a consistent positive attitude of gratitude toward life.

Granddaddy built rocket engines and tested them in firing pits most of his adult life and enjoyed each day of his job. Still, when he retired he had a lot of people thinking he'd miss it and have a hard time adjusting to the change. Granddaddy always met such concern with his usual wit and used to say, "Lots of folks told me I'd have a hard time getting used to being retired. I retired on Friday, by Monday morning I was used to it."

You ever see folks whose faces are all pinched up like they are just waiting for an opportunity to complain or find fault in something? My granddaddy was just the opposite. He was one of those folks who was always ready to smile, laugh, and tell a joke. One glance could tell you that about him, too.

But a career testing rockets doesn't exactly bode well for a body's health and my granddaddy was one of the first among his former coworkers to be diagnosed with cancer, on his birthday no less. He took it with such stride that one by one, as each of his coworkers received their diagnosis, they always turned to him with their fears and worries over the toll of the disease. "Jay, they say they don't know how much longer I got left. Reckon how much longer you got?" Granddaddy got questions like this a lot and his answer was always the same: "Aw, I got lots of time, I'm not planning on dying from this. I'm gonna live a long time. I still got lots of fishing to do."

I'll never forget that first Christmas after cancer had become a part of our family. The doctors told us to have our holiday early because Granddaddy wouldn't be with us come December. So we had a bittersweet celebration in November . . . and spent the next several years teasing Granddaddy about the lengths he went to in order to get his presents early that year.

At a time when Granddaddy's friends were taking to their beds, he and my grandmother finally built their dream house on a little piece of riverfront land known as "a fisherman's paradise" in Alabama.

Later, when the chemotherapy made Granddaddy too weak to walk to the river, my brother brought him his four-wheeler and Granddaddy used it to ride down and fish off the pier several times a day with his trusty Labrador, Sweetie.

Granddaddy did just what he planned on doing, he lived a long life, outliving the doctors' expectations by many years and, sadly, outliving his friends as well. He had times of extreme health, where he'd gain weight and set off traveling with my grandmother. Sometimes he'd have to get treatments again and spend a little time in the hospital, where the nurses always left his room laughing and looked forward to seeing him again on their next shift.

I'll never forget a doctor's visit he told me about once. There was a man about his age in there, obviously nervous, and Granddaddy got to talking to him. Turns out, he'd just been diagnosed. After hearing my granddaddy had been diagnosed over ten years prior, he asked him, "What did you do when you found out?"

"What do you mean what did I do?" Granddaddy had asked.

"I mean, did you get your will in order, did you make arrangements for your funeral?"

Granddaddy enjoying his work

Granddaddy looked surprised and shook his head with a smile, remembering that birthday all those years ago. "Naw, I ain't never planned on dying from this."

Granddaddy lived his long life and he got his fishing in, just like he had always planned. A man who was told he was dying by year's end spent the next decade showing us all a thing or two about living. ♥

Chocolate Meringue Pudding

SERVES 6 TO 8

This is a layered pudding (similar to the Picnic Banana Pudding on the following page), with a rich chocolate flavor. A golden baked meringue topping finishes it off perfectly, but you can leave it off to save time or if you have any folks who don't care for meringue. I make the pudding while I'm cooking supper, then pour it over the wafers and get the meringue browned just before we sit down to eat.

1 box (11 ounces) vanilla wafers, such as Nilla

¾ cup sugar

¼ cup all-purpose flour

½ cup cocoa powder

3 large eggs, separated

2 cups milk

½ teaspoon pure vanilla extract

1 Place the vanilla wafers in a layer in a large oven-safe casserole dish.

2 Combine ½ cup of the sugar, the flour, and cocoa powder in a medium-size saucepan. Add in the egg yolks and milk and cook over medium heat, stirring constantly with a wire whisk to prevent scorching, until thickened, about 15 minutes. Remove the pudding from the heat and stir in the vanilla. Immediately pour the pudding over the wafers in the casserole dish. Allow the pudding to set for 5 minutes.

3 If you wish to top the pudding with meringue, preheat the oven to 325°F.

4 In a clean, large bowl, beat the egg whites with an electric mixer on high speed until foamy. Gradually add the remaining ¼ cup sugar and continue beating on high speed until stiff peaks form. Pour the meringue on top of the pudding and spread to the edges with a rubber spatula to seal well.

5 Bake until the meringue is golden on top, 15 minutes. Serve warm.

The pudding will keep for up to 3 days when stored, covered, in the fridge.

Picnic Banana Pudding

SERVES 8 TO 10

I'm a banana pudding purist. For me, the ultimate banana pudding is cooked on the stove from eggs, milk, and flour, then poured over a heaping bowl of vanilla wafers and sliced bananas, topped with homemade meringue and served warm. In fact, that is the recipe that started my whole career and I featured it as the first recipe in my first book.

Sometimes, though, we need a variation that travels a little better and keeps a little longer. The bananas quickly brown in cooked banana pudding and the meringue just doesn't hold up that well for a long car ride or in the hot summer sun. I think this picnic banana pudding comes in a close second for its taste (even many purists admit to loving it), and it travels a lot better for big events. I once made enough for two hundred people when my friend Jyl's daughter got married, and I received many requests for the recipe.

Special thanks to my friend Heather for introducing me to this wonderful concoction. I especially love that she introduced it to me by making me an entire banana pudding to take home and enjoy! Here it is, in all its glory and ease.

1 package (8 ounces) cream cheese, softened

1 can (14 ounces) sweetened condensed milk

1 package (5 ounces) instant French vanilla pudding mix

3 cups milk

2 teaspoons pure vanilla extract

1 tub (16 ounces) frozen whipped topping, thawed, or 1 recipe Homemade Whipped Cream (page 281; about 2 cups)

1 box (11 ounces) vanilla wafers, such as Nilla

5 to 7 bananas, peeled and sliced

1 In a large bowl, beat the cream cheese with an electric mixer on medium speed until fluffy. Add the sweetened condensed milk, pudding mix, milk, and vanilla and mix until well combined and smooth. Gently fold in 1 cup of the whipped topping.

2 Place one third of the vanilla wafers in a layer on the bottom of a trifle dish

Picnic Banana Pudding

or a large clear glass bowl. Layer on top one third of the bananas, then one third of the pudding mixture, and then one third of the remaining whipped topping. Repeat the layers two more times, ending with the whipped topping.

❸ Cover and refrigerate for at least 1 hour or up to 1 day before serving (you want the pudding to chill completely).

The pudding will keep for up to 3 days when stored, covered, in the fridge.

Bill Gentry's Apple Cream Cheese Cobbler

SERVES 6 TO 8

This is a wonderfully simple cobbler using canned crescent rolls as a significant shortcut. Unlike other recipes using them, though, it's hard to tell this crust isn't made from scratch! The addition of cream cheese gives it a wonderfully smooth, creamy texture and flavor.

Switch this up by using different types of pie filling—I have used peach and blueberry with great results. I often use Splenda or Ideal sweetener in this dish as well.

Special thanks to my dear friend Bill Gentry for sharing this recipe with me.

Cooking spray

3 packages (8 ounces each) cream cheese, softened

1½ cups sugar

1 teaspoon pure vanilla extract

1 teaspoon ground cinnamon

2 cans (8 ounces each) crescent roll dough

2 cans (21 ounces each) apple pie filling

½ cup (1 stick) butter, melted

❶ Preheat the oven to 350°F. Coat a 9- by 13-inch pan with cooking spray.

❷ In a large bowl, beat together the cream cheese and 1 cup of the sugar with an electric mixer on medium speed until fluffy. Mix in the vanilla and ½ teaspoon of the cinnamon, scraping down the side of the bowl, until well blended.

❸ Open one can of crescent rolls and lay the dough in a single layer, pressing the seams together, in the bottom of the prepared pan. Spread the cream cheese mixture over the dough, then top with the apple pie filling.

④ Open the second can of crescent rolls onto a piece of wax paper and press the seams together to form a crust. Carefully remove the wax paper and lay the dough on top of the filling to form a top crust.

⑤ Stir together the remaining ½ cup sugar and ½ teaspoon cinnamon in a small bowl and sprinkle the mixture evenly over the dough. Pour the melted butter over all.

⑥ Bake the cobbler until the top is brown and the filling is bubbly, 30 to 40 minutes. Serve hot.

Faux Pecan Pie

SERVES 6 TO 8

This is a fun dish to feed people who haven't tried it before. At first glance, it looks like a pecan pie and folks usually don't take a second glance before digging in for a bite and telling you how good it is. My husband's exact words were "That is the *best* pecan pie I've ever tasted!" It's always amusing to watch the looks on people's faces when you explain that there are no pecans anywhere in this recipe.

This is a fabulous pie for those with nut allergies but I initially developed it as a way of saving money when the cost of pecans went too high.

FOR THE PIE

4 large eggs

1¼ cups sugar

½ cup (1 stick) plus 2 tablespoons unsalted butter, melted and cooled

¾ cup light corn syrup

1 teaspoon pure vanilla extract

1 store-bought 9-inch deep-dish pie shell

FOR THE TOPPING

1½ cups crushed pretzels

3 tablespoons butter, melted

2 tablespoons sugar

Who Are the Most Important
People in Your Life?

Chances are pretty good that we share a common heart on this matter, so I doubt you're going to say clients, colleagues, or employees. Yet the demands of our everyday life often call us to spend the majority of our waking hours with work associates instead of the people who matter most to us. I'm not saying we're bad people for having commitments, I'm just saying that it is important to do an inventory from time to time and ask yourself, "Who are the most important people in my life?"

Then follow up with "Do they know it?"

That's the secret. Making it known. We can't just do it with our words, we absolutely have to follow up with our actions.

So you have to work late? We understand, but make coming home a priority. If you say you're leaving at five and will be home at six, realize that some of those people, the ones who are most important, will be watching out windows and holding their breath.

My sister and I used to play Next Car's Mine while we waited on Daddy to come home from his job at the police department. We'd sit on the couch on our knees as we watched out the window, taking turns calling cars. "Next car's mine!" If the next car was Daddy, you won. If it was a neighbor, the other one would call out, "Next car's mine!" as soon as they drove by.

Daddy had to work late hours sometimes but when he said he was coming home, he came home. Oftentimes he'd only be able to come home for supper and then his patrol car would pull out of our driveway once more, but he and my mother showed us that sitting down to supper as a family was important, it was a priority.

Some schedules are trickier than others. But by working together there is always a way to show someone their importance. Letters are easy to write. Emails are free. Phone calls are cheaper than ever before.

When you think of the people who are special to you, do something, right then, to let them know.

I may be here. I may be away. But you are the most important people in my life. ♥

1 Preheat the oven to 350°F.

2 Assemble the pie: Place the eggs, 1¼ cups sugar, ½ cup plus 2 tablespoons melted butter, the corn syrup, and vanilla in a large bowl and mix with a wire whisk until well combined. Pour the mixture into the pie shell.

3 Make the topping: Combine the pretzels, 3 tablespoons melted butter, and 2 tablespoons sugar in a medium bowl and stir well with a spoon until the pretzels are coated.

4 Sprinkle the topping evenly over the pie and bake for 30 minutes, then cover the pie with foil and bake until the center is set, 30 minutes more.

5 Allow the pie to cool completely before serving.

The pie can be made up to 2 days ahead of time and stored, covered, in the fridge.

Basic Chocolate Cake

MAKES TWO 9-INCH LAYERS OR
ONE 9- BY 13-INCH CAKE OR
24 CUPCAKES

This is a couldn't-be-easier chocolate cake, made with ingredients you likely have on hand. It can easily be used in place of any recipe calling for a chocolate cake made from a mix.

Floured cooking spray or
  shortening, for greasing the
  pan(s)
1¾ cups all-purpose flour, plus extra
  for coating the pan(s) if using
  shortening
2 cups sugar
¾ cup cocoa powder
1½ teaspoons baking powder
1 teaspoon baking soda
1 teaspoon salt
2 large eggs
2 cups milk
½ cup (1 stick) butter, melted and
  cooled
2 teaspoons pure vanilla extract

Cake Basics

So many of life's celebrations are marked by serving cake: birthdays, weddings, anniversaries, graduations . . . Of course, the possibilities with cake combinations are limited only by our imagination, which is why I've put together a few foolproof recipes that I hope you'll consider a starting point. My two standard cake recipes—Basic Chocolate Cake (opposite) and Basic Yellow Cake (page 264)—don't require special flours or fancy ingredients but yield moist cakes that can be used in place of boxed mixes in most every recipe. I've also included my favorite classic frosting recipes and hope you'll mix and match them with the cakes to round out your dessert repertoire. Since they offer so many possibilities, I consider these the perfect additions to any recipe collection.

1 Preheat the oven to 350°F.

2 Spray or grease and flour two 9-inch cake pans or one 9- by 13-inch cake pan or line 24 muffin tin cups with paper liners.

3 Stir together the dry ingredients in a large bowl. Add the wet ingredients and beat with an electric mixer on medium speed until combined, 2 to 3 minutes.

4 Pour the batter into the pans (for cupcakes, fill each liner two thirds full) and bake until a toothpick inserted in the center comes out clean, 30 to 35 minutes (15 to 20 minutes for cupcakes).

5 If planning to turn the cakes out of the pans or frost them, allow to cool for 10 minutes before doing so.

The cake will keep for up to 3 days when stored, covered, at room temperature and for up to 5 days in the fridge.

How to Frost a Cake

Allow the layers to cool completely before frosting. Or better yet, put them in the fridge for an hour to chill (refrigerated cake layers are easier to ice than ones at room temperature).

When ready to frost, brush loose crumbs from top and sides of the layers, and place one layer, rounded side up, on a serving dish. Spread approximately half a cup frosting to within one-quarter inch of the edge. Place the second layer, rounded side up, on top of the frosted layer. Spread the frosting on the sides of the layers and then put the remaining icing on top. Use a long offset spatula to spread the icing to the sides, making sure it completely covers the sides and top. Swirl the icing or leave the top smooth in order to apply decorations. Supereasy and beautiful!

Basic Yellow Cake

MAKES TWO 9-INCH LAYERS OR ONE
9- BY 13-INCH CAKE OR 24 CUPCAKES

This is my favorite from-scratch yellow cake since I usually have all the ingredients on hand. It bakes up light and wonderfully moist and can be used in place of a boxed cake mix. The batter isn't as thick as store-bought but results in a beautiful cake. It mixes up in almost the same time as a cake mix but saves having to go out to the grocery store (which I hate when I am all ready to make something!).

Cooking spray

2¼ cups all-purpose flour,
    plus extra for coating
    the pan(s)

1½ cups sugar

½ cup (1 stick) unsalted butter,
    at room temperature

3 teaspoons baking powder

1 teaspoon salt

1 teaspoon pure vanilla extract

1½ cups milk

3 large eggs

1 Preheat the oven to 350°F. Spray and flour two 9-inch cake pans or one 9- by

13-inch cake pan or line 24 muffin tin cups with paper liners.

② Combine the sugar and butter in a large bowl and cream together with an electric mixer on medium speed.

③ In a medium-size bowl, stir together the flour, baking powder, and salt. In a separate small bowl, stir together the vanilla, milk, and eggs until combined.

④ Add the wet and dry mixtures to the creamed butter mixture, alternating between each and mixing well with an electric mixer on medium speed between each addition, until fully blended and smooth, 2 to 3 minutes.

⑤ Pour the batter into the prepared pans (for cupcakes, fill each paper liner two thirds full) and bake until a toothpick inserted in the center comes out clean, 30 to 35 minutes (15 to 20 minutes for cupcakes). Allow to cool before frosting or turning out of the pan.

The cake will keep for up to 3 days when stored, covered, at room temperature and for up to 5 days in the fridge.

Basic Cream Cheese Frosting

MAKES ENOUGH FOR TWO 9-INCH LAYERS OR ONE 9- BY 13-INCH CAKE OR 24 CUPCAKES

This cream cheese frosting is wonderful on anything from cakes to brownies, cinnamon rolls to cookies. You can customize it by whipping in a teaspoon of cinnamon or even a cup of crushed fruit (such as strawberries) to the finished recipe.

1 package (8 ounces) cream cheese, softened
¼ cup (½ stick) butter, at room temperature
3 cups confectioners' sugar

Combine all of the ingredients in a large bowl and beat with an electric mixer on medium speed until smooth and creamy.

The frosting will keep for up to 1 week when stored, covered, in the fridge.

If a Cake Breaks . . .

No need to cry over broken cake! If you ever have a cake that falls apart or sticks to the pan, it's easy to salvage. Simply allow it to cool completely, break it into bite-size pieces, and layer it in a trifle bowl or large, clear glass bowl with sliced fruit and Homemade Whipped Cream (page 281). You may find yourself hoping your cakes stick!

Basic Buttercream Frosting

MAKES ENOUGH FOR TWO 9-INCH LAYERS OR ONE 9- BY 13-INCH CAKE OR 24 CUPCAKES

When most people think of birthday cake, they think of this frosting. It's the time-honored standby for very good reason. Just the smell always brings back childhood memories of blowing out candles and opening presents. If you have such wonderful memories, you are blessed indeed!

½ cup (1 stick) butter,
    at room temperature
2 teaspoons butter flavoring
    (see Note, opposite page)

3 cups confectioners' sugar
2 to 4 tablespoons milk

1 In a large bowl, cream the butter with an electric mixer on medium speed until light and fluffy. Add the butter flavoring, 1 cup of the confectioners' sugar, and 2 tablespoons of the milk and beat well on medium speed until combined, 1 minute.

2 Add the remaining sugar and beat, scraping down the side of the bowl, until well blended, about 2 minutes. If the frosting is too thick, add 1 to 2 tablespoons more milk and beat again until light and fluffy.

The frosting will keep for 1 week when stored, covered, in the fridge.

NOTE: Butter flavoring is sold alongside vanilla extract in the spice aisle of the supermarket. If you can't find it, use vanilla instead.

_____

Basic Chocolate Frosting

MAKES ENOUGH FOR TWO 9-INCH LAYERS OR ONE 9- BY 13-INCH CAKE OR 24 CUPCAKES

My husband is a simple guy. I give him my Basic Yellow Cake (page 264) topped with this chocolate frosting and he's happy indeed! My kids especially love this on cupcakes.

½ cup (1 stick) butter,
    at room temperature
3 cups confectioners' sugar
⅔ cup cocoa powder
6 tablespoons milk
1 teaspoon pure vanilla extract

1 Place the butter, 1 cup of the sugar, the cocoa powder, and 2 tablespoons of the milk in a large mixing bowl. Beat with an electric mixer on medium speed until mixed well and no longer lumpy; it will be thick.

2 Add the remaining sugar, vanilla, and remaining milk, a tablespoon at a time, and beat until smooth and creamy, scraping down the side as needed.

The frosting will keep, covered, in the fridge, for 1 week.

_____

Peanut Butter Cream Cheese Frosting

MAKES ENOUGH FOR TWO 9-INCH LAYERS OR ONE 9- BY 13-INCH CAKE OR 24 CUPCAKES

Special thanks to Mrs. Pecola Norris, grandmother of our dear family friend Kate Burhop, for sharing this wonderful recipe with us.

For a family of peanut butter lovers, this take on cream cheese frosting elevates our cakes to a whole other level!

Desserts on Deck

Refrigerator cakes are some of my favorite kinds of cake to make! You can bake them as many as three days ahead of time, so I store them in the refrigerator and pull one out whenever I need a quick dessert for the family or company. With a small family, this is an easy way to make a dessert and have little after-meal treats all week long.

1½ cups creamy commercial
    peanut butter
1 package (8 ounces) cream cheese,
    softened
4 cups confectioners' sugar
2 to 4 tablespoons milk

1 Place the peanut butter and cream cheese in a large bowl and beat with an electric mixer on medium speed until fluffy, about 1 minute.

2 Add the confectioners' sugar and 2 tablespoons of the milk and mix on medium speed, scraping down the side of the bowl, until smooth and creamy, about 2 minutes. If the icing is too thick, add 1 to 2 tablespoons more milk and mix until well incorporated.

The frosting will keep for 1 week when stored, covered, in the fridge.

Chocolate Sundae Cake

MAKES ONE 9- BY 13-INCH CAKE

This refrigerator cake (see box, page 270) is a celebration cake to me. It even looks festive. My husband says it reminds him of the chocolate fudge cake he used to get on his birthday when his parents took him out to eat.

It's supereasy to throw together and the cool mix of chocolate syrup, chocolate cake, whipped cream, and bright red cherries will make any day feel like it's a special occasion! I also love to add toasted chopped nuts to the top just before serving to give it a little crunch.

You can easily make this cake several days ahead of time—it keeps well.

1 recipe Basic Chocolate Cake
(page 262) or 1 box
(16 ounces) chocolate cake mix

1 bottle (20 ounces) chocolate
syrup, such as Hershey's

1 tub (16 ounces) frozen whipped
topping or 1 recipe Homemade
Whipped Cream (page 281;
about 2 cups)

Chopped nuts, such as pecans,
for garnish (optional)

Maraschino cherries, for garnish
(optional)

1 Prepare the cake in a 9- by 13-inch
pan and bake as directed.

2 While the cake is still hot, poke holes
all over the top with a fork. Pour the entire
bottle of chocolate syrup over the cake
and allow it to soak in while the cake cools
completely. Spread the whipped topping
over the cake and refrigerate, covered,
until chilled, 2 to 3 hours.

3 Cut the cake into 20 squares (see
Note) and garnish each with chopped
nuts and a cherry, if desired.

The cake will keep for up to 5 days
when stored, covered, in the fridge.

NOTE: You can also leave the cake
whole and garnish the top with nuts and
cherries.

Miss Patsy's Easy Coconut Cake

MAKES ONE 9- BY 13-INCH CAKE

Miss Patsy McGough and I go to the same church. When she came to a meeting with this cake I just had to ask her for the recipe! She replied, "Aw, honey, I hate to tell anyone the recipe because it's just too easy!" I assured her that the recipes I always thought of as "too easy" were the ones that were the biggest hits, and she was kind enough to give me permission to share her recipe with you. I know you're going to enjoy the ease and amazing coconut taste of this light cake.

1 recipe Basic Yellow Cake
(page 264) or 1 box (16 ounces)
yellow cake mix

1 can (12 ounces) sweetened
condensed milk

1 can (15 to 16 ounces) cream of
coconut (see Note)

1 cup sweetened flaked coconut

1 tub (16 ounces) frozen whipped
topping, thawed

1 Prepare the cake in a 9- by 13-inch pan and bake as directed.

2 Turn the oven to 350°F. While the cake is still hot, poke holes all over the top with a fork.

3 In a medium bowl, whisk together the sweetened condensed milk and cream of coconut until well combined. Pour the mixture over the hot cake and let cool.

4 Meanwhile, spread the coconut on a baking sheet and bake, watching carefully and stirring often, until lightly browned, 10 to 15 minutes.

5 Spread the whipped topping over the cooled cake and sprinkle with the toasted coconut. Cover and refrigerate until fully chilled, 2 to 3 hours.

The cake will keep for up to 5 days when stored, covered, in the fridge.

NOTE: Cream of coconut is usually found near the liquor section in stores. It has no alcohol in it but is often used in mixing cocktails, thus the placement.

Cappuccino Cake
MAKES TWO 8-INCH LAYERS OR
ONE 9- BY 13-INCH CAKE

We used to have a great restaurant in my hometown of Huntsville, Alabama, whose signature dessert was cappuccino cake. They always brought out a huge wedge of it for birthdays and special events and served it cold (I think it is better that way) with a side of chocolate ice cream and a generous drizzle of chocolate syrup.

After the restaurant closed and I spent over a decade pining away for the cake, I decided it couldn't be that difficult

Cappuccino Cake

to duplicate it. Since I couldn't find the actual recipe anywhere on the Internet, I went by memory and a basic starting point of dark chocolate cake with coffee-infused buttercream. I was thrilled when my cappuccino cake tasted every bit as wonderful as the one in my memory. This is my absolute favorite cake for birthdays—especially when I can get my mother to make it for mine!

For the cake, simply prepare the batter for my Basic Chocolate Cake (page 262) or use a box of dark chocolate cake mix. It works very well in a 9- by 13-inch pan if you'd like to save some time!

Vegetable shortening

Cocoa powder, for dusting the pan(s)

1 recipe basic chocolate cake batter

½ cup milk

3 teaspoons instant coffee (this may seem like a lot but it's right!)

1 cup (2 sticks) butter, at room temperature

5 cups confectioners' sugar

1 teaspoon pure vanilla extract

Chocolate ice cream, for serving (optional)

Chocolate syrup, such as Hershey's, for serving (optional)

1 Preheat the oven to 350°F.

2 Grease two 8-inch cake pans or one 9- by 13-inch cake pan with shortening and dust with cocoa powder.

3 Pour the cake batter into the prepared pans and bake as directed.

4 If using 2 cake pans, let the cakes cool in the pans before turning them out to cool completely; if using a 9- by 13-inch cake pan, allow the cake to cool completely in the pan.

5 When the cakes have cooled, make the frosting: Place the milk in a small bowl and stir in the instant coffee granules until dissolved.

6 Place the butter in a large bowl and beat with an electric mixer on medium speed until fluffy, 1 minute. Add the confectioners' sugar and vanilla and beat until smooth, about 2 minutes. Scrape down the side of the bowl and continue beating until the frosting is fluffy and whipped, 5 to 7 minutes more.

7 Immediately frost the cake and refrigerate for several hours to chill. (I think it's best if served cold with chocolate ice cream and drizzled with chocolate syrup.)

The cake will keep for up to 5 days when stored, covered, in the fridge.

Elvis Presley Cake

MAKES ONE 9- BY 13-INCH CAKE

This is supposedly a cake that Elvis Presley enjoyed on many occasions. I have no idea if it is true or not but after you taste it you'll sure be able to see why people would think that. It contains crushed pineapple, which was rumored to be one of his favorite flavors. The crushed pineapple addded inside and on top of this cake makes it a very special dessert.

1 recipe Basic Yellow Cake
(page 264) or 1 box (16 ounces)
yellow cake mix
1 can (16 ounces) crushed
pineapple in juice

1 cup sugar
1 package (8 ounces) cream cheese,
softened
½ cup (1 stick) unsalted butter,
at room temperature
3 cups confectioners' sugar
½ cup chopped pecans (optional)

1 Prepare the cake in a 9- by 13-inch pan and bake as directed.

2 While the cake is baking, stir together the pineapple and sugar in a small saucepan over medium heat. Bring to a boil, stirring constantly, until the sugar is dissolved, 2 to 3 minutes. Remove from heat and wait on the cake to finish baking.

3 While the cake is still hot, poke holes all over the top with a fork. Pour the warm pineapple mixture over the cake, spreading with a spatula as needed to cover. Let cool.

4 In a large bowl, beat together the cream cheese and butter with an electric mixer on medium speed until smooth, 2 minutes. Gradually add the confectioners' sugar, beating until the frosting is smooth and creamy. Add the pecans, if desired, and mix in well.

⑤ Drop the frosting by dollops onto the cake until the top is mostly covered, then smooth and spread it to coat. Cover and refrigerate the cake until fully chilled before serving, 2 hours.

The cake will keep for up to 5 days when stored, covered, in the fridge.

Strawberry Angel Dessert

SERVES 8 TO 10

This is from my dear friend Heather. She's one of the kindest and most loving people I know and I think that is why her food always tastes so good—she puts her heart into everything she does. For those who love strawberries and cheesecake, this is a delightful blend of those flavors combined with the airiness of angel food cake. It's great for springtime.

1 ready-made 10-inch angel food cake

2 packages (8 ounces each) cream cheese, softened

1 cup sugar

1 tub (8 ounces) frozen whipped topping, thawed

1 quart fresh strawberries, hulled and sliced

1 container (18 ounces) strawberry glaze

① Tear the cake into bite-size pieces and place them in a layer on the bottom of a 9- by 13-inch dish.

② In a medium bowl, beat together the cream cheese and sugar with an electric mixer on medium speed until light and fluffy, 2 to 3 minutes. Gently fold in the whipped topping.

③ Press the cake pieces down with your hands to compress them, then spread the cream cheese mixture over them.

④ Stir together the strawberries and glaze in a medium-size bowl until the strawberries are well coated. Spread the strawberries over the cream cheese layer. Cover and chill for at least 1 hour or overnight before serving.

The dessert will keep for up to 3 days when stored, covered, in the fridge.

Frozen Banana Puddings

SERVES 18

While the kids have their Popsicles and ice cream cones on hot summer days, we can have these little beauties. Homemade banana puddings freeze wonderfully in individual serving sizes and let you have this decadent Southern classic anytime you want. They're great to keep on hand for last-minute guests or the afternoon unwind.

This recipe makes about eighteen servings, but you can also freeze half and use the other half to make a small warm banana pudding for two.

If you love banana pudding—and I mean real, honest-to-goodness homemade banana pudding—you've just got to make these!

½ cup sugar (see Notes, page 276)

⅓ cup all-purpose flour

⅛ teaspoon salt

3 large eggs (see Notes, page 276)

2 cups milk

½ teaspoon pure vanilla extract

4 to 5 bananas, cut into ½-inch slices

1 box (11 ounces) vanilla wafer cookies, such as Nilla

1 tub (8 ounces) frozen whipped topping, thawed

1 Place the sugar, flour, salt, eggs, and milk in a medium-size saucepan (or double boiler) over medium-low heat. Stir well with a wire whisk to combine and cook, stirring constantly to prevent scorching, until thickened, about 15 minutes. Remove the pudding from the heat and stir in the vanilla.

2 Pour the pudding into a heatproof bowl, cover with plastic wrap, and refrigerate until cooled, 30 minutes or up to 24 hours.

3 Line 18 muffin tin cups with paper liners and place about 4 banana slices in each. Pour a small amount of pudding over the bananas, just enough to fill each cup halfway or three-quarters full.

4 Push 4 vanilla wafers around the inner edges of each cupcake liner to form a "crust," keeping the banana slices in the center to help hold the wafers up. Add a dollop of whipped topping to the center of each one and spread it gently with a rubber spatula until it touches the wafers.

5 Freeze the puddings in the muffin tins until completely frozen, a few hours. Insert a knife into each cup between the tin and the paper liner to pop the puddings loose.

6 Store the puddings in the freezer in a ziplock bag or airtight container until ready to serve, up to 3 months.

NOTES: You can also use Splenda in place of the sugar, if you like. I use Splenda a lot and really can't tell any difference in flavor.

Normally we separate our eggs for banana pudding, but since this recipe doesn't call for meringue you can just use the entire egg.

Ice Cream Grahamwiches

MAKES ABOUT 30 GRAHAMWICHES

These pretty little graham cracker sandwiches are easy to make and low in sugar compared to many treats. I like to dip the sides into colorful rainbow jimmies for the kids and then I dip mine in chopped salted nuts for a bit of a salty crunch. You'll find that once frozen, these taste just like ice cream sandwiches, but with a bit more flavor and a lot less guilt.

3 cups milk
1 box (2.1 ounces) sugar-free instant
   chocolate pudding mix
1 tub (8 ounces) frozen sugar-free
   or light whipped topping, thawed
About 30 graham cracker sheets,
   carefully broken in half widthwise
Sprinkles, for garnish (optional)
Chopped nuts, for garnish
   (optional)

1 Combine the milk and pudding mix in a large bowl and beat with an electric mixer on medium speed until thick,

1 minute. Gently fold in the whipped topping and stir until smooth.

2 Place a large dollop of the pudding mixture on a graham cracker and top with another graham cracker to make a sandwich. Lightly squeeze the graham crackers together until the filling spreads to the edges, then dip each edge into the sprinkles and/or nuts, if desired.

3 Place each sandwich in an individual ziplock sandwich bag and freeze for at least 2 hours or up to 3 months.

Mandarin Orange Freezer Pie

MAKES 2 PIES; EACH SERVES 6 TO 8

This fruity and creamy pie is just the thing on a hot summer's day. It's also a convenient ending to any meal because the recipe makes two pies, which you store in the freezer until needed (or until you realize you forgot to make dessert!).

1 can (14 ounces) sweetened
 condensed milk
½ cup bottled or fresh lemon juice
1 tub (8 ounces) frozen whipped
 topping, thawed
1 can (20 ounces) crushed
 pineapple, drained
1 can (15 ounces) mandarin oranges,
 drained
2 graham cracker piecrusts
 (6 ounces each)

1 Stir together the sweetened condensed milk, lemon juice, and whipped topping in a large bowl until smooth and creamy.

2 Stir in the drained fruit and divide the mixture evenly between the piecrusts. Wrap the pies in aluminum foil and freeze for at least 2 hours or up to 3 months.

3 Remove the pies from the freezer about 10 minutes before serving.

Front Porch Salads

MAKES ABOUT 36 SALADS

These individually frozen fruit salads are so handy when folks drop by or when you just find yourself needing a little treat. Freezing them in cupcake paper liners helps keep them separated and makes for a pretty presentation. Eat them with a fork or like an ice cream bar—preferably on a shady porch!

1 can (12 ounces) frozen orange
    juice concentrate with pulp
1 can (20 ounces) crushed
    pineapple in juice
1 can (15 ounces) apricot or peach
    halves in juice
½ cup sugar
3 ripe bananas
1 bag (24 ounces) frozen sweetened,
    sliced strawberries
1 tub (16 ounces) plain Greek
    yogurt or regular yogurt or
    frozen whipped topping, thawed
    (optional)

1 Place the can of frozen orange juice in a small bowl and allow it to thaw slightly, 30 minutes.

2 Drain the juice from the pineapple and apricots into a measuring cup. Carefully dice the apricots and set the fruits aside in a small bowl.

3 Place the reserved fruit juices in a small saucepan over medium heat, add the sugar, and cook, stirring constantly, until the sugar is dissolved, 2 minutes. Remove from the heat and set aside to cool.

4 Peel the bananas, place them in a large bowl, and mash them well with a dinner fork. Add the reserved apricots and pineapple, the strawberries (juice and all), the orange juice concentrate, and the yogurt, if using, and stir well until fully mixed. Pour in the cooled juice mixture and stir until well combined.

5 Line 36 muffin tin cups with paper liners and divide the fruit salad mixture among them. Freeze the salads in the muffin tins until firm, several hours. Insert a knife into each cup between the

tin and the paper liner to pop the salads loose.

Store the salads in the freezer in a ziplock bag until ready to serve, up to 3 months. Serve frozen.

Bananas in Red Stuff

SERVES 6

If you are familiar with the Shoney's breakfast bar, you know how wonderful this stuff is. It's the belle of the ball. Light tasting, slightly sweet, filling, and refreshing, I longed (literally, *longed*) for the recipe for this banana-strawberry salad for years.

Then a little while back Mama and I found ourselves talking about it yet again. We'd gone over all sorts of theories about what the red stuff was, from diluted Jell-O to a grenadine-based sauce. The thing is, though, we knew it had to be simple for a restaurant like Shoney's to turn it out on such a large scale, and we knew that restaurants are notoriously creative when it comes to inventing dishes from what they have on hand. Then it dawned on us: What is Shoney's specialty? Strawberry pie. So what would they have on hand at all times? Strawberry glaze!

Oh, goodness, we hit pay dirt! Here's the recipe—I hope you make it soon. It sure is good!

1 tub (about 12 ounces) strawberry
　glaze
4 to 6 medium-size bananas

❶ Place the glaze in a medium-size bowl and fill the empty glaze container with water; pour that in the bowl as well. Mix with an electric mixer on medium speed until completely blended.

❷ Cut the bananas in thick slices into a large bowl. Pour the glaze over the bananas and stir to coat.

❸ Cover the mixture and place it in the refrigerator for several hours to chill. Serve cold.

The strawberry-banana salad will keep, covered, in the fridge for up to 2 days.

10

Pantry

This chapter contains the sauces and basics that are the backbone of so many of my recipes. Many of these have shortcut counterparts available at the grocery store that work really well, but if you want to go the extra mile or save yourself a trip to the grocer's when you've run out of an ingredient, you'll find what you need here—including my favorite sweet tea! A simple sauce, marinade, or gravy can turn any meal into a mouthwatering adventure.

Homemade Whipped Cream

MAKES ABOUT 2 CUPS

There is nothing like a dollop of this on top of pies, slices of cake, or even in your coffee! If you have a need for whipped cream at supper, it is perfectly fine to make it earlier in the day and store it, covered, in the refrigerator. The secret to making whipped cream is getting the cream, bowl, and beaters chilled ahead of time. This helps the cream to whip up faster. After you see how easy it is to make and how very delicious it is, you may never buy store-bought whipped cream again!

    1 cup heavy (whipping) cream,
       chilled
    3 tablespoons sugar

1 Place the cream in a chilled medium-size mixing bowl and add the sugar gradually to taste. I suggest starting with 2 tablespoons and adding more later if you like.

2 Beat the cream with an electric mixer on high speed until soft peaks and ripples form, 1 to 2 minutes.

Cover and refrigerate until ready to use, up to 2 days for best results.

Meringue

MAKES ENOUGH FOR 1 PIE OR PUDDING

This is a basic meringue recipe that can be used to top a variety of pies and puddings. Any custard pie always benefits from the addition of a high, fluffy meringue. It also provides a wonderful finishing touch to desserts such as banana, pineapple, or coconut puddings.

    3 large egg whites
    ¼ cup sugar
    1 teaspoon pure vanilla extract

1 Preheat the oven to 325°F.

2 In a large bowl, beat the egg whites with an electric mixer on high speed until soft peaks form, 2 to 3 minutes. Gradually add the sugar and vanilla and continue beating on high speed until the sugar dissolves and stiff peaks form.

3 Pour the mixture on top of a pudding or pie and spread it to the edges with a rubber spatula to seal well. Bake until the top is golden, 15 minutes.

Cream of Chicken Soup

MAKES 2¼ CUPS; EQUIVALENT TO 1 CAN (10 OUNCES) OF CREAM SOUP

This delicious homemade cream soup, and the variations that follow, can be used in any recipe calling for canned cream soup. Richly flavored and velvety, they work beautifully as substitutes in modern recipes. And while I do love the extra *oomph* this homemade soup adds to any recipe, I'm the first to save time and reach for canned when I have it on hand.

3 tablespoons butter

3 tablespoons all-purpose flour

½ cup milk (I use whole, but 2 percent is okay)

½ cup chicken broth

Salt to taste

Ground black pepper to taste

Melt the butter in a small saucepan over medium-low heat. Add the flour to the pan and stir well until no lumps remain. Add the remaining ingredients and stir constantly until thickened, about 10 minutes. Use immediately as a replacement in any recipe calling for 1 can of cream of chicken soup.

Cream of Mushroom Soup

Substitute beef broth for the chicken broth. Add ¼ cup finely chopped mushrooms to the melted butter in the saucepan, before adding the flour, and sauté until tender, 3 to 5 minutes. Add the flour and proceed as directed.

Cream of Celery Soup

Vegetable or chicken broth can be used for this variation. Add ½ cup finely chopped celery to the melted butter in the saucepan, before adding the flour, and sauté until tender, 3 to 5 minutes. Add the flour and proceed as directed.

Life Really Isn't Fair

If you're reading this, you, like me, probably have luxuries like a home, electricity, a computer, running water, a heater for that running water (heaven forbid a cold shower, right?), access to medicine, clothing, shoes, food, and maybe even a car.

Did you know that this makes us wealthier than the majority of the world's population?

So next time we find ourselves thinking "Life's not fair," we should immediately and humbly answer, "No, it sure isn't." ♥

Quick Pizza Sauce

MAKES ABOUT 2 CUPS

I love the ease and flavor punch of this simple pizza sauce. This recipe can be used in place of store-bought pizza sauce in any recipe.

1 can (15 ounces) tomato sauce

1 can (6 ounces) tomato paste

1 tablespoon dried oregano

1 teaspoon dried basil

1 teaspoon sugar

½ teaspoon garlic powder

Place all of the ingredients in a medium-size saucepan over medium heat and cook, stirring, until the mixture is smooth and heated through, 5 minutes. (Alternatively, place the ingredients in a medium-size microwavable bowl and heat in the microwave, stirring occasionally, on 100 percent power for about 1½ minutes.)

Simple Marinara Sauce

MAKES ABOUT 3 CUPS

If you've gotten this far in the book it shouldn't come as a surprise to you that I love this sauce! This is my homemade marinara sauce that can be whipped up in a flash. It's delicious over spaghetti, in lasagna, as a sandwich topping, and even in soups (for example, the Spaghetti Lover's Soup on page 34). This also freezes well so feel free to make a double batch to have some handy whenever you might need it.

½ pound ground beef

½ cup chopped onion

1 can (16 ounces) diced tomatoes,
    with their juice

1 can (6 ounces) tomato paste

1 tablespoon dried Italian seasoning

1 teaspoon garlic powder

1 Place the ground beef and onion in a large skillet over medium-high heat and cook, stirring occasionally, until the beef has browned, 8 to 10 minutes. Drain off any grease.

2 Add the tomatoes, tomato paste, Italian seasoning, garlic powder, and ½ cup of water to the skillet and stir well to combine. Reduce the heat and simmer until heated through, 10 minutes. Serve hot.

All-Purpose Marinade

MAKES 1 PINT

You can whip up this homemade marinade recipe in the time it takes for you to gather the ingredients from your pantry. It contains less salt than the store-bought versions and is delicious on everything I've ever put it on—pork, chicken, and beef, as well as grilled, baked, or steamed vegetables. You can make it right when you need it, or you can prepare it ahead of time and store it in the refrigerator in a sealed jar.

½ teaspoon garlic powder

2 tablespoons apple cider vinegar

1 tablespoon ground ginger

1 cup soy sauce

Combine all of the ingredients with 1 cup of water in a jar, cover, and shake to mix well. Store any unused marinade in the refrigerator (be sure to discard any that has touched raw meat, of course).

This marinade will keep for 3 months (if it lasts that long!).

Basic Beef Gravy

MAKES 1½ CUPS

This is very similar to higher-priced store-bought canned gravy. I pour it over a roast before cooking it in the slow cooker or heat it up and serve it over mashed potatoes. It is equally good alongside your favorite roast beef sandwich as a dipping sauce. My husband loves it served over beef tips.

I originally came up with the recipe to save a last-minute trip to the grocery store. It seems I could never remember to buy gravy on my regular shopping trip. Once I came up with this recipe and realized how easy it was to make, I never bought canned again.

¼ cup (½ stick) butter
¼ cup all-purpose flour
1½ cups beef broth

1 Melt the butter in a small saucepan over medium heat. Add the flour and stir constantly until smooth, 1 minute.

2 While stirring, slowly pour in the broth and continue to cook, stirring, until the mixture is smooth, completely mixed, and thickened, about 10 minutes.

My Go-to Milk Gravy

MAKES 1½ CUPS

Basic white gravies, like this delicious version, are an excellent accompaniment to eggs, mashed potatoes, pork chops, chicken, biscuits, rolls, or beef. We even love it served at breakfast over sliced tomatoes. While my grandmother has been known to reheat it, it is definitely best served right after it's made, while it is still hot.

3 tablespoons bacon grease, butter,
or vegetable oil (bacon grease
is best)

¼ cup all-purpose flour

½ teaspoon salt

¼ teaspoon ground black pepper

1½ cups milk, plus extra as needed

1 Heat the bacon grease in a medium-size skillet over medium heat. Stir in the flour, salt, and pepper and cook, stirring constantly, until the flour begins to brown, 3 to 4 minutes.

2 Slowly pour in the 1½ cups milk, stirring constantly with a wire whisk to break up any lumps. Reduce the heat to low and continue cooking, stirring constantly, until the gravy thickens enough to coat the back of a spoon, about 5 minutes. If you prefer a thinner gravy, stir in more milk.

White Barbecue Sauce

MAKES 2 CUPS

Usually found only in north Alabama, this white barbecue sauce is wonderful over chicken and pulled pork, or as a dipping sauce for French fries. It has a tanginess that perfectly complements barbecued chicken. Whenever you order barbecued chicken, this sauce is always served alongside in either a small plastic cup or in squeeze bottles on the table.

2 cups mayonnaise

1½ tablespoons salt

2 tablespoons ground black pepper

6 tablespoons white vinegar

6 tablespoons lemon juice

¼ cup sugar

Combine all of the ingredients in a medium-size bowl and stir well to dissolve the sugar. Refrigerate, covered, for several hours before serving.

This sauce will keep for several weeks when stored, covered, in the fridge.

Come Back Sauce

MAKES 1 CUP

Good with fried chicken, French fries, vegetables, and all kinds of other finger foods, Come Back Sauce is quick to throw together, which you'll appreciate because your guests will be *coming back* to sample it until it's all gone! It is also a handy dipping sauce to have for parties where chicken nuggets or popcorn chicken arc being served.

½ cup mayonnaise

½ cup ketchup

1½ tablespoons ground black pepper (see Note)

Combine all of the ingredients in a medium-size bowl and stir until well combined. The sauce can be served immediately but is best if it's refrigerated for several hours before serving.

It will keep several weeks when stored, covered, in the fridge.

NOTE: This seems like a lot of black pepper but the other ingredients keep the sauce from being spicy.

Barbecue Sauce in a Hurry

MAKES 2 CUPS; EQUIVALENT TO 1 BOTTLE (16 OUNCES) BARBECUE SAUCE

When I don't have a bottle of barbecue sauce or some of my home-canned sauce handy, this recipe works great! If you're in a bind, it'll taste just as good as the real thing.

1 cup ketchup

1 cup Coca-Cola

Stir together the ketchup and Coca-Cola in a small bowl until well combined. Use as directed in a recipe to replace 1 bottle of store-bought barbecue sauce.

Self-Rising Flour

MAKES 1 CUP

Occasionally a recipe will call for self-rising flour, which already has the leavening agents mixed in so you don't need additional baking powder. To make your own, you can follow the recipe below. It is also handy to make up a larger batch to keep in your pantry if self-rising flour is not available in your area. It can be kept in a labeled sealed container alongside your all-purpose flour.

It's easy to increase this recipe: Just measure out the cups of flour you need and add one and a half teaspoons of baking powder and half a teaspoon of salt per cup.

1 cup all-purpose flour
1½ teaspoons baking powder
½ teaspoon salt

"We tend to forget that happiness doesn't come as a result of getting something we don't have, but rather of recognizing and appreciating what we do have."

—*Frederick Koenig*

Place the flour in a medium-size bowl and whisk in the baking powder and the salt.

The self-rising flour will keep in a sealed container for up to 1 year.

Buttermilk Substitute
MAKES 1 CUP

This is an easy way to make your own buttermilk when you don't have any in the fridge and can't run out to the store. It works well in any recipe as a substitute. The lemon juice or white vinegar has a reaction that causes the whole milk to sour, which results in buttermilk. If you have any left, it can be stored, covered, in the refrigerator for several days.

1 cup whole milk
1 tablespoon lemon juice or white vinegar

Pour the milk into a small bowl and stir in the lemon juice. Let the mixture sit until it begins to thicken, 5 minutes. Then use it wherever buttermilk is called for.

Sweet Tea

SERVES ABOUT 6

I've had iced tea with pretty much every supper I've ever eaten in my entire life. In fact, the first thing I do after clearing the breakfast dishes each day is make a gallon of tea. This Southern classic is expected at all family meals (beyond breakfast) regardless of formality or occasion. If you see us sitting down to supper, regardless of what is on the table, iced tea is in the glasses!

> 5 regular-size tea bags (see Note)
> ¾ cup sugar, Splenda, or Ideal
>   Sweetener (more if you prefer)

1 Remove and discard the tags from the tea bags and place them in a small saucepan. Add 4 cups of water and bring to a boil over medium-high heat. Boil for 1 to 2 minutes, then remove from the heat and let sit while you prepare your pitcher.

2 Fill a 2-quart pitcher halfway with cold water and add the sugar. Pour the hot tea into the pitcher, using a strainer to remove the tea bags. Stir the tea until the sugar is dissolved.

3 Fill the remainder of the pitcher with cold water. Serve over ice.

NOTE: We use orange pekoe tea, but you can experiment with other teas as well. Earl Grey is also delicious!

Acknowledgments

IRST AND FOREMOST, I WANT TO THANK GOD for never-ending love and grace. He has put up with a lot from me over the years, and I'm gonna do my best, but I suspect He'll put up with more still in years to come.

I am so very grateful to each and every single member of the Southern Plate family for sticking with me, believing in me, and being a wonderful presence at our little virtual supper table. One of the greatest joys of doing what I do is getting to spend time with wonderful people like you.

My parents and grandparents, for walking the straight and narrow, even in times when winding roads and offshoot paths would have made for easier travel.

This year I learned that one of the drawbacks of having so many wonderful grandparents in your life is that you will eventually have to say good-bye to them. I lost two grandparents who were very dear to me at the beginning of 2013, my mother's father and mother.

My grandmama Lucille left us quite suddenly in April. Grandmama, I don't think any of us will ever get over losing you, but heaven sure has a treasure now. Some people step lightly through your life, but others burst in, wrap their arms around you in a big old bear hug, and never let go. Grandmama was such an integral part of our everyday lives with her wisdom, her joy, and her laughter. She was the only person I could call at 4:30 in the morning and know she'd be up just like I was. I loved our morning chats before the sun came up, visiting over cups of coffee and telephone lines. She taught us that it was better to do something to help rather than stand around and complain, that there is always a bright side to every situation, and that hard work will get you a whole lot further than wishing ever will. I lost Grandmama, but I also lost one of my dearest friends. While the world is not the same without you, we will carry on in your absence with the character qualities you instilled in us. If God ever wants to send you back to us, though, you tell Him we're ready anytime!

Papa Reed faded in and out with his memory for several years, but he finally went home to his mama and nine brothers and sisters in January. Thank you for all of the tractor rides, walks on the farm, rides on the four-wheeler, and visits to the creek. Thank you for letting me throw in the biggest rocks I could find and for standing there and laughing when the splash soaked your worn overalls. Thank you for letting me gather the eggs, feed the pigs, and chase cows on the four-wheeler. Okay, maybe you didn't know about me chasing cows . . . but if you did, you never fussed. Thank you for teaching me to drive and for responding with "Yeah, boy!" to practically every idea I ever had. You're missed here, but I know your mama is proud to have all ten of her children around her table once more, and there is gonna be some awfully good

home cooking to look forward to for the rest of us.

Special thanks to Mama and Jyl. The two of them are saints just for answering their phones each time I called them in the course of writing this book. Every recipe I developed, I'd serve to my family one night and then have Jyl make it for her family the following night. If we both liked it, I knew it was good.

My mama is a homemaker, mother, grandmother, quilter, champion Sudoku solver, and most likely a saint. With this book she added "editor" to her long list of credits, and believe me, she earned it! I still want to be like her when I grow up.

To all my friends, when we're in heaven together I promise to: Be organized, always be available, be better at putting outfits together, do my best to stay awake after 9:00 p.m., try not to force-feed you gargantuan amounts of food out of my unnatural fear of you starving, and have a house where you can drop in anytime, without having to give a one- to two-week notice. In spite of all of this, thank you for loving me anyway.

To my husband, there is no way you could have ever fathomed the amount of dishes you would have to wash being married to me. You're a good man. I love you and I'm blessed to be your wife. But seriously—on the dish thing—I sure wouldn't want to be married to me!

Again, I want to dedicate this book to my two wonderful children. Brady, your heart amazes me. God has equipped you to be a man of honor and integrity with compassion for those around you. I can't wait to see how you make the world a better place. Katy Rose, you are just joy in human form, and His light shines so brightly through you! I would keep you a girl forever if I weren't looking forward to having you as a best friend once you are grown.

I'm also thankful for old stoves, warm hearts, worn hands, twinkling eyes, and easy smiles. Folks who have spent their whole life loving their families, where

sacrifice is never a question, but an immediate reaction whenever possible. People who have chosen to love others more than themselves, and to stop the world if a neighbor is in need. I'm thankful for neighbors and front porches and rocking chairs and the steady tick-tock of old clocks. I'm thankful to chipped serving platters and dishrags and drying towels. And all of those cleaners that smell of lemons, because they remind me of sunshine.

I'm thankful for sunshine.

Just in case my dog ever learns how to read: Zoey, you rock. *ARF!*

Gratefully,
Christy
Num. 6:22–27

Index

Page references in boldface refer to photographs of prepared dishes.

C